Shannon Danford

Manufactured in the United State of America

ISBN: 1470159902
ISBN 13: 9781470159900

Dedicated to everyone who encouraged me on this path—, my life partner, family, tribe, and friends. And to those friends I haven't yet met who appreciate the value of laughter. Special thanks to Marie Donahue, Deputy Superintendent, Boston Police Department, for sharing her knowledge of law enforcement procedures. And thanks to Faith Fleming for her wit and whimsy.

BRIDGE CLUB
Blues

Chapter 1

THE HIT

"When do you plan to start taking those meds?" Hector jabbed an index finger in the direction of the pharmacy bag sticking out of Tess Fontana's purse.

"Mind your own damn business." She took one more drag off the last two inches of her cigarette before thumping the butt away. It spun over the translucent light blue hood of her new Audi Cabriolet and rolled a few inches before the glow died. It was December, and while nearly every state in the union was experiencing winter weather, Naples, Florida, was a pleasant seventy-seven degrees. The sun was out and the humidity was low, which was why the snowbirds were flocking there in droves and why Tess had the top on her convertible down.

Tess tipped her head to the right for a better look at her reflection in the side mirror. Her thick wavy hair was mostly gray now, with a few streaks of black, and her last face-lift was holding nicely. She worked out regularly with weights and practiced the rigid posture she learned from the nuns in parochial school. Good diet and genes made it possible for her to enjoy a cocktail or two before

1

dinner every night. And she always scheduled time for Hector in the sack, so Tess felt she was fairly well-rounded and aging gracefully for a sixty-five-year-old. And not many women her age could wear a black pantsuit with such confidence.

"I'm just sayin' it's been a week already. I just think you need to get proactive with this. You need to start the meds," Hector prodded.

Tess grabbed the purse from the Audi's floorboard and parked it in her lap. The oversized bag was new, a white leatherette knockoff she'd picked up at the flea market. She'd tucked the newly filled prescription in the side pocket a week ago. Tess Fontana was not ready for a diagnosis of Parkinson's. A week earlier, Dr. Fish had broken the news. It wasn't what she had expected. In fact, it was the last thing she had expected. She thought the symptoms were from a lingering flu bug, a bad can of Ensure, but not this, of all things. Hector had the prescriptions filled that day. He was handling it better than she was.

But it was easier for Hector. He wasn't the hitter. He didn't make the decisions, and he didn't have the pressure riding on him. He was the damn caddie; Tess was the game. She clutched the purse, relieved that her worry, at least, was safely hidden behind her sunglasses. Not that Hector was judgmental in any way. He was more of a dull-eyed oaf. A dull-eyed oaf with long black lashes and a rugged five-o'clock shadow, all of which were traits she required in her men.

"I'll take one as soon as we finish the job."

Wordlessly, Hector took his soda can from the cup holder and held it out to her.

She tore the prescription instruction sheet from the package and began to read. "Did you look at the side effects? I can't take this now. You big *goomba*. Causes drowsiness…I'm not gonna take one of these till we're finished here. And this diazepam, are you kidding me? Don't operate heavy machinery or drive? And what is this? Liquid? Really?"

"Fish thought you'd prefer drops. And you should know I took the liberty of filling out the paperwork for your drug plan, so you won't have to order again for three months. If you want I'll do it for you on the computer."

They stared into each other's reflective lenses until Hector turned away.

"You tell the boss?" Hector had to ask.

"Who are you, my mother?" It was an ironic question, considering that Tess was nearly old enough to be Hector's maternal parent. "Back off." Then, as an afterthought, she added, "I'll let you know."

Hector nodded. Nothing good would come from an argument. He had a future to worry about and didn't want the old broad to take him down if she lost her position in *the club*. He'd spent the last few days wondering if he ought to stand up to her and prove himself. First, he had to prove himself to the guy looking back at him in the mirror every morning. The fact was, Hector was afraid of her and afraid of their boss. Tess was a nice broad most of the time, and he didn't mind banging her a couple of times a month. He considered it part of his job description. But he couldn't help feeling intimidated when the two women were together.

Unbeknownst to Tess, Hector had been seeing a girl from the other coast pretty regularly. It was getting intense, too. Hector wanted it to get more serious. The only thing that stood in the way of advancing his relationship with Christie was the very real possibility of how Tess would react if she found out. Initially, Hector had hoped that Tess's diminished capacity would force her into retirement, leaving the position open for him. But the dame was hard and stubborn.

Tess looked at her watch, moving it away from her eyes until the numbers came into focus. Although she seemed to be losing her sight on top of everything else, she noticed her hand was surprisingly steady. "It's time." She slipped out a pair of black gloves, tucked them into her waistband, and gingerly eased the revolver into her pants pocket. She climbed out of the coupe and patted the door. "Let's do this."

Tess, aka Smiling Tess Fontana, started counting as soon as the gate at the mouth of the underground parking garage began to slide open. It ran on a chain that eased along like a tortoise, slow and steady so as not to intimidate the residents, who did not appreciate being rushed. Forty-five seconds passed between the time the Phantom Coupe Rolls-Royce first appeared and when it glided into its designated parking space and came to a complete stop.

This isn't right, Tess thought as she watched the driver climb out.

The driver of the Rolls was supposed to be its owner, Anita Lemoyne. The nonagenarian had her hair done every Monday afternoon: shampoo, blow-dry, and style. She had allegedly worn the same hairstyle for over fifty years. Every six weeks, Chez Coupe gave Anita a trim. Today, of all days, had to be different, Tess fumed. Pressing her back against the cold concrete pillar, she listened to the footsteps echoing in the garage.

She chanced a quick look and saw that the driver was a young woman, and she was headed toward the elevator. The car sat idle. Presumably Anita was inside, but it was difficult to tell with such a dark tint on the windows.

The plan was spiraling out of Tess's control, something she could not afford to have happen. There was too much riding on this hit, not to mention her personal reputation hung in the balance. And there was no way of alerting Hector, who was stealthily pulling out of position and moving toward the gate where the car had just entered. He obviously hadn't seen the driver walk away. There was no time to call his cell and have him abort the plan. The video camera on the gate was recording Fontana's car and tag as it left, providing her with an airtight alibi. Everything was already in motion and couldn't be stopped.

"*Maron.*" Tess growled the familiar Italian word through clenched teeth as she hurried from behind the cement pillar to the Phantom and tapped on Anita's window. Fontana would salvage the plan, and no one would be the wiser. But she had to work fast now because the driver would no doubt return shortly. There was no room for error in her business. She attempted a smile, aware that her new dentures were slightly larger and more pronounced than her old ones, giving her the appearance of a horse reaching for an apple through a barbed-wire fence. She interlaced her fingers, pressing the gloves into the tightest possible fit on each hand before reaching for the door handle.

Anita was polite enough to return the smile when she recognized the face of her neighbor. And she gladly popped up the lock when Tess gestured that she wanted to talk.

"Yes, dear?" Anita edged over and invited her neighbor inside the climate-controlled leviathan.

In a flash Smiling Tess was inside the gray Phantom. "Listen up, because I'm only going to say it once. Ooh, nice upholstery." Tess was distracted by the soft leather seat. "Like a baby's bottom."

"I picked out the cows myself," Anita said, and proudly patted the seat.

"Okay, this is how it's gonna go down. You're gonna tell me the names of the board members you've been talking to."

"Wait a minute. I think the batteries on my hearing aids are going." Anita plucked the aid from her right ear and examined it.

Tess drew the thirty-eight from her waistband and pointed it at Lemoyne. "I think you've been talking out of school. And I want to know who you've been flapping your gums to." The accusation ended abruptly in a respiratory spasm as a cough wrenched loose from Tess's lungs, leaving her nearly breathless. A long-time smoker, she knew better than to yell, but her temper often won out over her sense of reason.

Even with the barrel pointed at her, Anita was ever the gentlewoman; she took a lace handkerchief from her linen blazer and handed it to Tess.

Smiling Tess Fontana took it and covered her mouth as she hacked. Finally, when she was able to regain her breath and composure, she pointed the revolver between Anita's eyes.

"You're very rude, Miss Fontana. I certainly expected better of you, but then again, you don't have the best reputation, do you? Everyone knows you slept with Mr. Gerard when his wife was having her hip replaced. And you run around with that man who is young enough to be your grandson."

"Oh, yeah," Smiling Tess hissed. "Let me show you rude…" But before she could finish the sentence, Anita Lemoyne's eyes grew wide and the stately woman's face contorted. She gasped twice. Her birdlike hand grabbed a fistful of navy blazer and squeezed as her head fell back against the seat. Her mouth crimped into a grimace that left little doubt she was in trouble.

"You've got to be kiddin' me." Tess shook her head. Clearly, her victim was going to die before she had the opportunity to whack her. "This is just great," Tess murmured as she stashed the revolver. It was beginning to look like she wasn't going to shoot anybody.

From her handbag, Tess withdrew a blonde wig; one that closely resembled Anita Lemoyne's hairstyle and color. She slipped it over her own hair and carefully tucked in the loose ends. Next, she wrestled Anita's blazer from her lifeless body and rolled the corpse onto the floorboard out of sight. Then, she squirmed into the jacket as best she could, even though it was several sizes too small. She was winging it now, free styling. *Just like the old days*, Tess thought, and felt like a twenty-year-old again.

She cautiously climbed out of the Phantom, looked left and then right. Hunching slightly to make her arms appear shorter, as the blazer rode up nearly to her elbows, the sixty-five-year-old hurried as fast as her wiry legs and nicotine-stained lungs allowed, to the elevator, where she could see the numbers blinking as they counted down.

When the door opened, Tess stood with her back to the wall until the driver stepped into view. With one good swing, she drove the thirty-eight's butt into the young woman's head and watched her drop to the ground with a gratifying thud.

"Son of a…" Tess heard the blazer rip when she reached down to grab her victim's ankle.

This latest stooge was too heavy to drag, so Smiling Tess attempted to nudge the unconscious woman with her foot. Same results, but now Tess was winded. Time was running out.

Suddenly, Tess remembered the large rolling dolly Hector had used to move her old TV. She found it in the community storage space between the assortment of stolen grocery carts and red wagons. With great effort, Tess was able to scoot the lip of the dolly under the driver's upper body. She pushed her load to the farthest corner of the garage, behind the Trumans' Bentley. The Trumans were in France for Christmas and wouldn't be back until January. No one was likely to stumble across the driver until Tess was in the clear.

The hit woman climbed in behind the wheel of the Phantom and dropped it into reverse. The engine whispered, and the Phantom felt like it was gliding instead of rolling. As Tess neared the sliding gate, she slunk down in her seat, in an effort to appear like the late Mrs. Lemoyne, of the Connecticut Lemoynes, out for a drive.

Tess was doing a fine job of acting until she sideswiped the ID reader just outside the gate. "I'm not believin' this shit," Tess groused, and eased the behemoth out of the complex.

Still creeping along as she adjusted to the Phantom's temperament, Tess straightened in her seat. While she still had her license, Hector did nearly all the driving, so she was not accustomed to maneuvering a vehicle twice the size of her Audi.

Her cell phone began to play the theme from *The Godfather*. Still cruising along at a safe twenty-five miles per hour, she leaned down and retrieved her bag from the floor. Rooting through her collection of makeup, cards, condoms, and over-the-counter pill bottles, she could not find the phone. Not until she clipped a mailbox did Tess look up. The passenger side mirror was now bumping along the asphalt.

"I'm trying to drive here, Hector. What do you want?"

"Where are you?"

"I'm coming already." She could hear the man popping his gum on the other end.

"You don't sound like yourself. Are you okay?"

"Let's just say things didn't go exactly as planned."

"Is she...?" Hector asked solemnly.

"Of course, you douche bag. Where are you?"

"Near the toll booth. I just wanted to make sure you were okay."

"Look, I'm gonna pull over for a second, so hold on." Tess put the cell in her lap. She slowed down and turned the wheel to ease the land barge up to the curb, but accidentally rolled clear onto the sidewalk. The screech of the

6

Phantom's underbelly scraping over concrete was unnerving, not to mention the sudden shock to Tess's nervous system, which was something she could have done without.

"What was that?" Hector called from the floorboard, where her phone had landed after the collision with the curb.

Tess put the car in park and rolled down the passenger window. She walked around the vehicle. The mirror lay in the grass, still attached to the Rolls by two cables. Tess found the battered side mirror surprisingly heavy as she lifted it through the window and dropped it in the seat beside her.

"You still there?" She shifted the car into drive and guided its front tires back onto the asphalt.

"What was all that?"

"Don't worry about it."

"Tess, this isn't part of the plan." Hector couldn't resist admonishing his partner.

"You don't make the plans, Hector. You follow them." Tess hit the end button and tossed the phone into the backseat. "I make the plans," she assured herself, and glanced in the rearview mirror to make sure the coast was still clear. "I make the effing plans."

Chapter 2

THE ASSIGNMENT

Monday, December 22, 2008 – 11:50 a.m.

Agents Winnie and Pell sat obediently in the chairs their boss pointed to, as though they had a choice of chairs or whether to take a seat. The chief pressed his tie down as he sat across from the pair in his own impressive, without being ostentatious, executive leather swivel. "We have a situation in Naples."

"Cacho?" Winnie leaned forward, her eyes suffused with anticipation.

A year had passed since the two agents had apprehended the drug kingpin and several members of his gang without firing a single shot. Despite their work, Cacho Rodrigo had escaped the following day, when the van he was being transported in overturned in the Everglades. He was last seen heading southeast toward Miami, hands and feet shackled, hobbling in earnest toward freedom.

Agents Winnie and Pell received promotions and their reputations in the male-dominated profession were gilded in gold. The two women had been invited to join the more elite Organized Crime Unit of the Florida Bureau of Investigation (FLABI). Even as they moved up the ladder, neither woman lost sight of the fact that Cacho was still on the loose, with their names and faces only a year old in his memory.

"No," the chief said bluntly. "But it's big...very big. This is what we know so far." He shoved a pair of identical manila folders across his desk.

The women flipped through a series of surveillance photos, notes, and a mob-related hierarchy chart, which they had to turn sideways to view. Like a drill team, they finished their assessments at the same time, laid down the folders and looked up.

"I want you two to head up the investigation." He paused to measure their reaction but only got robotic stares. "You know the area. You know the local police...and they know you."

Winnie's eyes shifted the slightest bit, remembering the episode a year ago. Although no bullets were wasted in the capture of Cacho Rodrigo, the incident had not gone smoothly. The local sheriff had attempted to steal their collar. Sheriff Shoat lived for camera time and was quick to realize just how valuable the capture would be for his own career when he landed in the national spotlight.

The agents had hijacked Shoat's news conference, leaving the man humiliated and nursing a grudge.

"I don't know if they'll cooperate with us this time around," Pell noted.

"Of course we'd prefer their cooperation, but we don't need it. You can call in reinforcements as needed. You'll have the full support of this office. So?" The chief didn't mince words, nor did he expect an argument once his mind was made up.

Winnie nodded and turned to the other agent, who nodded with less enthusiasm.

"Good." The chief clapped his hands together and spun his chair to face the rear wall. He stood and tugged at a cord dangling behind his desk. A projection screen unfurled. In the next moment he aimed a remote at the lights as faces appeared on the screen.

A photo from their package appeared first. "Meet Ralph Bustamante, alias Piano Man. He got that name because he likes to play the piano in one of his own nightclubs. He's pretty good, I understand, but he's second-generation mob, so he probably didn't get to pick his own career. So far we know he's at least second down from the top. He runs with Vinnie Ragusa, Johnny the Saint Marcola, Little Joey Bondi, and Butch Columbo. They're all Jersey boys, born and raised there. Couple of them have records, but they all changed course and headed south. They run Boca, Palm Beach, and the upper Keys."

"What about Miami?"

The chief sighed heavily. "They stay clear of Miami's gangs, and won't go near Lauderdale either. And they've protected their operation for nearly three decades without the bullets and drama. If they're killing, we don't have any evidence, not one body. Either they aren't spilling blood, or they have one hell of a button man. That's part of the reason they haven't come up on our radar more often. They don't leave a bloody trail and they stay out of the press. The only reason we know anything is a big shipment of pharmaceuticals was stolen from a delivery truck en route to the V.A. in Key West. Then pills from one of the batches suddenly start turning up in Naples. We think they're branching out, trying to cultivate new territory on the West Coast."

"But there are no gangs and no real infrastructure in Naples or the Ft. Myers area. I don't even see how they could get a toehold there," Pell noted.

The chief nodded, "Exactly. They're contained right now, we don't want them spreading across the Everglades corridor. The drugs I mentioned came from a high school kid who claimed he bought them from his friend's mother, and the other pills were discovered by a pharmacist in an upscale nursing home, of all places. You two already have the lay of the land. We'll be setting up our strike force on the East Coast. You will synchronize your movements with us, and we'll see if we can cast a net to take everyone down at the same time. That's best-case scenario, which is always the objective. Worst case, we'll make it difficult for them to expand into the Naples area and we'll bring some real force to bear in their own turf. The big gangs take each other out faster than we can arrest them. This mob is scary because they are biding their time, waiting for the right moment to make an inside play and take all the territory." The chief stressed the word *all* to make his point. The implications were clear.

It was a terrifying thought. If one gang had the muscle to control the entire southwestern part of the state, the agency's job would grow exponentially. So would their mortality rate.

Chapter 3

CRUKINSHANK SECURITY AT THE STONE CRAB FLEA MARKET AND MARINA

Monday, December 22, 2008 – Noon

"Milo?"

Milo Purdie plucked the walkie-talkie out of the cup holder on his golf cart. "This is Purdie, over." He modulated his voice for optimal professionalism.

"Milo, we have a situation in Perky-eight."

Although he had been on assignment at the flea market for less than a month, Milo knew that this was code for Ms. Perkins in booth 448 had cornered some kid who got underwear-happy in her store. Only natural, he thought. A young man being interested in ladies lingerie was hardly unusual; in fact, he thought it was a rite of passage. Milo remembered being seduced by the mannequin in the window of Victoria's Secret at the mall. He had his face mashed against the glass when the sales clerk came up behind him. Black. He smiled coyly at the recollection of the panties in the window. Black with lace.

"I'm on my way." Milo deftly wheeled his golf cart around and headed down the loading dock alley which ran behind and between the stores. At booth 448, Milo hopped out, remembering to take the keys with him so the golf cart wouldn't get hijacked again.

Pranksters had taken his cart for a joyride two weeks ago and left it in a Publix parking lot with the lights on. It didn't take long for the battery to die, forcing Milo to push it all the way back to the flea market. The spectacle of him in his uniform pushing the cart beside one of Naples's main thoroughfares landed his photo in the community newspaper. Taking the keys was a lesson he wouldn't soon forget.

Indeed, Ms. Perkins had a captive. A quivering young man tried to protect his head and then his groin as the fifty-some-year-old retiree swatted at him with a plastic hanger.

"Ms. Perkins," Milo said in the commanding voice he'd been practicing on his dog, Boomer. "Ms. Perkins, I'll handle it from here."

Ms. Perkins whipped the hanger back for a good swipe and thwacked Milo between the eyes. She wasn't a big woman, maybe five feet tall and no more than a hundred pounds, but she was clearly deadly with a hanger.

He blinked several times before slowly sinking to his knees.

"Oh, Milo! I'm so sorry. I certainly did not mean to hurt you." She reached for him, taking his face in her hands. "Milo, can you hear me?"

Eyes tightly shut, he gently felt along the bridge of his nose; mercifully it was not broken, but a welt was rising between his eyebrows. He felt her hands under his armpits as she struggled to lift him. With his butt just clear of the floor, the shopkeeper suddenly released her grip and he was back on the indoor/outdoor carpet of her booth.

"You get back here!"

Her voice sounded surprisingly similar to the call of a mating screech owl, Milo thought, as he rolled onto his side to get up. Through blurred vision, he saw the boy make his move and leap out the back of the store, where Milo had parked the golf cart minutes earlier.

"Never mind. The little pervert got away." Ms. Perkins whipped the hanger at the fleeing boy and Milo heard it connect with something other than its intended target.

"Well, he might have gotten away, but I seriously doubt he'll ever bother you again," Milo noted in his voice of authority, which was now largely nasal.

He felt something hard against his shoulder and grabbed onto it for support. Hoisting himself up, the Crukinshank man swayed slightly and bent forward to regain his balance.

"Look over here," Ms. Perkins said. When Milo turned, he saw a bright burst of light as the flash on her cell phone went off, capturing his photo.

He squinted, still unable to stand up.

"Milo, that's a great shot of you and my Ken mannequin. I'll probably blow it up and put it by the register. You know, give customers a little chuckle." She pulled up the photo and nodded approvingly. "Yeah, that came out good."

Still leaning forward, hands on hips, Milo looked over his shoulder and spotted the life-size mannequin standing directly behind him. The six-foot, flesh-colored, lifelike Ken doll was proudly sporting nothing but a leather thong. His arms were slightly raised as if inviting everyone to enjoy his masculine fashion sense. The way Milo was unwittingly backed up didn't leave much for the imagination.

"I better get going, Ms. Perkins. It's time to make my rounds." Milo knew he had to move on before she got it in her head to take another photo.

Chapter 4

SLEEPING WITH THE FISHES

Monday, December 22, 2008 – 12:20 p.m.

Tess slowed the Rolls slightly when she saw the sign for the I-75 toll plaza. She took a moment to look in the rearview mirror, making sure the wig was on straight and her sunglasses concealed the upper half of her face. As she drew even with the booth, Tess purposely kept her gaze straight ahead, carefully extending the dollar bill toward the collector while hoping no one took notice of the fact that the passenger side mirror was missing and all that remained were raw wires and chipped paint.

"Have a nice day," a female voice said perfunctorily.

Tess attempted the regal nod she had seen Anita give the wait staff in the Highland Terrace dining room. She did not dare turn and give the toll collector a frontal view of her face. Smiling Tess Fontana was no amateur. Her days as a button man might be numbered, but she was still a pro.

The green light came on, and she controlled her urge to floor it. The Phantom pulled forward into a light flow of Miami-bound traffic.

Hector had said he was one-point-six miles from the booth and would watch for her. Tess had every intention of setting the trip meter, but she could not look away from the road long enough to figure out the dashboard. A horn blew, but she did not jerk the wheel. Instead, she gave the irate driver a polite queen-like wave, as though she was passing by peasants in her horse-drawn carriage. Although she had never seen Anita do this, Tess thought she would have under the same circumstances. She would have to estimate the distance and hope there was some sign of Hector off the side of the road. The traffic was surprisingly light, but she still wished they could have taken care of business at night. However, given Anita's schedule, there weren't many opportunities after dark. The woman was in bed by seven every night.

Tess cruised along, watching the mile markers, realizing just how comfortable the seat was. She reached for the radio dial and another horn blew. Although she still had the presence of mind not to jerk the wheel, she very nearly clapped one hand into her elbow while saluting with her fist. Instead, she waved once again and muttered, "*Tie vaffanculo*," a less than endearing expression she had heard from her parents at least once a day.

Two minutes passed and Smiling Tess pulled off onto the shoulder. There was no sign of Hector in the rearview mirror. Sighing, she reached behind her and felt around on the floorboard where she had tossed her cell phone. She was sweeping the floor when someone tapped on the window.

Hector stood outside, his arms lifted. She saw him mouth, "What?" He already had on his latex gloves and looked very irritated. He tried the handle and discovered the door locked. Tess finally located the lock control and Hector slid in beside her.

"Where you been? Oh, nice seats." Remembering where he was, Hector turned and spotted the body in the floorboard. "What? No blood?"

"Don't worry about it." Tess pulled out a handkerchief and went to work wiping down all the surfaces she'd come in contact with.

"I mean it, how did you whack her without a drop of blood? Where's the blood?"

Tess struck like a snake, pinching Hector's nose between her thumb and forefinger. "Shut your hole. I'm not gonna tell you again, you understand?" The man's eyes watered. He nodded.

Satisfied the Phantom was clean and none of her prints remained, Tess waited for a lull in the traffic before getting out and making her way down to a thicket of vegetation by the canal. She could see the hole in the fence now, gaping wide; it would easily accommodate the Rolls. She also saw two sizeable alligators on the opposite bank idling in the sun. The reptiles looked harmless from this far away. Tess hoped they hadn't eaten in a while.

The sound of the Rolls trundling over the grass and down the embankment caused her to spin around and jump back in time to avoid the oncoming car. In the process, she fell backward, landing on her tailbone in a patch of vegetation. "You bastard," Tess growled, as she collected herself and rose onto all fours. The wig was knocked sideways and blonde bangs now covered her eyes. She slapped them away before tearing the thing off her head.

The car had picked up enough speed in its descent and had plunged in well away from the bank. Brackish water was rushing into the open windows. The luxurious vehicle would be underwater in minutes.

Hector hurried down the embankment, going as fast as he could, which wasn't fast at all since he couldn't get an inch of purchase with his smooth-bottom loafers. He doubled over when he reached Tess's side.

"Are you okay?" he gasped. He had aimed the steering wheel perfectly with the intention of clipping her and cleaning up the hit at the same time. It would have worked if she hadn't moved. Now he was faced with an angry hellcat who packed a weapon and wasn't afraid to use it. He didn't think it was the best time to tell her that she was up to her elbows in poison ivy.

She reached up, extending her hand for assistance, but when Hector came close enough, she rabbit-punched him in the face. A searing pain shot through his nose. He felt the trickle of blood between his fingers as he tried to protect himself from another blow.

"You motherless bastard, son of a bitch. I should shoot you and tie you to a tree until those lizards swim over and eat you. You could have killed me, you moron."

Hector wasn't penitent, but he knew the only way to stop her rage was a convincing act of supplication, so he launched into a stream of apologies.

"You're sorry? You're sorry? I should shoot you, *cazzo*! I should shoot and watch you bleed to death."

Hector peeked through his fingers to see if she was winding down and decided it would be a good idea to turn on the tears. The philosophy was to overwhelm her drama with his own.

"I could have killed you." He moaned and dropped to his knees. "I'm so sorry."

Hector continued his histrionics until he realized Tess had grown quiet. He found her standing over him. She leaned toward him and he flinched.

"I'm not gonna hit you, you big gorilla. C'mon, let's get going. Where did you leave the car?"

On the way back to Highland Terrace, Smiling Tess Fontana started her prescription.

Chapter 5

CARMEN BUSTAMANTE

Monday, December 22, 2008 – 12:42 p.m.

"Looking good, Carmen." Dr. Fish closed the file that contained the last decade of Carmen's health records. "Aside from a slight elevation in blood pressure, you're in excellent health. Keep an eye on that. Check it from time to time, either here or when you pick up your prescriptions. Let me know if anything changes. I do wish you'd quit smoking. I'd be happy to write you a scrip for a patch or gum right now." He clicked an expensive ballpoint pen and grinned expectantly.

The sixty-six-year-old turned her small dark eyes on the doctor. She smacked her meaty lips. "What, and take away my one joy in life?"

"You have grandkids," Dr. Fish noted. "Enjoy them."

"Aw," she growled, and waved her hand. "They will be the death of me. Besides, so what if I enjoy a smoke from time to time. I refuse to die from something that brings me so much pleasure."

"Well, unless something changes, I'll see you in six months." Fish slipped the pen into the breast pocket of his lab coat, tucked the file under his arm and bowed out of the exam room.

"Ugh." Carmen scooted to the edge of the exam table until her feet hit the tread on the stool at the end of the table.

"I thought the one joy in your life was your four o'clock martini." Muscia Bolineaux, a freakishly large Dominican woman, slowly rose to her full five-feet-eleven-inch height before gently taking her employer's elbow and helping Carmen onto her feet. She held her a second longer.

"Okay, I guess I got two joys in life. You can let go. I'm good," Carmen told her, when she was sure of her footing.

They made for a strange couple: Carmen; a squat, pale Sicilian quick with invective versus Muscia; subtle, quiet, and breathtakingly thick. Muscia had answered an ad for a private-duty CNA a decade earlier. The original tour of duty was only supposed to last six weeks, the standard recovery time for hip replacement surgery. But Carmen's hip had not healed as planned. Whether it was the result of a botched surgery or the fact that Carmen refused to actively participate in her physical therapy, the pain remained, her range of motion was limited, and Carmen was unable to walk without assistance. Upon meeting her, Carmen instantly realized the possibilities. Devoted, fearless, and willing to throw herself in danger's way if Carmen was threatened, Muscia was an ideal bodyguard as well as a nursing assistant. And she was so compact; Carmen suspected armor-piercing bullets would be no match for her dense, muscular body. After ten years together, Muscia realized she would never find another Carmen, and Carmen knew she could not break in another Muscia. Theirs was a relationship of complete balance, Carmen's yang to Muscia's yin; they were symbiotic companions of the highest order.

Just as Muscia pulled around in the powder blue Seville, Carmen felt the vibration of her cell phone in the pocket of her cardigan.

"Yes?" she answered.

"It's done." The voice at the other end of the line had the same Jersey accent as Carmen. Everyone in her circle of friends and associates shared the dialect that was distinct to North Jersey, to the extent that everyone else sounded oddly out of place.

Carmen flipped the phone closed and climbed into the rear passenger seat, then waited patiently as Muscia buckled her in and laid a plaid blanket across her legs.

"Let's swing into Publix. I gotta get some snacks for the girls. We got bridge club tonight." Carmen slipped on her wraparound sunglasses as the car rolled onto U.S. Highway 41, the Tamiami Trail.

"The grandkids are coming too," Muscia reminded. Her deep monotone was perfectly matched to her physique.

"Little bastards." Carmen made a hissing sound as she sucked air through her dentures. "What time?"

"April said the nanny will stop by after dinner."

Carmen's daughter-in-law, April, had married into the family a decade earlier. She was the daughter of a prominent banker who found himself in arrears with a substantial gambling debt to the Bustamante family. His daughter's hand in marriage was considered payment in full. Upon learning of her father's betrayal, April had started a career in binge drinking. Ten years and two children later, April was a high-functioning alcoholic.

"Get 'em a box of Yodels. No, get Twinkies. I feel like a Twinkie." The old woman ran her hand over the white leather upholstery while the Caddy idled in the Publix parking lot, air conditioner on and Frank Sinatra in surround sound.

Carmen had picked up her first Cadillac the day her late husband was laid to rest. The Fleetwood Brougham Elegance Coupe had been ordered the week before his death, shortly after Carmen had put a quarter teaspoon of rat poison pellets in his prune juice. The other two tablespoons dispensed over the course of six months were too slow acting, so she went ahead with a change in dose. Everyone expected him to die soon anyway. He had returned to bed complaining of nausea, drawn the sheets up to his chin and broken out in a sweat. Carmen, twenty-three years his junior, alighted on the bed beside him.

"What are you doing?" Ralph had awakened to find his wife's fingers pressing the side of his neck, cutting off his carotid's circulation. Pale and perspiring, he was gasping for air; a milk-like substance oozed from the corners of his mouth.

"I'm putting you out of my misery." Carmen tilted her head to one side, watching the spectacle with frighteningly cool detachment. "Now shut up and die already."

Ralph's eyes closed and he began to laugh. He laughed all the way to the gates of Hell, his hand weakly gripping Carmen's wrist. It was over in less than five minutes. Carmen shook his bony fingers free and lit up a Virginia Slims. "Rest in peace, ya bastard."

The thought suddenly occurred to her that Cadillacs were one of the few things she had ever been faithful to.

Muscia tapped on her window. Carmen pulled down the switch the way she pulled a trigger, with controlled precision.

"Here." Muscia stuck an unwrapped Twinkie through the opening.

One corner of her lip turned up and she smiled for the first time that day. "Thank you," she said, and bit into the sponge cake, savoring the moment while Muscia loaded the groceries into the trunk.

Chapter 6

EMERGENCY ROOM DRAMA

Monday, December 22, 2008 – 3:00 p.m.

Sonny ran up to the emergency room doors and would have powered through them if they hadn't parted for her. She spotted her parents right away and headed in their direction. They both stood to meet her.

"They're doing X-rays right now, but we were able to talk to her before she went in," Cole said, as he hugged his middle daughter.

Elizabeth Delaney sandwiched her daughter. "Oh, honey," she comforted.

"What did she say? Have the police found anything? I can't breathe."

Elizabeth and Cole backed away. "There is no sign of Anita or her car, but it seems pretty clear that they wanted her, not your sister." Cole planted his hands on Sonny's shoulders. "She's going to be all right."

All three turned to the sound of Bethany, the oldest Delaney sister, whose sobbing forewarned of her arrival. She had apparently entered the hospital through the main entrance and was just now winding her way through the corridor leading to the emergency room. Her face was already puffy from crying and swearing, a hormonal condition that happened monthly.

"*Ack, ack, ack*," she wept into Elizabeth, then turned to her father and continued. "*Ack, ack, ack*."

"Beth, you need to stop. You're making a spectacle of yourself," Elizabeth noted softly.

"I can't help it. My baby sister's been hurt. I can't...*ack, ack, ack*."

Sonny folded her arms over her chest and rolled her eyes upward, scanning the fluorescent bulbs overhead. She glanced at the clock on the wall, yawned, and picked up a dog-eared magazine from the closest table.

All the while, Elizabeth patted her firstborn the way she had when the girls were infants and needed burping.

"Okay, Mom. I bruise easily," Bethany sniffed, and dabbed her eyes with a wad of tissue. "How is she?"

Sonny tossed the magazine back on the table. "She's getting X-rays right now."

"Have you all heard from the police? Do they know anything?"

Sonny was about to answer when she noticed the television in the waiting area, where a live account of the assault was being filmed at Highland Terrace. Everyone followed her gaze and strained to hear the report. A current photo of Anita Lemoyne suddenly filled the screen.

"Crime Alert is asking for your help this afternoon in locating Anita Lemoyne. Mrs. Lemoyne, a senior from the Highland Terrace community, went missing just hours ago. Police became involved when Mrs. Lemoyne's caregiver was found in the parking garage here at Highland Terrace, unconscious, the apparent victim of an assault. Mrs. Lemoyne is a well-known philanthropist and highly respected member of this community. Viewers might recall that she funded the Cityscape Park project last year. That facility opened this month and Mrs. Lemoyne was on hand for the ribbon-cutting ceremony. She is not in good health and requires medication for a heart condition. Police are asking for your help in finding her, and the family is offering a reward for information leading to her whereabouts. If you have any information that might be helpful, please call Naples Police at five-six-six-zero-nine-seven-five. I'm Katie Ingstrom. Now, back to the newsroom."

As if on cue, Sheriff Troy Shoat appeared. Two years ago, he had been new on the force, freshly minted, barely out of the academy. But his father, Sheriff Shoat Senior, had suffered a stroke nine months ago, and Troy had been promoted. He strode over to the clutch of Delaneys and drew out a small pad and a pen.

Giddy with a sense of importance, he sucked in a breath and stood an inch taller. "I need to ask y'all some questions."

The ER nurse, a young woman dressed in smart blue scrubs, made eye contact with Elizabeth and took a step in the clan's direction.

Elizabeth bolted from the group, followed by Bethany and Sonny; Cole brought up the rear, leaving the young Shoat alone and rather irritated.

"She has a skull fracture," the nurse said, and paused for effect. "They're stitching her up right now, but her doctor wants to keep her a few days for observation, just to be on the safe side."

Shoat was behind the group, listening in with feigned interest. "I'd like to ask a few questions—"

Elizabeth shot him a hairy eyeball, and he took a step back.

Cole wrapped an arm over her shoulders, a gesture meant to protect the pesky cop from his wife. "When can we see her?"

"I can take one of you back right now. As soon as we have her situated upstairs, I'll get you all a room number."

Elizabeth didn't wait to get an invitation. She slipped from under her husband's arm and disappeared with the nurse into the belly of the ER.

Chapter 7

WINNIE AND PELL RETURN TO NAPLES

Monday, December 22, 2008 — 4:54 p.m.

"This is a waste of time, Pell." The shorter of the two agents rolled her shoulders and flexed her fingers in and out of fists as she stood by the dark blue Ford Taurus waiting for her partner.

"Chief said to at least try and make nice with the sheriff. And it's protocol, so suck it up." Agent Pell drew up beside Winnie. "Put on your happy face and let's get this over with."

At age twenty-five, Agent Pell still had the look of the high school athlete who lettered in track, basketball, and tennis. She stood just over five feet eight inches tall, and under her sunglasses, startling light blue eyes hinted at her Germanic ancestry. Her gait was measured and alert, the result of hours of disciplined study in jujitsu and tae kwan do. With honey-blonde hair and a cool demeanor even in the heat of a Florida summer at high noon, Pell was learning how to parlay her good looks and cold, calculated vision into an instrument ideal for her line of work. Unlike her male counterparts, Pell had no difficulty holding a suspect's attention during an interview. Lulled into a sense of testosterone-driven bravado, the accused was usually so consumed with the sight of Agent Pell that by the time she peeled off her dark glasses, he was already under her spell. Her laser-like stare could extract information and confessions with surgical precision. It was a gift she was just beginning to appreciate and cultivate.

While most Floridians wore sunglasses to protect their eyes from the sun, Pell wore them to protect the innocent from her penetrating gaze.

Agent Winnie was one of the few people immune to Pell's eyes. And for the frigid temperature cast by Pell, Winnie was the polar opposite.

Agent Winnie, also in her mid-twenties, was the night to Pell's day, with the sun-bronzed skin of her Mediterranean ancestors, dark eyes, and black hair. She was slightly shorter than her partner and exuded the energy of something untamed that belonged in a cage, or at least on a leash. Easily as attractive as her partner, Winnie saw no benefit in using her looks on the bad guys when she could just as easily Taser them or punch them into submission. Suspects seemed to sense this and looked to the Nordic agent for protection.

They shared a love of jazz music, preferred their coffee black, and had a nearly obsessive need for heavy starch in their oxford shirts and khaki pants. And after sharing a room at the academy followed by two years paired as partners, there were few secrets between them.

After their brush with Shoat a year earlier, neither woman was anxious to see the man again. Had they not been given orders to make their presence known to the chief of police and remind him that their badges exceeded his jurisdictional authority, they would gladly have avoided contact with the man.

Winnie held the door and then followed her partner into the Naples Police Department headquarters. The receptionist was painting on lipstick when the agents appeared at her window.

"Oh my goodness!" The receptionist clapped her hands. "It is so good to see you all. Come on back here so I can give you all a hug."

Winnie grimaced when the receptionist turned away to release the door into the main part of the building.

"She's on our team," Pell reminded her. "Suck it up."

"Wait till I tell the sheriff you're here." In her exuberance, the receptionist had accidently left a streak of Passion Fruit Red on one of her front teeth. Each time she smiled, which was often, the streak seemed to scream *look at me.* "You all wait right here, I'll be back in a flash." *Look at me.*

"Sheriff?" they heard the receptionist yelling. She pronounced the word *sheriff* as one syllable, so it rhymed with *Smurf.* She returned moments later still wearing her smile, front tooth still screaming *look at me.* "I thought he was in the little boy's room, but I guess not. Anyway, a lot has gone on since y'all were here." She leaned toward the agents and lowered her voice, although her tooth continued to be disruptive. "Sheriff Shoat had a stroke round about a month after y'all were here. So Troy got promoted and the election is still on hold. He's trying to fill his father's shoes. I'm sure y'all figured out he's not the brightest bulb, but he tries hard. He'll have to run to keep the seat next May once his father's term is up. Troy feels like he's got a good chance. I guess there's still no word on that Cacho fellow?"

Both agents solemnly shook their heads.

"And we just got a call this afternoon about a missing person, but Troy is treating it like a possible kidnapping."

"Really?" Pell tilted her head. Now she was interested.

"Well, it started when someone called and said there was a body in the parking garage over at the Highland Terrace. That's one of those upscale nursing homes. Every unit in there starts at a million five. Can you believe that? But all those places on Gulf View are pricey. A penthouse can go for ten. *Look at me.* I read that Naples has one of the largest communities of millionaires in the country. And I believe it. If I had that kind of money I'd get me one of those places on the Gulf—"

"And then what happened?" Pell interrupted.

"Well, Troy went over and found this woman lying between a couple of cars. She wasn't dead at all, but she got the daylights knocked out of her. The poor thing has a fractured skull or a concussion—something bad. She's in the hospital."

Winnie focused on the receptionist's eyes, making a concerted effort to ignore the lipstick-stained tooth. "Well then, who is missing?"

"Apparently the young woman just got hired to look after a woman named Anita Lemoyne. All those people have private caregivers, cooks, maids, and all. So Anita's car is gone and Anita with it. Thing is, the security camera caught Anita's car driving away, and one of the valets said he saw her driving off. Actually, he heard her hit one of the gate posts. She tore off a side mirror."

"What kind of car was she driving?" Pell had out a pad and pen.

"It was one of those Rolls-Royce luxury automobiles. You want to take a look at the report?" The receptionist glanced toward Troy's office, suddenly uncertain. "Or maybe I should bounce it off Troy first."

"We're all on the same team, right?" Pell gave her a practiced smile. "Don't worry, I'll take full responsibility."

"Highland, as in Highland Terrace?" Winnie noted confidentially as soon as the receptionist was out of earshot.

"As in, where the stolen drugs turned up?" Pell continued.

"Could be a connection."

"Could be." Winnie nodded.

When she returned with the file, Pell opened the jacket and began to read. "Listen, you've got a smear of lipstick on your tooth," she said, and pointed.

The receptionist turned to look for something to wipe off the lipstick. In an instant, Pell had removed the contents of the file and handed it behind her, where she knew Winnie was standing. Without a word, Winnie took the pages and secreted them in her blazer. "Do you mind if Agent Winnie uses the copy machine to make copies of our receipts? Our supervisor is a real stickler for accuracy, and we always like to have a backup in case we lose one."

"Oh, sure, help yourself. You all know where everything is." She rubbed feverishly at the tooth. "You want me to put you on some coffee?"

"Not for me. How about you, Winnie?"

Agent Winnie was already in the copy room scanning in the first document. "I'm good, but thank you anyway."

"Did that get it?" The receptionist gave Pell the smile she had used to win the Miss Swamp Apple crown some forty years earlier.

"That's about it," Winnie called from the copier.

"On second thought, I could go for a cup of your coffee. Don't make a whole pot, though." Pell picked up the baton.

No sooner had the receptionist turned around than the agents exchanged the pages once again. In the same instant, Troy Shoat appeared in the doorway, smiling and swaggering; practicing, no doubt, to hit the campaign trail. He had on cowboy boots and was removing a wide-brimmed, high-crowned white Stetson that gave him an air of edginess and old-fashioned simplicity.

When he spotted the agents, his smile disappeared, leaving in its place a tight, thin line. "Where'd you get that?" Troy reached for the file.

Pell allowed him to snatch it away. "Found it on your desk. We were waiting for you in your office, but there were no magazines."

"What are you two doing here? Did you lose Cacho again?"

"Don't be mad 'cause you all got caught trying to steal a collar." Winnie took a step toward him and stuck her bottom lip out. "And then the bureau gave you a spanking...in front of the press." She mimicked wiping tears from her eyes.

"We're with the Organized Crime Unit. We've got a case down here. Consider this a courtesy visit to let you know we're in town."

"Fine. I know you girls are here." Troy did his best Dirty Harry imitation, complete with facial expressions.

"We'll set up base in our hotel. We're staying at the Residence Inn again. Don't hesitate to call if we can be of help in your kidnapping case. And I know we can count on your full cooperation for our investigation." A business card had magically appeared between Pell's second and third fingers.

"You can leave that with the receptionist on your way out." Troy turned, the sound of his boots ominous on the linoleum as he headed back to his office.

"I'm sorry about that," the receptionist said. "He was raised better. But his mama said he's been suffering with hemorrhoids. I had them after the birth of my last child, so I can tell you they're painful—can't walk, can't sit, can't..."

Winnie waited for Pell to give her signature two-fingered salute, which Winnie always followed with a curt nod.

"Take a look at page three," Winnie said as they slipped into their sedan.

Pell read the copy and nodded. "If there isn't a connection, I'd be very surprised."

"I think we should interview this witness, Charlotte Delaney. Let's see if she knows anything."

"So, what we've got so far are stolen pharmaceuticals and a missing senior. What links the two?"

"Highland Terrace." Winnie slid the seat belt across her lap.

EZ-Go Golf Cart

Chapter 8

MILO SPOTS SOME INTERESTING ACTIVITY

Monday, December 22, 2008 – 6:10 p.m.

Just before Thanksgiving, Edwin Winslow, the manager of the Stone Crab Flea Market, thought it would be a good idea to hire extra security.

"With the economy in the doldrums, we've had a number of shoplifting incidents. The holidays are coming and I suspect things are gonna get worse. I'd like to beef up security a bit, Mr. Purdie. We have Roy, but technically he was hired for maintenance. And he's only got one leg, so he has a helluva hard time catching shoplifters. In fact, the only one he ever caught actually tripped and knocked himself out, so Roy was able to tie him to the EZ-Go golf cart and drag him down to the office." Edwin sighed heavily. "Roy is fine with electrical problems. And he can fix the golf carts and rig shelving. He's a hard worker. And then we have a guy on weekends, but Jorge has been calling in sick a lot. I think he might have another gig somewhere. The point is, Mr. Purdie, I need a man I can depend on."

Milo Purdie was trying to listen, but the chair he was sitting in had a sprung spring, making it impossible to get comfortable. He found himself leaning first to one side and then the other, but quickly realized his movement resembled the actions of a man trying to deal with last night's Mexican food. Finally, he leaned forward, squared his shoulders, and tried not to appear annoyed as the metal coil goosed him for the hundredth time.

"And I was there that night last year at the Ballyhoo with my family. We were eating one of those appetizer platters, you know with the nachos, wings, and cheese sticks? I saw those guys come in and didn't think much about it till they shot that bottle of blue gin behind the bar. That got everyone's attention. I grabbed my kids, and we did a duck and cover under our table." Winslow leaned back in his leather chair; he looked very comfortable and did not seem to be aware of the disagreeableness of the seat Milo was in. "I saw you tear into those boys with nothing more than a tire iron and a bad temper. You likely saved some lives that day, Milo. And any man brave enough to take on two armed gangsters is someone I want on my team. Now, I know your company charges eight an hour, but I'm prepared to pay you an extra dollar in Stone Crab money if you'll agree."

Milo pretended to consider the proposition, even though he secretly longed to work at the Stone Crab. As a Crukinshank security guard, his services were highly sought after, but spending eight hours a day checking IDs at a gated community was no place for a man like Milo. He wondered if he would be entitled to employee discounts.

Winslow mistook Milo's silent daydream as reluctance. "Look, I'll give you two Stone Crab dollars an hour and free lunch every day." He pulled open the top drawer of his desk and produced a stack of purple cash. Holding Milo's gaze, Winslow riffled through the wad of Stone Crab dollars. "They spend anywhere on the property, just like hard cash."

Milo often thought back on that day a month earlier. His first sight of Winslow with his stringy comb-over and the wandering eye that kept Milo shifting from one leg to the other as he tried to figure out which eye exactly was looking at him. Yes indeed, Milo was thriving at the *Crab*. Since he started, Milo had been responsible for capturing three shoplifters. Winslow had already given him an official raise, another quarter an hour in genuine minted money. The possibilities were limitless, Milo thought, as he started patrolling the closed market on his last rounds of the night. He had even started toying with the idea of opening his own booth.

His stopped his golf cart at the loading dock near Perky's booth. He flipped on his penlight and found his clipboard. Milo made a note that one of the overhead light bulbs needed to be changed. He went over to the garage-style door and gave Perky's combination lock a tug. It was getting dark early, so Milo was doing two rounds a night instead of just one, since the opportunities for theft and vandalism seemed to increase in the dark. So far the job was working out well. Besides free lunch at a restaurant of his choosing, Milo was meeting all sorts of interesting people and learning all manner of trade secrets and tricks. Mr. Hassam at the Coin Trader booth showed him how to appraise vintage coins. The Lucas brothers told him how they went from working in a chop shop to owning a successful parts business that sold American car parts overseas. And William Ruckles, a retired horticulturalist, grew exotic plants and knew all there was to know about herbal remedies.

Milo looked forward to getting up in the morning and going to work. He particularly liked his perfectly pressed khaki uniform and wide-brimmed hat. The ladies blushed and smiled when he tipped the hat in their direction and used the word *ma'am*.

And each day he logged in at the Stone Crab put him further away from the sins of his past year. The summer of 2007 was one Milo would just as soon forget. Besides losing the love his life, Milo had agreed to shoot a young woman in return for ten thousand dollars in cash. At the time of the transaction, he was toasted and brokenhearted, and the idea had sounded pretty good. While that was bad enough, he felt even worse about being duped into believing the target was extorting money from an elderly man. In fact, Lilah, the young woman in question, was cute, kind, and personable once Milo got to know her. Less than a week after seeing her for the first time in his rifle crosshairs, he had fallen in love, or lust; Milo always had difficulty telling the two apart. The season finale of his summer ended with a brief romance with Lilah. What remained of the ten thousand, after the purchase of chrome rims and fog lights for his truck, was still in his bank account. His newly realized moral code forbade him from touching this blood money, although it tempted him on a daily basis.

The memory of that week was bitter and sweet all at the same time. But Milo was anxious to put as much distance as possible between the present day and that week in August 2007.

He had tried his hand at a few other jobs before getting into security work. The job at the Stone Crab enabled Milo to pay his monthly bills, put gas in his truck, and have a beer with his friends on weekends. And for the first time in his life, he was able to put a few dollars into savings every month.

As he maneuvered the EZ-Go golf cart around the dumpsters at the end of building three, Milo was reminded of the fact that, unlike Roy, his appearance seemed to be a deterrent to crime. Shoplifting was down by half, and Mr. Winslow had given him a fifty-dollar Christmas bonus to boot. He definitely had a foot on the ladder of success and was climbing higher every day.

He drove around the corner of building four and scanned the alley. He thought he heard voices and turned his vehicle in that direction. Halfway down the row, a door went up, filling the alley with light. He couldn't picture the booth, only that it was near the discount nail salon where several cute Asian girls worked. He had his eye on one who had wavy black hair and blue eyes. Milo knew the eye color came from contacts, but she looked exotic all the same.

The gravel under the golf cart's tires crunched as he crept forward. He sat up when a head popped out and looked directly at him. Still forty feet from the loading dock, he could see she was an older woman with bluish gray hair. Milo gave her a reassuring wave as he approached.

"You all need some help?"

"No, we all are just fine." The old woman's surly reply was delivered in a sharp northern accent.

Milo's first thought was to remind the vendor that there was no call for rudeness, he was just trying to be helpful, but Milo knew that right now he was the face of the Stone Crab. So instead, he said, "Well, all the loading is supposed to be done by five, so we can close up. There is a fifteen-minute grace period, but it's after six now. I won't write you all up this time, but please try to remember in the future." Milo was trying to place the woman's face, but he had no recollection of her. But there were hundreds of vendors. Between her grating accent and rudeness, Milo had already made a mental note to keep an eye on her.

Suddenly, there was another woman standing on the cement lip. She was slightly shorter. Milo tipped his hat and nodded politely, but both women just stared at him without emotion as though he were an insect. He felt their eyes on him as he drove around the corner, but would not allow himself to turn around and acknowledge them. Out of sight, he pulled out the clipboard and made a note in his shorthand—an eye with the number 408. Tomorrow he'd be back to check on booth 408 to see what kind of business went on there. Mr. Winslow was getting his money's worth.

Ten minutes later, Milo finished his rounds. He parked his EZ-Go golf cart and was closing up the shed when his cell phone began to vibrate.

"Whassup?" Milo answered his buddy's call.

"Whassup? Dude, you want to meet us for a beer?" Sheldon was getting into his car. Milo could hear the door slam and the ignition crank to life.

"Where are you?"

"Just leaving work, dude. Are you still at the Stoned Crab?" Sheldon always used the pejorative when talking about Milo's place of employment.

"Just leaving. What time and where?" Milo had his truck keys in hand and was loosening his tie. "I've got to feed Boomer first."

"How about like seven at the Ballyhoo? We can split some nachos or something."

"Sweet." Milo cranked the pickup and reached for the lights.

Headlights swung around the other side of the building, and Milo could see the two women from 408 as they passed under a streetlight on Vanderbilt Beach Road. They turned south.

"It's ladies night, Milo. Lose the uniform, dude, or I'll act like I don't know you."

"Yo, I'm thinking about getting a tat. We got a guy here who says he'll give me thirty percent off any design. I'm thinking chicks like tribal stuff."

"Dude! Seriously, forget the tribal. Get a stallion or a shark, something cool you won't mind looking at when you're old."

"How about something in Japanese, like mighty warrior or—"

"No! No, Milo. You can't have something in another language because no one but you would know what it meant. You need something that shows who you are, so you don't have to explain yourself. Let me know when you go to do it. Maybe I'll get one, too."

Milo laughed, "Yeah, maybe he has one of those marijuana leaves from the sixties."

"Asshole. I'll see you in a few."

"Roger that," Milo snorted, and closed the cell phone.

Chapter 9

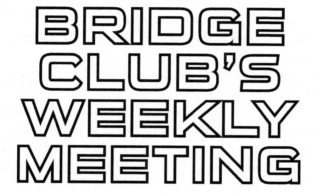

BRIDGE CLUB'S WEEKLY MEETING

Monday, December 22, 2008 – 6:40 p.m.

The smell of fresh garlic, onions, yeast, and coffee wafted into the hallway outside unit 802. There wasn't much that could be done to aroma-proof units, but contractors at Highland Terrace had gone to great lengths to soundproof each unit. Even so, Frank Sinatra's vocals could be heard by anyone passing by 802, with or without hearing aids.

Carmen waddled toward the table carrying a plate laden with antipasto and freshly baked garlic rolls. "Okay, ladies. Let's get started." This announcement was viewed by all present as the dimming of the lights at the theatre when the first act is about to begin.

Connie the Clown Columbo trailed behind Carmen. Florence Bondi, known as Flobo, was already seated, with Smiling Tess Fontana on her right.

"Yo, Muscia. Bring me another one of those rolls," Flobo barked, even as she was swallowing the last bite of her third roll. She chased it with half a glass of Chianti.

"It's like pouring bacon grease down a PVC pipe. You're barely a month from your bypass. Are you trying to have another?" Muscia was used to taking orders, but she seemed to be the only one who paid attention to Florence's health.

"Whadda you care?" Flobo sucked her teeth noisily.

"That was me holding you up when you could hardly walk to the bathroom after your surgery." Muscia wrapped the roll in a napkin and clapped it down on the table where Flobo was eating her way through a plate piled three inches deep.

"How 'bout a refill?" Flobo lifted her wineglass.

"Doctor said you need to drop at least fifty pounds. How about a glass of water?"

"Fine." Flobo rolled her eyes. She leaned toward Tess and growled in a low voice, "She's been bustin' my chops since I woke up in the recovery room."

Tess Fontana pursed her lips and eyed the woman she'd known since parochial school. "With all due respect, you're a pig. Muscia is trying to keep you alive. It would be nice if you cared about your health even half as much as she does."

"Oh, just 'cause you got a nice young piece of ass, you think you're all that." While Flobo's tone was not exactly aggressive, she was clearly getting irritated. After the birth of her son, she had somehow managed to gain between one and two pounds every year. Now in her mid-sixties, Flobo had given up on ever seeing her figure again. She just wanted to be happy, and hot garlic rolls were definitely a cause for celebration.

"Everybody ready to get started?" Carmen the Nose Bustamante pulled up to the card table next to Flobo. "Muscia! The cards?"

"Carm, this is really a good idea. You get tired of the same old routine. It's nice to get out and do something different." Connie lifted her glass and tapped Carmen's.

"What? Don't I always put out a nice spread?" Both palms turned up, Carmen gestured at the buffet on the bar.

"I'm just saying this is a treat from coffee and cold cuts every week. That's all."

"So is Delaurentis's going to start carrying these rolls?" Flobo asked, her cheeks stuffed to their limit. A piece of debris left her open mouth and landed on the side of Tess's saucer.

Tess wordlessly picked up her napkin, wiped the saucer clean, and folded the napkin over.

"Sorry, Princess." Flobo swallowed and lustily sucked her teeth.

"You two knock it off. Muscia picked up two dozen, so help yourself."

"Muscia, would you put a couple in a bag for breakfast?" The sides of Flobo's mouth were shiny with garlic butter.

"No." Muscia handed her employer a fresh deck of cards. "More decaf?" In the early days of her employment, the Dominican's accent had sounded odd in a room of Jersey natives, but they were all family now.

Tess nodded and handed her cup and saucer to the Amazon.

"Don't you want something to eat?"

"No, Muscia. Thank you for asking. I had dinner before I came over."

"So?" Flobo smiled, and cackled, clearly pleased with herself. "Yo, Muscia. I want you to know I'm grateful for your help. Don't get me wrong, but right now I'm really grateful for this spread."

"Like I said earlier." Tess leaned back and crossed her legs.

"How many cards do I deal?" Carmen looked to Muscia for the correct answer.

Muscia shrugged. "Does it matter?"

"You're right." She held the deck up to get everyone's attention.

"Deal 'em, Carm." Flobo made her bimonthly announcement, and like a judge's gavel, the Bridge Club was now in session.

The women had actually made a serious attempt to learn the card game after moving into the Highland Terrace. Before bridge, there had been pinochle, mahjong, and shuffleboard. Carmen had even tried watercolor painting. But no amount of dedication to new hobbies could deter them from practicing their natural abilities.

All four had grown up in the same neighborhood, Newark's first ward. Carmen's house was a two-story brick on Sixth Street, Connie lived around the corner on Seventh, and Florence grew up on Fifth. Tess's family home was located on Bloomfield Avenue, which ran perpendicular to the other three streets. They attended elementary through high school together, had their first communion together, and spent their first night in jail together. It was an overnight stay intended to scare the teens after they were caught with cans of orange spray paint that happened to match the color of the wet graffiti on the brick walls of the other parochial school in town. Connie had left for college after high school while the other three stayed behind, matriculating into Newark's workforce. Against a backdrop of blue-collar working families, summers at the Jersey Shore and their second-generation Italian neighborhood, the women seemed destined for the mediocrity that defined their parents. Were it not for the aspirations of the four women, they likely would still be living on the same block where their parents were born and raised.

Besides their history and friendship, the other constant that united Carmen, Florence, Connie, and Tess was a neighborhood organization. Calling themselves the Eye, a handful of local men met for the first time in the early 1900s. Their original gathering met for the sole purpose of protecting their part of the city from foreigners. But over the decades, the group turned into a small-time gang which held a certain luster for the area's young men. The women were aware that their brothers and cousins, boyfriends, and even their fathers were involved with the Eye. From armored truck hijacking to murder for hire, the collection of petty criminals evolved into a loosely structured gang headed by Carmen's late husband, Ralph.

After high school, the women began to grow apart. Florence was the first woman arrested in connection with the Eye, after she was caught behind the wheel of a station wagon used in an armed robbery days earlier. Her boyfriend, Joey, asked her to wait outside the bank while he went inside. She knew what Joey was up to when he reached into the glove compartment and pulled out a gun instead of his checkbook. But Joey was an olive-skinned Adonis with eyes like Cary Grant.

Flobo had intended to marry her partner in crime, but things hadn't worked out. Joey died a month after starting his sentence, leaving Florence behind bars and pregnant with Joey Junior.

Connie graduated from Fairleigh Dickinson with a degree in accounting and opened a storefront on the outskirts of the neighborhood. She struggled most of her career to prove herself in a world where men dominated the financial sector.

And Smiling Tess Fontana began an affair with a military-trained sharp-shooter. Her soldier was conveniently married and absent for extended periods. Even so, Tess learned to appreciate his infrequent and spontaneous visits.

Marked by their intense intimacy and gifts, Tess lost any desire to marry. After leaving the service, the young warrior taught his paramour how to shoot, clean, and care for a weapon. She surprised him with a keen interest in sharpshooting and a genuine talent. Tess fell in love for the first time on her thirtieth birthday. Her soldier took her away for the weekend on a trip to the Pine Barrens, a disquietingly dark and isolated forest in mid-state New Jersey. Alone, deep in the woods, the soldier set up a variety of targets and then presented Tess with her first rifle. She couldn't wait to try it. So she shot him. The barrel was still warm when she closed her eyes and kissed the metal.

Though they never lost touch completely, the women reconstituted their friendship again in the mid-seventies. Carmen took over her late husband's florist shop in New Brunswick. The storefront was ideal for laundering all the proceeds from her illegal activities. Naturally, she hired Connie to keep the books. After serving twelve of her fifteen-year sentence, Flobo also went to work at the flower shop, in the collection department. Between her creative arrangements and her talent for making people disappear, Tess drew a handsome salary at the shop as well. The women made a joint decision to sell the business and retire in 1997.

To mark the new century, the four had every intention of enjoying their golden years without the stress from the old business. They also hoped to walk away from the sins of their past and any possibility that one of those sins might resurface. Each knew she was too old to spend her last days behind bars. They took their cash and one by one headed south.

Carmen was the first member of the gang to move into the Highlands. She had been a widow for decades, there was nothing holding her to New Jersey. That, and the winters grew crueler with each passing year. Between her arthritis and eczema, Carmen needed a warmer climate. She had vacationed with her son in Lauderdale when Ralph Jr. was growing up. She was not at all surprised when he set up house there. Despite his protestations that she should be close to family, Carmen liked to keep the miles between them. It took just over two hours for her son to drive across Alligator Alley. Two hours was plenty of time to childproof her condo from his sticky-fingered brood.

Florence Bondi arrived in Naples the week after her final meeting with her parole officer. Flobo had never been to Florida and was anxious to go on an extended retirement vacation.

Tess bought a unit sight unseen, based on Carmen's recommendation. Without her two best friends, Tess was lost and feared becoming a casualty of retirement boredom. In 2001, Connie had reluctantly joined the others after selling her accounting business. She told her childhood friends she was keeping her house in the old neighborhood for sentimental reasons, but everyone knew Connie always needed an exit strategy just in case.

Flobo leaned forward in her chair so that her massive gut rolled onto her thighs. "So, we have an in at the flea market on Vanderbilt. It's beautiful."

"I have to admit it is pretty clever." Connie pushed a pad of yellow lined paper into the center of the table. "Distribution of the product will take a couple of months, but we're in touch with the front end in case the opportunity for another—"

"Heist," Flobo interjected.

Connie shrugged and tapped the pad. "The product is in the bags that are sold at the flea market. You want a nickel bag? You call the night before and it's in the inside compartment. You pay the cashier, and we've got a sale and clean money."

Carmen cleared her throat, slipped on her reading glasses and pulled the pad closer. "How do you know one of the pocka books won't accidentally end up being sold to the wrong person?"

"The little Chinee girl who owns the place is scared shitless. She don't touch the bags unless we give her the nod," Flobo explained.

"Don't we have at least two men in that part of the organization?"

"Carm, please. You ain't gotta worry. They get a black fanny pack. It's easy." Flobo suddenly grimaced and rested one hand on her ever-expanding stomach. "*Agida*." She belched with purpose.

"*Porcaccione*," Tess said under her breath, and fanned the air between them.

"Are we paying the Chinee?" Carmen frowned.

Flobo smiled wolfishly. "No, we're protecting the Chinee."

"Where do we stand with the project in the building?" Carmen pressed on, indicating she was satisfied with the new distribution arrangement.

Examining her fingernails, Tess did not look up. "All obstacles have been removed."

Using her index finger, Carmen read down the page, nodding. "Numbers game looks good, real good."

Connie nodded modestly. "It's all about the spread."

"Who would have thought?" Carmen finished reading and slipped off her glasses. "Numbers game took what? Maybe two weeks to set up? Now this operation is going through the roof. Who would have thought four Jersey girls could pull all this off?" Carmen picked up her mug and lifted it.

Flobo held out her wineglass and the other two women followed suit. "The Bridge Club," they said in unison.

Without any warning, the door to Carmen's unit suddenly opened.

Muscia was the first to move. Her hand flew to the waistband of her scrubs, where a pocket large enough to accommodate her revolver was sewn into the fabric. In two steps, she had moved to block Carmen from whoever was coming through the door.

Connie reached for the pad, while Flobo and Carmen lifted their plates. At the same moment, Tess yanked off the tablecloth to reveal a bridge setup with four innocent hands of cards.

"Well, hello, ladies. I thought you might be able to use some pie for your party!" Mr. Phillips, Carmen's neighbor to the left of her unit, stood in the foyer proudly displaying a store-bought pie in one hand and a carton of ice cream in the other.

Muscia stood between the man and the table. Carmen leaned wide to see around her tree-sized CNA. The Bridge Club remained silent.

"Well, what do we have here?" Mr. Phillips approached the group. "Cards? I don't care what we're playing, just deal me in."

Muscia discreetly withdrew her hand from the butt of her weapon and extended her open palm toward the old man the way a bouncer removes drunks.

"Don't hurt him," Carmen said in a low voice.

"Boy, you're a big one," Mr. Phillips observed, as Muscia bore down on him. "You can cut me a big piece. I love apple pie. My wife used to make them all the time. There's nothing better than apple pie a la mode."

"This is a private party." Muscia gently but firmly refused to accept the pie or ice cream and smoothly turned the elderly gentleman back toward the door. "Mrs. Bustamante will call you later."

"You sure?" Mr. Phillips called over his shoulder, but the words seemed to be absorbed by the sound barrier of Muscia's torso.

As the door closed, Muscia was the only one who heard the faint voice in the hall outside the door. "Well, that was a total waste of a blue pill."

"As if my stomach wasn't burning already." Flobo grabbed her gut and made a face.

Connie asked, "Are you having another heart attack?"

"No." Flobo pushed her plate away and said, "I got gas, is all."

"Muscia, just lock the freakin' door and let's get back to business." Carmen motioned for Tess to continue. "This is why I have to drink decaf?" she offered to no one in particular.

"Mrs. Anita Lemoyne of the Connecticut Lemoynes won't be at the next homeowners association meeting. I doubt anyone else will offer any resistance." Smiling Tess Fontana revealed how she came by her nickname, with a broad grin that consumed much of her face.

Chapter 10

SAUCHA - THE SECOND NIYAMA

Tuesday, December 23, 2008 – 8:25 a.m.

Sonny was sitting on the side of her sister's bed, reading an article in the latest issue of *Yoga Journal*. She had been there since visiting hours started, watching Charlotte sleep between articles. Sonny kept a loose grip on Charlotte's right fingers, more to reassure herself than her sister.

"No touching."

The sudden sound of her sister's voice caused Sonny to jump. "You scared me."

"You scared me," Charlotte mimicked in her quirky robotic voice, the one she used when she was nervous.

"How do you feel?" Sonny rearranged herself to better see the patient.

"I feel hungry."

"I thought you might be. I brought you your favorite, a chicken biscuit."

Charlotte yawned. She reached for her remote and winced as her head came up.

"Still a lot of pain?"

Charlotte nodded. "Move," she said.

"You don't have to throw up, do you?" Throwing up made Sonny very uneasy. It hadn't been that long ago that she worked as a Certified Nursing Assistant (CNA). Back then, she was constantly cleaning up bodily fluids and performing menial tasks that involved human waste. Most caregivers adjusted to the odors and lack of modesty, but Sonny had gotten worse. She suffered from an exquisitely fine-tuned gag reflex. Even as a child, she had not been able to go on class outings to petting zoos with her classmates. The odors produced by a typical barnyard set her vomiting seconds after getting off the bus. There were even days when the smell of the school cafeteria's lunch triggered her gag reflex and she had to eat alone on the playground.

"No, I'm not going to throw up. I want to brush my teeth." Charlotte swung her feet over the side of the bed and let them dangle.

"Listen, why don't you just sit right here and I'll get you the stuff from the bathroom?"

The younger Delaney agreed, and waited patiently until Sonny returned with her toiletries and assisted with her morning ablutions.

When Charlotte at last unwrapped her chicken biscuit, it was with great care. She smoothed the foil flat and stared down pensively. "Have they found Anita?"

"No, Char. I'm really sorry."

"She was my friend."

"I know. I know you liked her."

"Have you heard how much longer I have to stay here?"

"No. I imagine a doctor or someone will come by today. They have to do their rounds at some point. I do know there is a note on your chart to call Mom and Dad. They'll make sure you have a ride home. Hopefully you'll be home for Christmas."

"I'm going to lose my clients." Charlotte sighed loudly.

"People will understand. You've got a cracked skull. You can't work for a while."

Charlotte picked up a crumb and sampled the biscuit. "They won't wait for me even if they want to. You know they'll call someone else to drive them or buy groceries. I'll have to start all over when I get out of here."

Sonny closed her eyes and hung her head as if defeat was imminent. "I'm going to hate myself for asking. Where is your schedule book?"

"Well, it was in my back pocket with my wallet." Charlotte considered for a second. "And I had some Kleenex in that pocket, too."

Sonny went to the dresser on her sister's side of the room and opened both drawers. They were empty. In the closet above, she found the missing clothes neatly hanging, along with the penny loafers Charlotte had worn the day before.

A year earlier, Charlotte and Sonny had worked together caring for one of Naples's wealthiest men. The job had lasted over four years until the gentleman sailed off into his last sunset. During that time, professionalism dictated they wear scrubs and white tennis shoes every day. But now that Charlotte was on her own, she rarely wore scrubs, preferring instead khaki pants and colorful Hawaiian shirts. She insisted they were her trademark, setting her apart from the average caregiver.

"Got it." Sonny held the slim book up.

"Bring my Kleenex, too."

Sonny rolled her eyes but complied. The wad was unused and folded but frayed and turning to lint. Charlotte had clearly been packing the Kleenex for a while. Sonny handed over the wad, saying, "Classy."

"It's my lucky Kleenex."

"I'll probably regret asking, but why is this Kleenex lucky?"

"I got it from Anita's bathroom."

Sonny nodded empathetically as though she understood her sister's logic, and then turned her attention to the pocket calendar, where she hoped things made more sense.

Sonny flipped to the month of December and saw that there were only five names on the schedule for the rest of the week. Three of the appointments were before Christmas. The other two were on the twenty-sixth.

"This isn't too bad. Assuming that you won't be in much longer, do you want me to fill in for you the rest of the week?"

Charlotte patted the crown of her sister's head, a gesture she reserved for special occasions. "Yes. Yes, I would."

"Do you have to do that?" Sonny ducked, hoping to make Charlotte stop, but the hand remained.

"Yes. Your head feels like a coconut. It's one of the things I like about you."

Sonny acquiesced, allowing her sister to leave her hand in place while she read the schedule. "You have Mrs. Sheridan down today at two o'clock?"

"Yes. She has an appointment at the Retina Center. It's her semi-annual appointment, so she really has to be there."

"I hate that place. They make you just sit there and wait for hours."

Charlotte nodded. "Yes, but you get paid twenty-five an hour to sit and wait."

"Good point. What about Mr. Phillips on Christmas Eve at ten?"

"He just needs a haircut. It's that place at the corner of the Trail and First Avenue, the one with the red and white sign. It usually takes about an hour. Sometimes he likes to get an ice cream afterward. Mint chocolate chip."

"One scoop or two?"

Charlotte cocked her head. "You're trying to be funny, aren't you?"

"I am funny," Sonny retorted.

"I'm not laughing," Charlotte replied innocently.

"Deep, cleansing breath." Sonny closed her eyes and breathed like a professional.

A man in white scrubs and clear latex gloves entered the room carrying a pair of trays.

"Sorry, ladies. We're running a little behind this morning. Mrs. Kirchner?"

The elderly woman in the bed by the door lifted her hand and croaked, "That would be me."

He set the tray on her bedside table. "So you must Charlotte," the nurse said. He smiled benevolently and placed her tray on the table, ignoring the half-eaten biscuit in Charlotte's lap.

Sonny lifted up the plastic lid covering the plate, grimaced, and shuddered violently.

"You're not going to throw up, are you?" Charlotte asked, clearly amused with herself.

Slamming the lid back down, Sonny snapped, "Not as long as I don't have to eat here. Listen, I got you hash browns in there and a coffee with extra cream. Mom and Dad said they'd be by later. Here, let me help you with that." Sonny reached for the coffee, which was dribbling on the sheet while Charlotte struggled to get the lid open.

"No, I can do it."

"I could use some help," Mrs. Kirchner noted weakly. Her voice was thick with phlegm and she struggled to breathe.

"I'll be right here if you need me." Sonny put the bag of takeout in her sister's lap and went to minister to Mrs. Kirchner.

"Thank you, dear," the old woman said appreciatively, when Sonny finished raising the head of her bed.

"No problem. Let's get the tray closer so you can reach it." Sonny pulled the tray under Mrs. Kirchner's chin, unwrapped her silverware, and collected the plastic lid off the entrée and put it near the sink. Holding her breath, Sonny said, "Let's see, eggs and toast. Coffee, and I think these are tubes of jam. Mmm, looks good," Sonny lied, and made a hasty retreat back to the sink.

These days, Sonny worked as a yoga teacher, but she never minded using her skill as a nursing assistant when the occasion arose.

"Do you need help eating?"

"No, doll. But would you mind getting me my teeth? They're over on the sink. And bring me a cup with tap water so I can rinse them, please."

Sonny was also a germaphobe, one of many issues in the obsessive-compulsive category. She swallowed, exhaled and relaxed slightly. The knowledge that there was a sink nearby with an endless supply of antibacterial soap calmed her until she spotted the box of latex gloves. The feel of protection on each finger gave Sonny the mettle she needed to complete the mission. She slipped on a pair and smiled, clearly pleased with herself.

Mrs. Kirchner's teeth were in the bottom of a plastic cup containing a cleaning solution that was foggy with debris. Sonny retrieved the teeth, and with the use of controlled breathing, gracefully set the plastic cups on Mrs. Kirchner's tray with a smile.

"Thank you, honey." A painfully thin arm reached for the dentures but collided with the container, knocking it over.

Sonny watched in horror as the unthinkable happened. The murky water rose up in slow motion before raining down on her shorts and bare legs. Sonny stood as though skewered to the floor, unable to move, even to breathe. She grew lightheaded as the liquid slithered down her legs into her socks. As Sonny's chicken biscuit grew restless in her stomach and teased her diaphragm, she longed for a stunt double.

The dentures came to rest on Mrs. Kirchner's tray. "No harm, no foul," the older woman said, and expertly dipped her teeth in the fresh water before popping them into her mouth. She snapped a few times to make certain they were secure before tackling her runny eggs.

"No good deed goes unpunished," Charlotte quoted their father's favorite expression. "You can probably ask the nurse for a clean gown."

Wordlessly, Sonny went to the bathroom and commenced a cleaning ritual that lasted nearly ten minutes.

Pell was the first one in the room. She looked at the old woman in the nearest bed and scowled. "Charlotte Delaney?"

Mrs. Kirchner shook her head and jerked her thumb in Charlotte's direction.

"Charlotte Delaney?" Pell was looking at Charlotte now and could see that her head was bandaged from the assault. "Can we talk?" Both agents reached for the badges like gunslingers go for their six-shooters. With practiced skill, the badges were revealed and quickly disappeared back into their leather carrying cases.

"Yes, you can talk." Charlotte was sincere.

Hearing different voices, Sonny finally gave up on complete sterilization and came out of the bathroom. She found two women in blazers and khaki pants standing by her sister's bed.

Winnie felt someone before she actually saw Sonny. Her head snapped around, eyes locked on the other Delaney. She had her badge out again. "I'm Agent Winnie. This is Agent Pell. We're with the Florida Bureau of Investigation." Although neither asked, it was clear that the two agents expected some sort of introduction from Sonny.

"I'm Sonny, Charlotte's sister. She already talked to the police yesterday."

"Yes, we have their report. We'd just like to ask you a few more questions." Pell was talking to Charlotte, her back to Sonny. "Would that be okay?"

"What kind of questions?" Sonny frowned.

"Unless you were there, we'd like to talk to your sister."

"You don't think she had anything to do with the kidnapping?" Sonny felt herself drawn into the role of defender.

"Who said anything about a kidnapping?" Pell slipped off her sunglasses and aimed her blue eyes at Sonny.

"Look, I don't want to fight with you. My intention is to protect my sister. That's all."

"I think Charlotte here can answer for herself. Why don't you step outside, and we'll come get you when we're finished," Pell said, and gestured to Winnie to escort Sonny out. Winnie was devoid of expression when she took Sonny's elbow and urged her forward.

"Don't you hurt her, she's a nice girl." Mrs. Kirchner was stronger with a little food in her. "I'll call security…"

Sonny lifted her free hand and patted the older woman's feet through the blanket. "It's okay."

Winnie let go and watched to make certain Sonny was outside before she closed the door. Pell had already drawn the curtain that separated the beds.

Sonny didn't even make an effort to listen in on the conversation. She pulled out her cell phone and pushed number one on her speed dial.

"Hey." Tricia caught it on the first ring.

"Hey."

"How's Char?"

"Well, she's fine, but two special agents just went in to interview her."

"Shouldn't you be in there?" Tricia asked.

"I would be, except one of them escorted me out when I tried to tell them that Charlotte is in no way involved in this."

"So they don't know about her condition?"

"Conditions plural. Actually they're syndromes, if you want to get technical. Tourette's and Asperger's fall under the category of syndromes," Sonny explained.

"They'd probably think you were making it up. I'd love to have a hidden camera in there."

"Tricia, I just pray she doesn't blurt out something and get herself arrested."

"Honey, you should be more worried about the guys than your sister. Char can take care of herself."

"Women. They're women."

"You're not supposed to be using a cell phone in here," a no-nonsense nurse said as she rolled by with a pill cart. "It interferes with the electronic equipment."

Sonny turned her back to the nurse. "Listen, before I hang up, will you please find a sub for my classes the rest of the week? I'm going to help Charlotte out. I'll call you when I leave."

"Okay, honey, I'll see what I can do and we'll talk shortly."

Sonny had given up wearing a watch when she became involved in yoga and aware of the movement of energy in the body, so she couldn't be sure how many minutes passed before the door opened. Pell's head popped out.

She and Sonny eyed one another, each conducting her own inventory of the other woman. "C'mon," Pell said, jerking her head.

Sonny found the shorter agent sitting in the leatherette chair under the window, a faraway look in her eyes.

"Is she crying?" Sonny asked Pell.

"No, I'm not crying," Winnie snapped, and looked away.

"What did you say to her?" Sonny pressed her sister for an explanation.

"I just told her——," Charlotte began.

"Nothing. She said nothing," Winnie interrupted, then stood and turned to the window.

"Why didn't you tell us about your sister? You could have saved us some time." Pell had her sunglasses on again and was rolling a piece of chewing gum from one side of her mouth to the other.

"I tried. You didn't give me a chance."

"Let's start over," Pell offered by way of apology. "I'm Agent Pell." A business card appeared as if by magic.

"And that's Agent Whiny," Charlotte said demurely.

Pell jabbed her index finger at her partner as Winnie gripped the armrests of her chair and prepared to launch herself at Charlotte. "Do you need to go wait outside?"

Winnie exhaled and sank back down. Pell extended the business card between her index and third fingers, "Keep this handy just in case you think of something helpful." Turning to her partner, she said, "Agent Winnie, are you sufficiently recovered to join the conversation?"

Winnie waved a hand, indicating they should carry on without her. She placed both hands on the windowsill and pressed her forehead to the glass, where water was condensing from the flow of cool air from the vent below.

"All right. Char was diagnosed around age three with a hybrid case of Tourette's and Asperger's syndromes. She just says whatever is on her mind. She has no filters. She is what they call high-functioning, she can drive, hold a job. Actually, she's a certified genius, so she can pretty much do anything she wants, unless it involves people and social skills. She has very little impulse control. The only other relevant fact is she is incapable of lying."

"But I try," Charlotte inserted.

"She tries, but she just can't," Sonny echoed. "And she hates human contact, especially with strangers. You didn't try to shake her hand, did you?"

Pell shook her head. "We don't think she had anything to do with the kidnapping. But we need to know if she remembers anything. There is an eighty-year-old woman out there who needs our help. Can you translate or get her to talk?"

Sonny went to her sister's bedside. Charlotte reached over and deftly swung the side rail into place. "Don't worry, I'm not going to touch you. I just want you to tell me one more time what exactly you remember about yesterday."

"Anita told me to leave the car running while I went up to her condo. She wanted a coupon. She cut it out of the newspaper but forgot to pick it up when we were leaving. She was going to take me to lunch. Have they found her yet?"

Pell rested her hands on the foot rail at the end of Charlotte's bed, and watched as the patient drew her feet up and away until her knees were tucked into her chest. "I don't know you, Charlotte, but I know she's counting on you to speak for her right now. You were one of the last people to see her yesterday."

"I heard her blazer, and then the lights went out," Charlotte said stoically, before taking the last bite of her biscuit.

"What do you mean, you heard her blazer? I don't understand."

"Seven, eight, nine...," Charlotte began to count.

"She's counting," Sonny explained. "She has to chew each bite thirty-six times—thirty-five times for good digestion and one more for luck."

Pell deflated a little, then shrugged her shoulders the way a boxer does before entering the ring.

"Thirty-five, thirty-six. The buttons clicked. I know how the buttons sounded when they touched. They clicked. I heard the buttons click."

Pell nodded. "And then the lights went out."

"Yes." Charlotte reached for her coffee.

"Charlotte, is there any way that Anita could have gotten out of her car, come to the elevator, and hit you with something?"

Charlotte cocked her head and blinked. "Her crutches were in the trunk. She sprained her ankle Saturday and has to use crutches. She sprained her ankle Saturday. She sprained her ankle. Uh-oh ..." Her voice trailed off.

Everyone followed Charlotte's gaze to the TV screen on the wall opposite her bed.

"This just in. Police are on the scene of a car being pulled from the canal along I-seventy-five. It is believed to be the vehicle of Anita Lemoyne, who you may recall was reported missing just yesterday. Police officials say a body was pulled from the car, but they are withholding the name pending family notification. Folks, you are seeing this live."

The tail end of a gray Rolls-Royce was slowly making its way up the bank of the canal, pulled along by the winch line of a wrecker. A body encased in a black bag was being carried to a waiting emergency vehicle.

"Police also say they have divers searching the area. Apparently they are looking for clues in the disappearance of Mrs. Lemoyne. They did add that the search is slow going because this part of the canal is infested with alligators and snakes. Stay tuned for more on this breaking story."

The newscaster was supplanted by a young mother proudly sniffing a pair of socks, presumably an advertisement for laundry detergent.

Chapter 11

STONE CRAB'S NEWEST VENDORS

Tuesday, December 23, 2008 – 9:00 a.m.

"Come on in, Milo." Edwin Winslow was sitting on the edge of his desk. "Meet Mr. and Mrs. Delaney."

"Cole and Elizabeth," Cole noted as he accepted Milo's handshake.

"I was just explaining that we're open longer this time of year. Usually we're just open on the weekends, but folks are watching their pennies and we here at the Stone Crab Flea Market are experts in helping our customers save money.

And we're doing our part to help folks stretch their dollars during the holidays by expanding our hours."

Edwin turned his face in Milo's general direction, but Milo couldn't be certain if Winslow's wandering eye was looking at him, or Cole, or both of them simultaneously, though they were standing at least six feet apart.

"They're opening a storefront on the A wing." Edwin preferred the term *storefront* to *booth*, thinking it added an element of class to the enterprise. "I wanted you to show them around, give them the lay of the land, so to speak. And lend a hand if they need anything setting up. You can call Roy if you need the forklift or whatever." Edwin ran his left palm over his hair, making sure the few precious locks of his comb-over were in place before he offered his right hand to Mr. and Mrs. Delaney.

"Well, thank you, Mr. Winslow, but I was just going to back my truck up to the loading dock and unload directly from the bed."

"What about shelving? We have some nice bamboo shelves the martial arts store left behind, and acrylic. And if I'm not mistaken, there are a couple of display racks in storage."

Cole was politely backing out of the office. "I think we've got everything we need, but thank you. Let's get going, Lizbeth."

"Well, at least take Milo," Edwin Winslow called as the Delaneys left the yurt that doubled as an office. The structure had been left behind by the previous owners, a group of environmentalists who lost their lease on the acreage. In an effort to recoup some of the losses, the property owners wasted no time erecting a mall-sized indoor-outdoor flea market on the land.

Milo trailed after the couple for a few feet. "I'll just follow you down in my EZ-Go."

"That sounds like a laxative," Elizabeth noted.

"It's actually an earth-friendly vehicle. The truth is, it's an electric golf cart. We all call 'em EZ-Gos. There is a solar panel on top of the maintenance shed that charges up all the carts on the premises." Milo stood a little straighter when he said the last word. It felt good to use big words. Then he frowned and stroked his mustache, wondering if he had used it correctly.

"Would you mind going first and we'll follow you?" Cole gestured to a well-used Ford F-150. "That's me."

Milo pointed to his dog-eared golf cart and said, "That's me." He liked the man already. Anyone who drove a Ford F-150 was his kind of people.

They pulled up to the dock outside number 411. Milo removed the Universal lock and lifted the overhead door. "Do you all have a lock?"

"Yeah, Edwin suggested we bring two, for the front and back." Cole came up beside him and hoisted his jeans up his wiry torso.

Milo skillfully tossed the lock into the front seat of the EZ-Go and hoped no one else saw it hit the seat and bounce out the other side. "Can I help y'all unload?"

Cole sauntered into the unit and stood with his hands on his hips. "I think I can handle this, Lizbeth. If you want to look around, go ahead. I'll probably be here a while putting up shelves."

"Let me get you a map, Mrs. Delaney." Milo retrieved a layout of the marketplace and handed her one corner. "This is a nice jewelry shop. They make the beads themselves out of special clay. And Weiner Max has excellent hot dogs and sausages if you like that kind of thing. But my all-time favorite is the produce stand outside this wing. They make fresh smoothies to order."

"What about kitchen things, like placemats and such?" Elizabeth Delaney's eyebrows peaked with excitement.

Milo jabbed a finger, stating, "Right here. And if you like perfume, you can buy just about any imitation here in seventy-four. There isn't much we don't have here at the Crab."

"Take your time, Cole. I might be a while." Elizabeth folded the map in quarters and tucked it into her purse. "Call if you need anything. I'll have my cell on." Elizabeth practically tingled with anticipation as she stood outside 411 and looked up and down the row of storefronts. Goods overflowed their stalls, spilling into the aisles, hanging from hooks, anything to get the shoppers' attention. She turned right and drew in a breath at the sight of hundreds of purses, flip-flops, wallets, and scarves.

"Milo, would you mind if I called you back after a while to help me unload a couple of boxes? I'd like to put these shelves up before I get all the inventory in here."

"Call me on my cell and I'll be right over." Milo reached into his breast pocket and drew out a business card he had printed in Mr. Wang's shop the week before. He had selected a print-ready muscle-bound man for his logo. Mr. Wang had given him a deal, but Milo later discovered a typo in his last name. The card read: *Milo Pudie Security Guard, #404-8249.* After Perky had asked him whether he pronounced his name Poodie or Puddy, Milo had corrected all five hundred cards with a felt-tip marker, and Mr. Wang had given him a full refund.

Cole looked at the card briefly and then tucked it into his pocket, "Will do. Shouldn't take me more than an hour to put these up. I brought my electric screwdriver."

"What do you sell?" Milo noticed a huge boxed labeled *Snakes*.

"I'm an amateur taxidermist. Those boxes"—Cole patted the top carton proudly—"contain just about every native species in the state along with some non-natives. Got a lot of connections in the hunting and fishing business, so my friends are always leaving me animals they find. You know, roadkill and such. I usually sell them on eBay, but I'm getting to the point that they come in faster than I'm moving them, so I thought, what the heck? I'll see if they move faster when people can see them in person."

Milo nodded pleasantly, although he thought the whole thing was a little creepy. "I'll just make my rounds, then, and wait for your call."

He discreetly tossed the heavy metal lock into the passenger floorboard before leaving his cart. For a change of pace, Milo started his daily rounds at the far end of the B wing.

The Stone Crab was laid out with one central aisle, D, that was intersected by three smaller aisles, A through C. The outside of the building was connected by a series of loading docks suitable for pickup and delivery trucks. Each wing had one hundred storefronts, fifty on either side. At the end of each wing there was a food court where restaurateurs from every corner of the globe cooked their native cuisines. Milo ate Tandoori chicken one day and Swedish meatballs the next. He considered this perk one more reason to love the Crab.

"Hey, Milo." A man he didn't know smiled and waved in Milo's direction. He smiled and nodded back, enjoying his celebrity status as much as his professional courtesy.

"Milo, you want to try some plantains? Hot and fresh." Rosita, a sophomore on Christmas break from the University of Miami, was working in her family's restaurant over the holiday. Milo had every intention of asking her out... someday.

As he reached for the paper plate, Milo felt himself blush. "Thank you, Rosita."

"Taste." She flirted with him, brushing his fingertips with hers as she handed him the paper plate.

"*Delicioso.*"

The sound of his shiny black shoes on the concrete walkway was muffled by the din of shoppers and the overhead sound system. A Jamaican steel drum band played "Jingle Bells." The tune provided the perfect ambiance for the shoppers, putting them in a party mood. Perky suddenly stepped out of the doorway where she had been standing and grabbed Milo for a quick dance. He did a few salsa steps with her and continued down the aisle with a tip of his hat. "You're getting good, Milo," she said, then waved and returned to her lingerie.

With the perfect job, the only thing missing from Milo's life was the love of a good woman. He considered turning around and asking Rosita out, but he didn't have the nerve. And too, there was a part of him that longed for something more than a two-week romance where the girl always left him behind for bigger things. Even the cute Asians in the nail store had ambitions of opening their own storefronts. Of course, it wouldn't hurt to get laid either, he thought. There had been a few one-nighters since Lilah. Girls from the bar, and the one he'd met on spring break at the beach—she'd given him crabs before returning to Michigan State University. Milo reckoned he'd have to go through a few more before he found the woman he would bring home to meet his mother.

He walked into 411 to check in with the new vendors. Elizabeth was back from her shopping foray and now she and Cole were busy installing shelves. Milo noticed the way Elizabeth regarded her husband. If the expression she wore on her face was what love looked like, Milo knew it would be worth the wait.

"How's it coming in here, Mr. Delaney?"

Cole looked up and used his forearm to wipe his brow. "It's coming. And it's Cole."

"All right, Cole." Milo nodded.

"Give me another hour and I'll be ready for a little help."

Milo continued on his rounds, recalling that he still had to pay a visit to 408 to remind the vendor about the Crab's policy regarding after-hours loading. He crossed the aisle before he reached the booth in order to get a feel for the place before he went in. His father, Gus, had taught him about recon. Gus fought in the jungles of Vietnam and prided himself on learning as much about the target as possible before deciding what action to take.

Had it not been for their surly behavior the night before, Milo would have had no reason to pay any attention to the storefront or its vendors. But they had left a bad taste in his mouth, and now it was his duty to conduct a little recon.

Handbags hung from hooks in the ceiling and were stacked high on shelves that divided the space into rows. There also appeared to be men's wallets and racks of colorful scarves. Milo took a notebook from his back pocket and jotted all this down, along with his first impression: *Nothing suspicious.*

Phase two of his plan involved browsing, so he crossed the main aisle and stepped inside. He smelled incense and turned to find the proprietor watching him from behind a fragrant stick. The woman was Asian, and timid, unlike most of the vendors at the Crab. She wore a turquoise silk jacket. Her lush black hair was drawn up in a tortoiseshell comb. She smiled.

"I'm just doing a little Christmas shopping. I'll holler if I have any questions," Milo noted peremptorily.

As he made his way to the far side of the unit, Milo paid close attention to every detail that came into his line of sight. And nothing appeared amiss. The merchandise was typical, leatherette knockoffs made in China for pennies on the dollar. And there was no shortage of goods. The store was completely stocked with new inventory. Milo moved out of the way when two women entered. He continued browsing, working his way toward the cash register. A large white bag caught his attention and he liberated it from the shelf. His mother would like something like this, Milo thought, examining the oversized purse more closely.

"You work here?"

Milo wasn't sure whether she was asking or stating a fact. "Uh, yes, I work here."

"Then you get an employee discount. You get ten percent off everything."

The vendor's accent was strong, revealing beyond a doubt that she was not from the states. Despite this, her English was surprisingly good, and she took her time pronouncing each word. Milo was playing close attention to her lips as she spoke. He estimated the woman was closer to thirty than he was.

"Well, thank you." Milo carried the bag and rested it on the counter before extending his hand. "Milo Purdie, security specialist."

"Grace Kwan." She reached over the glass case. "Good to meet you, Mr. Purdie." The woman was extremely polite, her hand gentle and light in his grip.

"Oh, call me Milo. Did you all get everything unloaded last night?"

The proprietor looked away. "Everything is good."

"You know, if you have a shipment that is coming after hours, just let Mr. Winslow know. We'll make arrangements for your people to get in and out. There is no sense in getting fined if you know you've got a load coming late."

Grace proceeded to interlace her fingers and bow her head. "I am very sorry. It will not happen again."

"Grace, you'd tell me if you needed help," Milo said in his most reassuring voice.

The woman nodded, but still did not allow her eyes to look at Milo. She rang up the purchase and started to put it in a plastic bag.

"That's okay, I don't need a bag. I'm trying to go green."

Grace tried to smile, but only managed an unconvincing grin. "Happy holidays, Mr. Milo."

"Okay, I'm going to finish making my rounds. I'll try to stop by later."

"Not necessary, but thank you." Grace bent down out of sight, suddenly interested in the arrangement of Buddha figurines in the glass case below the register.

Milo's walkie-talkie squawked. "Milo, there is a spill on A, and I can't raise Roy. Would you mind mopping it up?"

"I'm on my way," Milo replied, and turned on his heel. Looking back, he caught the frightened woman watching him as she lifted her cell phone to her ear.

As Milo passed 411, he noticed Cole was wearing a look of concern. His wife was standing nearby, wearing an equally grave expression as she spoke on her cell phone.

"They're pulling Anita's car out of the canal off Seventy-five. They have a body, too." Elizabeth's hand covered the cell phone and she closed her eyes. After a moment, the petite woman listened again and then continued with her report. "Sonny just left Charlotte's room. She said they gave Char something to calm her down and she fell asleep. Some agents came by to question her. According to Sonny, they tried to give Char a hard time and she reduced one of them to tears."

Cole shifted his weight and stretched. "I'm not surprised. That girl could make Mother Teresa lose her patience."

"Everything all right?" Milo asked, when they both noticed him standing just outside the doorway.

Elizabeth held up a perfectly manicured index finger; the nail sported a fresh coat of dynamite-red nail polish, no doubt from Nailed, the Vietnamese nail salon two doors down.

"We'll talk to you later." Elizabeth folded the cell phone closed. She angled herself so Milo could hear. "The woman who was reported missing yesterday was found about an hour ago. They haven't made it official, but who else would be in that car? Damn shame," Elizabeth noted solemnly, before turning her eyes up to meet Milo's. "One of my daughters worked for her. She's a little traumatized."

Milo nodded sadly. He didn't know Anita Lemoyne, but he felt a sadness for the woman's family. They would never have another normal Christmas after this.

"Nice purse, Milo. But I think khaki would go better with your outfit."

Milo snapped out of it and realized he was carrying his mother's gift. He blushed before he laughed. "It's for my mom."

The Delaneys were good people and getting better by the minute, he thought, as he dropped the bag in the passenger seat of his EZ-Go. Ordinarily he would have lingered to hear the whole story, but that spill would be all over the place if people started walking through it. He pressed the metal pedal all the way to the floorboard, pushing the cart to its top speed of fifteen miles per hour.

Chapter 12

OUR LADY OF PERPETUAL PRAYER

Tuesday, December 23, 2008 – 9:22 a.m.

Carmen the Nose Bustamante sat midway down the main aisle toward the end of the pew. She toed the kneeling bench, but knew better than to attempt to get down on it. Not only did she lack the physical strength to get herself back up, Carmen wasn't there to repent, contemplate her sins, or even pray. She wished she had taken the blanket Muscia had offered her when they came in. The church was always cold, even in the summer. Even the one in her old neighborhood was always chilly. Cold, she thought, like the roughhewn gray stones the old church was built with, and the sterile priests and nuns who ran the Catholic school she attended. Carmen had come by her nickname in that church. There to celebrate her confirmation, young Valentino Petrillo stepped in front of her, cutting in line to be near his friends. This had not set well with Carmen, who stepped on the back of his loafer, causing Valentino to trip. He recovered nicely and said, "Sorry, fellas. I tripped over Carmen's nose. Don't get too close to her, she could put your eye out with the schnozzle of hers." Her nose was in fact a most glaring feature, not surprising when viewed alongside her father, who had an even larger version. And so it stuck. Since the age of eight, Carmen Bustamante was known to one and all, friend and foe, as the Nose. In 1985, Val Petrillo left for work one morning at his father's salvage yard, but never showed up. As Carmen remembered the day, she interlaced her short, thick fingers over her belly and grinned with bitter satisfaction.

She heard a click off to her left and could not stop her first thought; someone had just racked a bullet into the chamber. But she was in Our Lady of Perpetual Prayer, so the sound was more likely caused by a door latch. She turned as far as her arthritic neck allowed and spied Smiling Tess Fontana fingering her rosary as she left the confessional.

Tess had also gotten her nickname in parochial school, when her front teeth were pushed forward to make room for her wisdom teeth. The scrappy child had toughened through all the teasing of classmates until the day she chucked a desk at one tormentor. The bully, caught by surprise, found himself on the floor, as Tess landed like a flying monkey on his chest. The entire time she pummeled him into unconsciousness, the little girl wore a smile of sheer pleasure. By the time she graduated from high school, Tess had a prominent overbite exaggerated by abnormally large front teeth. But unlike Carmen the Nose, no one dared speak the name of Smiling Tess louder than a whisper.

"You tell him?" Carmen asked, referring to Father Michael.

"Yeah. I couldn't help myself. I said, 'Father, forgive me. I just whacked this old broad and dumped her body in the canal off Seventy-five.'"

Carmen remained unruffled. "Seriously."

"Seriously, Carmen. I told him the old bitty wouldn't cooperate, so I had no choice."

"What did he say?" Carmen's thick lips were the only thing that moved. Her small pig eyes stared straight ahead, reminiscent of a coldblooded creature wired for basic survival.

"He said to say two thousand Hail Marys...whadda ya think?"

Tess's North Jersey accent could cut through timber, Carmen thought.

Tess shook her head wearily. She was enjoying this. "I told him I been boinkin' Hector. It's the truth."

"What about..." Carmen lifted her shoulders in a slight shrug, a gesture which was rich with unspoken meaning. "She say anything?"

Tess snorted. "The usual. Please, don't. Please, don't. I got grandkids. You know. So I says to her, *Listen, Lemoyne, this can go easy or it can get ugly...you choose.* Of course that shuts her up." Tess told the story with animated hands. From a distance she might have been sharing a recipe for meatloaf with her oldest friend. "I give her the juice. Bah-bing! She's gone." Tess had no difficulty lying. So far as she was concerned, the event happened like she said. Hector would never be able to work up enough brass to rat her out to Carmen. At the end of the day, no one would be the wiser.

"Where did you take her?" Carmen quizzed, looking straight ahead at the candlesticks on the communion table.

"Just past the toll booth. Hector found it. Fence was already down there, so we just pushed the car in. A couple of bubbles and she was gone."

"You know they got cameras at those things, the toll booths. How do you think they catch toll runners?"

"Carm, whadda ya think, I'm stupid? How long I been doin' this? C'mon, a little credit here. I wore a friggin' disguise. Besides, who is gonna care if a ninety-year-old falls asleep at the wheel and runs off the road? It's an accident. People drive into the canal all the time. If we're lucky, the alligators will get to her before the cops know she's missing. Please, you do your job, I'll do mine."

The two women were silent, reflecting. It was Tess who ultimately broke the reverie. Turning to her childhood friend, she planted a hand firmly on top of Carmen's. Carmen's thin-lipped, reptilian mouth curved into a grim smile. "Have you read this month's *Reader's Digest?* There is a very interesting article on how to get rid of varicose veins."

"Why, no," Tess winked, and took the large-print edition of the magazine from her friend. It bulged where the envelope of cash was secreted. "I'll be sure and return it when I'm done."

"See you this afternoon?" Using her cane, Carmen pushed herself up.

"If I can get through all of these." Tess held up her rosary beads, but made no move to follow Carmen.

"Aha." Carmen cleared her throat, and with painstakingly slow steps made her way to the end of the pew and hobbled down the aisle to where Muscia was waiting. "Let's get going. I feel like a salami and provolone. I'm treating today."

"Wait here. I'll go get the car," Muscia said in a baritone that was reminiscent of James Earl Jones's character in *Star Wars.*

She pulled the Caddy into the portico. Carmen did not move until Muscia started toward her. Winded and uncomfortable from the effort, she leaned on her cane and reached for Muscia with her free hand.

"You are too fat," Muscia noted as the older woman latched onto her muscular forearm. "Dr. Fish said you need to lose a few pounds."

"Screw Dr. Fish, and screw you, too," Carmen rasped as she ducked into the backseat.

"And when was the last time you had a b.m.?" Muscia pressed.

Carmen chuckled. "You know you're the only one I let talk to me like that."

"Yes, I know." Muscia was surprisingly gentle as she fastened the seat belt across Carmen's lap. "It wouldn't kill you to give up one martini a night."

"Remind me again why I hired you?"

"Watch your knee," Muscia said, and closed the door. When she sank into the driver's seat, the car seemed to list slightly in order to accommodate the large woman. "Because I am the only one who can stand you."

"But the thought of having just one martini," the older woman shuddered. "Let's face it, Muscia, if the alcohol don't get me, the pasta will."

"You don't have to give it up, just eat less."

Carmen stared at the back of Muscia's thick neck. The CNA wore her hair short, and from the rear, she looked like a linebacker.

"What do you know?" Carmen was defiant. "I'm not the only one who could stand to eat less."

"I burn it off in the gym." Muscia looked over the top of her sunglasses in the rearview mirror. "You could try swimming."

"Just drive already." Carmen folded her hands atop her ample belly. "Is that my phone again?"

"You want me to answer it?"

"No, Muscia, I want you to do the hokey pokey."

"We definitely need to get you some prune juice."

"Would you just answer the freakin' phone?"

"Hello?" She guided the Caddy into a 7-Eleven and put it in park. "May I tell her who is calling?" Muscia put her hand over the receiver. "It's Hector."

"Tess's Hector?"

Muscia nodded slowly and deliberately.

Carmen frowned but reached for the phone. "Yes?"

"I'd like to speak with you."

"Hector, you are speaking with me." Carmen's fleshy lips turned into a pout.

70

"Face-to-face."

"What is this about?" The old Sicilian looked bored.

"Tess."

Carmen nodded, considering the request. "When can you meet me?"

"Anytime."

"How long will it take you to get to Delaurentis's?"

"Ten minutes, tops."

"I'll be sitting on the patio." Carmen snapped the phone closed and handed it back to Muscia.

Muscia opened the tiny device, hit the off button, and returned it to her pocket. "You need to turn it off before you close it. Otherwise, the line is still open."

"Well, you heard. What do you think he wants?"

"Let's go and find out."

Chapter 13

WINNIE AND PELL AT HIGHLAND TERRACE

Tuesday, December 23, 2008 — 9:39 a.m.

The morning sunlight reflected off the dark blue paint on the hood of the Ford Taurus. The rental car had less than a thousand miles on it, practically new. The women sat for a moment, taking in their surroundings. Highland Terrace was twenty-four stories, one of the highest buildings in Naples. Its stately edifice bespoke of an elegant and timeless interior. Water danced in a terrazzo fountain located in the center of the brick-paved circular driveway. They exited the vehicle walking in their usual cadence, measured steps that sounded like a march.

In the cover of the portico, a man in Bermuda shorts came from behind a podium bearing the symbol of Highland Terrace, a Scot playing the bagpipes. He looked up and offered the women a sincere smile.

Winnie adjusted the collar of her white oxford shirt. "Feel good?"

"After almost two hours working out yesterday, hell yes. And I slept like a baby."

When they reached the valet, each woman flipped open her badge.

"I'm Agent Pell, and this is my partner, Agent Winnie. We're with the Florida Bureau of Investigation."

"You're here about the kidnapping." The valet's eyes were round with excitement.

Winnie removed a ballpoint pen from her pocket. She leaned in to see the name tag on the valet's shirt. "Mark, could you tell us where we can find a Mrs. Baxter?"

"I can do better than that. I'll call her office and have her meet you in the lobby."

"Thanks." Winnie nodded smartly. "Oh, and Mark, would you be available to answer a few questions later?"

"Sure."

Mrs. Baxter was a matronly woman with a bust big enough to carry a serving tray without using any hands. She wore a matching red boiled-wool skirt and jacket, with a tidy white blouse and a strand of pearls. Unlike the valet, her smile was anything but genuine. But that was largely due to her recent face-lift. While her foundation hid the pink incision, she looked like Gloria Swanson in the eerie final scene of *Sunset Boulevard*.

"Hello. I'm Eileen Baxter."

All right, Mr. DeMille, I'm ready for my close-up," Pell thought as Baxter extended her hand.

"I'm Agent Pell, and this is my partner, Agent Winnie."

"We were devastated to hear about Anita this morning. This whole affair has been very traumatic for the residents."

Pell cleared her throat. "Mrs. Baxter we're investigating the robbery of a truck that was carrying a shipment of pharmaceuticals. You reported that your pharmacist alerted you when a resident inadvertently tried to refill a phony prescription."

Mrs. Baxter nodded. "Would you two care for a cup of coffee? I was on my way to the dining room when I got Mark's page. If I don't have my second cup soon, I don't think I'll make it till noon." Without waiting for their reply, Mrs. Baxter turned and started down a hallway off the lobby. "It's after nine, so there shouldn't be any residents in there. The kitchen opens at six and everyone is usually finished by eight thirty at the latest. I'll tell you, this mess with Anita has everyone shaken up. And that poor girl they found in the garage. You know she wasn't one of ours."

"Wasn't one of your what?" Pell had to hurry to keep up with the bustling woman.

"Oh, she wasn't one of our aides. We have a pool of caregivers here. But residents are permitted to hire their own staff. They can hire whomever they want, but others prefer to let us do the work of screening, et cetera. Anita's caregiver was from the outside."

"I see." Pell watched the woman take a mug from an industrial dishwasher rack, and fill it from a silver urn. The agent took a mug and handed one back to her partner. They took turns at the tap and followed Mrs. Baxter to a nearby table.

"Is your pharmacist available?"

"No, I'm sorry. Dr. Zarlingo called in sick this morning. Before you ask, that is not unusual. He suffers with shingles from time to time. It's one of those times, poor man. But I can tell you about the incident."

Pell flipped open a notepad, clicked her ballpoint and nodded. "Go ahead."

"Well, one of the residents came in with an inhaler. He told Dr. Zarlingo that he had gotten it the day before but it was empty. So the doctor took it, but when he tried to pull it up on the computer, he couldn't find the scrip—"

"Scrip?" Pell interrupted.

"It's short for prescription," Mrs. Baxter explained. "So naturally he typed in the batch number, and that's when he discovered it was from a lot that had been reported stolen. This kind of inhaler is very expensive and so many of the residents have to use them. If they can buy them cheaper, they will. I mean, who wouldn't?"

"Mrs. Baxter, is that the only case you've had like this?" Winnie also held a notebook and pen, but instead of taking notes, she was jotting down a list of items she needed from the local gun shop.

"It's the only one." She wiped a lipstick print from her mug and took another sip.

"You know I have to ask who the resident was," Pell noted sternly.

"Yes, well, I'll certainly tell you, but you can't interview him."

"And why is that?"

"He's dead," Mrs. Baxter said sweetly. "He died last week—respiratory failure. It is not uncommon for residents to die. Highland Terrace is *the* most exclusive retirement facility in the area. We have a five-year waiting list. Many people pass away while waiting for a unit. Death is a part of life here at Highland Terrace."

A woman in black pants and a white shirt with the bagpiper embroidered on the pocket came to the table with a carafe and poured Mrs. Baxter a refill. "I'll be bouncing off the walls this afternoon," she noted joyfully, and dumped two packets of sugar into the black brew.

"How can we reach you if we have any more questions?" Pell smiled at the server and shook her head when she approached with the carafe.

Mrs. Baxter patted the side pocket of her jacket and produced a silver card case engraved with her initials. She handed each of the agents her business card. "Is there anything else I can do for you?"

"Would you mind letting us into Anita Lemoyne's unit?" Winnie asked.

"Is that also part of your investigation?"

Winnie replied, "We're not at liberty to say."

"I'm just asking because Sheriff Shoat said not to let anyone in. Would I be breaking any laws if I let you two in?"

Winnie seemed pleased. "No." Her lips curled into an unsettling smile. "And we'll take full responsibility if he asks."

The agents arrived at Anita's unit ahead of the manager, who had to retrieve the key from her office. Both women turned in the direction of the elevator when it opened, expecting to see Mrs. Baxter. Instead, they were met by the footrest of a motorized scooter, moving so slowly the elevator door closed and bounced open before the operator could get out. A tiny woman with a mop of downy white hair finally rolled out in a bright red Jazzy Scooter. She didn't seem to notice the women as she worked the throttle between her index finger and thumb. As soon as she cleared the threshold of the elevator, she pushed the lever forward and slammed into a letter table on the opposite wall. Her head snapped back, and a vase on the table wobbled perilously but did not fall. She backed away, turned in the direction opposite Anita's unit, and headed down the corridor, bouncing off one side of the hall and then the other, until she finally reached her own condo and vanished inside with a distant clatter.

"She no doubt drives one of those high-end cars we saw parked outside," Winnie noted sarcastically.

The elevator sounded again and this time Mrs. Baxter stepped off, dangling the key in front of her as she walked.

"Listen, we just observed one of the residents in one of those electric scooters going down the hall that way," Pell said, and pointed. "She slammed into everything, including the table across from the elevator. You might want to check on her make sure she's not having a stroke or something."

"Oh, that's Mrs. Guzeman. You think that's bad, you should see her behind the wheel of her Escalade. Clear the roads." Mrs. Baxter waved her hands. She meant to emphasize the statement with a look of fright, but recent Botox injections between her eyes made it difficult to control her facial muscles. Instead, her eyelids peeled back and her scalp appeared to move, an expression that was genuinely frightening.

Both agents stepped away from Anita's door wondering who was scarier, Mrs. Guzeman or Mrs. Baxter. It would be a close call.

Aside from the crime tape, the door was unremarkable and looked like every other door in the hall. The agents slipped on latex gloves before entering the condo.

The interior was straight out of *Architectural Digest*, with antiques and artwork the agents assumed were authentic. A Frank Lloyd Wright-style sofa faced a large window which overlooked the Gulf. The space was unnaturally clean, with magazines arranged in a perfect semicircle and placemats set at precise angles on the table and bar. A massive vase with an arrangement of tropical flowers stood in the center of the table.

"We'll lock up when we leave," Pell said. She left no room for argument from the manager, who took her leave with her caffeine buzz to go bounce off the walls. "What are you thinking?" Pell asked her partner.

"My gut tells me these two events are related. And I keep thinking about what the Delaney girl said. The buttons clicked." Winnie went to the window. "Can you believe this view?"

"It's hard to believe there are people who really live like this," Pell called from the kitchen.

"We need to call the ME and see if Anita had on that blazer."

Pell came over to stand beside her. "You're right. I think Anita knew something about those stolen meds." She handed a brown pill bottle to Winnie.

Winnie looked at the label. "Celexa. That's for anxiety, right?" She screwed off the lid and poured a handful of large blue pills into her palm. "Are these...?"

"Viagra." Pell finished her sentence. "I found a more recent prescription for the Celexa pills, and it has forty pills in a thirty-day supply, so she was probably hiding these Viagra pills in plain sight. No one, especially Shoat, would think to check her prescriptions."

"We need to see if there is a batch number."

"I'm going to take a look in the bathroom. Call the ME and ask about the blazer," Pell said as she dropped the evidence into a plastic baggie.

When Winnie returned, she found her colleague rummaging through the linen closet. "The body is definitely Anita's," Winnie reported. "She was wearing pants, a shirt, and one shoe. They pulled her from the backseat."

"Have they determined COD?" Pell stopped her search.

"Myocardial infarction," Winnie answered solemnly.

"Winnie, do you even know what that is?"

"No. I was kind of hoping you did."

"Heart attack. Anita died of a heart attack."

Winnie sucked air in through clenched teeth. "Well, I guess there isn't much doubt now that she was kidnapped. She probably died before they could demand a ransom."

"Or she died before they had a chance to kill her. Were there any ligature marks?"

"Nope," Winnie shook her head.

"TOD?"

"They don't know yet. The temperature of the water makes it difficult to determine her liver temp, so it's going to take longer to figure out when she died. But I keep asking myself about those buttons. It makes sense that someone else was wearing that blazer. I'm going to take a look in the master bedroom closet just for the heck of it, see what I can find."

After several minutes Pell joined Winnie in the walk-in closet. Shoes, purses, hats, and furs were matched up in one section, while another area held color-coordinated pantsuits and dresses. "Do people wear hats anymore?"

"We used to wear them on Easter Sunday." Winnie was bent over examining Anita's shoes. She slowly stood, her eyes narrow slits. "What if the drug ring is here?"

"You mean Highland Terrace?"

"Why not, Pell?"

"Because these people are rich already. They don't need money."

"But I imagine Viagra and all those drugs for erectile dysfunction would be pretty popular in a place like this."

Winnie considered this. "Why would you buy them illegally when you could just get a prescription from your doctor?"

Pell shrugged, "I don't know. Maybe they're cheaper or more readily available. Who can say? Mrs. Baxter said those inhalers were expensive. Who wouldn't want to save a few bucks? "

Winnie slipped a navy blue blazer off its hanger and let in dangle over her index and third fingers. "The buttons might have made a sound because of a quick movement. A movement like whacking someone with a two-by-four."

"Or a piece of rebar," Pell continued.

"A cane?"

Pell nodded thoughtfully. "A cane, a frying pan..." Her voice faded as she grew introspective. "I think we've found all the evidence that matters. I'm starting to see a picture."

"Maybe we should get that list of the hierarchy of the Bustamante Gang on the coast and see if we can match any names to the staff and management here."

Pell nodded, "Can't hurt."

"It would be nice to have someone on the inside."

"Yeah, too bad we've already been made."

"Let's roll. I'm hungry, and so is Betty." Winnie called her new Glock Betty. She called all her guns Betty. The agency issued Glock 23s to all graduating agents, but Winnie preferred the smaller 27 because it was easier to conceal.

"Didn't you just buy her a box of hollow points?" Pell checked the door one last time.

"She ate 'em. We were at the range over an hour."

When the elevator reached ground level, the agents disembarked. Ahead was the dining room where they had interviewed Mrs. Baxter. It was still empty, aside from the wait staff that was setting tables, complete with linen napkins and freshly pressed tablecloths. Outside, Mark was still beaming from his post.

Pell approached him, notebook in hand. "Just one question, Mark." She flipped until she found the page she was looking for. "Did you happen to notice what Anita was wearing when she pulled out?"

"I'm pretty sure she had on a black or blue jacket, maybe a blazer. I don't believe I ever saw her dressed in anything but pantsuits, maybe a skirt once in a while. But"—he looked up as though trying to recall—"yep, she had on something dark. I can picture her looking out the window when she sideswiped the ID reader. It had to be one of her blazers. Shame. She was a great tipper. And she always remembered me at Christmas. But all that should be on the film from the security camera."

Pell considered how to best approach this, since they had not been made aware of the film.

"You saw the footage from the security cam, right?" he asked.

"The film you gave to Officer Shoat?" Pell probed.

Mark nodded.

"Yes. Yes, we did. I just wanted to see what you might have recalled from that day," Pell lied, and made a mental note to get the film—with or without Shoat's assistance.

Chapter 14

HECTOR GETS HIS SIT-DOWN

Tuesday, December 23, 2008 –10:10 a.m.

Carmen was seated at an outdoor table for two, holding a colorful demitasse cup between her fingertips. A chocolate biscotti lay untouched on the lip of her saucer as she sipped her espresso.

Hector flashed an exaggerated smile in his rearview mirror and inspected between his teeth. He concluded this exam by blowing into the palm of his hand and smelling the results; his mouthwash was still working. From his console he produced a small brush, unbuttoned his shirt and fluffed his chest hair. He approached the designated meeting place wearing light green trousers and white loafers.

Muscia stood as he approached, while Carmen remained motionless, as befitting her position.

"Thank you for seeing me, Boss." Hector bowed slightly.

Carmen gestured for him to sit. Muscia took her place at Carmen's right elbow.

"Would you like an espresso? Lemonade?"

"No, thank you." Hector took a seat.

"What is it that we have to talk about?"

"Tess."

"Does she know you're here talking to me?"

"No."

Carmen took a moment to consider this. She sipped her espresso and took her sweet time swallowing, gauging his reaction throughout. "You may speak your mind, Hector," she said finally.

He bowed again. "Thank you. I think you need to know about the hit yesterday." Hector had planned his presentation. He tried to think through Carmen's responses, imagine what she would say, how she would think. "The mark wasn't killed. She died."

Carmen grew thoughtful. "Dead is dead. Why do you find this important?"

Hector frowned slightly, sniffed, and cleared his throat. He had not anticipated apathy. "Well, you pay your button man—woman—top dollar for a job. You paid for a job yesterday. But the vic was already dead."

Carmen's thick lips pressed together, giving her the dull-eyed look of a grouper on ice. She sipped noisily, again taking her time, knowing it made Hector nervous.

"I paid to get rid of something. Tess got rid of it. What do I care how it was done?"

"Have you seen the news?" Finally Hector saw a flicker of interest in the woman's eyes. "They have her body already."

Carmen's mouth tightened. Her heavy-lidded eyes blinked slowly. "She told me you picked the location. So this screw-up would be on you, Hector."

Hector nodded contritely. "I suppose you know about the Parkinson's?"

"What is it you're here for, Hector? Why are we here?" Carmen found her poker face and watched the man for his tell.

"I'm just saying." Hector exhaled and stayed locked onto the old woman's eyes. This was his moment.

Carmen sensed immediately that the man was trying to prove himself. Without breaking the connection, she snorted softly. "You break faith with Tess coming here."

Hector had anticipated this and was prepared. "My loyalty to Tess is important." He closed his eyes as he had practiced, saddened by the weight of the words he was about to say. "But not as important as my loyalty to you, Boss." A dramatic sigh completed the thought.

"I appreciate your candor." Carmen returned the cup to its saucer with a delicate *plink*. The sit-down was concluded.

Hector rose and bowed slightly one last time. "Thank you for seeing me. I am sorry to bring you this kind of news. I hope our next meeting is a happier occasion."

"What do you think?" Carmen asked when she was certain Hector was gone.

Muscia did not wait for an invitation. She returned to her seat across the table, the seat where Hector had just been appraised. "He has been an associate for nearly five years. He wants to be the next button man."

"So you think it's time to promote him?"

"When someone has the nerve to sit there and say what he just said, they're ready."

"And Tess?"

Muscia spoke without blinking. "Take her out."

"Just like that?" Carmen asked.

"You saw the news. Tess didn't call you and let you know the mark surfaced."

Carmen looked away. "Maybe she doesn't know yet."

"Even if she does know and just hasn't called you, the fact is we don't know how much longer she can operate."

"You don't think we should just cut down her workload?"

Muscia nodded. "She is not an earner."

"True."

Muscia continued, "Connie and Flobo, they bring in the goods, the cash. They keep the Bridge Club going. You need them."

"Tess has been with me since the beginning. So why don't we find something else for her?"

The big woman let out a short laugh. "This is all she's ever known. She doesn't know how to do anything else. She can't type, she can't file, she does not know how to use a calculator. All she knows is how to pull the trigger."

"Muscia, you've worked for me not even a fraction of the time I've been with Tess. I've known her since we were in pigtails. How do you know this?"

"You told me."

Muscia's deep voice reminded Carmen of Lurch from *The Addams Family* sitcom in the seventies. She imagined an organ chord being played at the end of each sentence. Carmen shrugged and nodded in agreement.

"And we both know no one ever really retires from this business."

"Do you want to handle this?"

Muscia slowly shook her head. "No. You should use your new man."

"Nice. If he pulls it off, we know where his loyalties lie. If he fails, Tess'll make sure he's fish food. Nothing lost, nothing gained."

"Are you going to eat that?" Muscia pointed to the biscotti.

"Take it." Carmen watched the big woman peel away the paper wrapper and bite the cookie in half. "You know, you're supposed to dip those in your coffee so it don't break your teeth."

Muscia chewed, her jaws crunching like tires on gravel.

"You know Tess is my oldest and dearest friend? We've been together fifty-some-odd years."

Muscia finished and swallowed. "Do you think she wants to end up in a wheelchair, sitting in a stinking room with someone like me feeding her because she can't hold her own fork? This way is respectful. This is what she would want."

Carmen considered this for less than a second, and then said, "Get Hector on the line."

Chapter 15

GRAHASTA - THE SECOND ASHRAM

Tuesday, December 23, 2008 — 4:50 p.m.

Sonny used the stairs instead of the elevator, hoping to burn off some of her nervous energy. She had her key in hand when she noticed the door to her unit was already open. Smiling, Sonny opened the screen.

She was greeted by an aroma of cilantro and lime. Tricia was standing over the stove with her back to Sonny.

"What are you making?" Sonny asked, wrapping her arms around the cook.

"I thought you would appreciate a home-cooked meal after what you've been through the last couple of days. Comfort food is very healing."

"You would be correct."

"Wash your hands and set the table," Tricia ordered.

'You come to my condo and boss me around." Sonny would have gone directly to the sink whether Tricia had been there or not.

"It doesn't matter, my condo, your condo, you never do what I say anyway," Tricia gamely noted.

"You want to eat in or out?"

"Deck. Definitely the deck." Tricia grabbed a spatula from a jar on the counter and examined it. Wrinkling her nose, she wiped the dust on a nearby bar towel before putting it to use. "This looks brand-new."

"Until now it was an ornament." Sonny carried the plates and silverware outside. Upon returning, she asked, "Where is the boy?" Sonny usually found Santiago curled up by the sofa or on one of the lawn chairs outside.

"Did you check your bed?" Tricia asked.

Indeed, Santiago, the wirehaired terrier mutt, was stretched out on his back atop the bed, his paws splayed to the side. As Sonny drew near, she could hear the little dog snoring. Returning to the galley-style kitchen she took a seat at the bar. "He's in there snoring."

"He must have learned that from you." Tricia flipped a piece of fish onto a stack of folded paper towels.

"Uh-uh," Sonny laughed.

Tricia was a first generation Cuban-American. Her family had narrowly managed to escape Castro's Cuba. They came to America with an Old World work ethic and enough cash to start a business. Sonny was the product of carnie and a local fisherman. Inspired by the love story of the carnival worker falling for the Florida cracker, Sonny's concept of an ideal love had seemed out of reach until she met Tricia.

Their paths had crossed under peculiar circumstances the year before. Sonny had helped Tricia chase a dog running for its life in the middle of a category three hurricane. They had traveled nearly half a mile down the beach before the frightened little animal surrendered. Santiago was named after the main character in Hemingway's *The Old Man and the Sea*. The two women shared him.

Since they had both experienced bad relationships in the past, neither was anxious to give up her home and autonomy to move in with the other. So it was mutually agreed that they would date for however long it took to make an informed decision about their future. After the first two months, Sonny was surprised how smoothly things were going. The next six months were even easier. After the first year, they were able to count their fights on one hand, and even those generally ended in laughter. Sonny liked to say, "Blame it on your ego."

While Tricia's summation was always, "That's not very yoga-like." Finally, Sonny stopped counting the passing months in favor of being in the moment.

Two months earlier, the couple had opened an eastern arts studio. They took turns teaching—Sonny, yoga, while Tricia was responsible for tai chi and qigong classes. The business was small but rich with promise. It had been Sonny's idea to open right before tourist season, and the strategy was paying off, as the number of students was growing weekly. They had already hired another part-time yoga teacher, so Sonny had more time to manage the business. Tricia was also employed part-time in an adult video store owned by her family. Neither doubted that someday they would combine households, but there was no point in rushing things.

"Tell me about your visit with Char."

Sonny helped herself to a serving of lightly battered whitefish topped with fresh salsa. "She is still in a lot of pain. When the news came on about Anita she got so upset. I don't know whether she's hurt more physically or emotionally."

"Every day brings her a little more closure and healing." Tricia covered her partner's hand with her own and squeezed.

"Her doctor wanted her one more night. At least she'll be home in time for Christmas. On that subject, what did you decide about where you'll spend the day?"

"I don't really want to drive to Miami and back in one day. I told my folks we'd get together for Christmas Eve and exchange gifts then."

"So can I tell my mother you'll be joining us for lunch?"

"Absolutely."

Santiago appeared at the slider, his button nose twitching as he sniffed the air.

"You know it's good if it wakes him from a sound sleep." Sonny patted her thigh, a signal for the dog to join them.

"It's the mojo, baby." The cook wiped the sauce off a bite of her fish and handed it to Santiago.

Sonny reached into her pocket where she kept packs of antibacterial wipes at the ready. She unwrapped one and handed it across the table.

"Dogs are cleaner than humans," Tricia pointed out as she accepted the wipe.

"Worms," was Sonny's one-word answer.

"I'm worried about you," Tricia suddenly said.

"Me?"

"Honey, I've seen you pick up litter someone threw out of his truck and throw it back in his cab at the next red light."

"Once. I did that once."

"Once was enough. I imagine you're still doing it, but with more discretion. My point is, your sister is in the hospital because someone knocked her unconscious on purpose. I know you're pissed."

"Honestly? What kind of yogini would I be if I let this get to me? My focus is on helping Charlotte heal."

"I gotta hand it to you, baby, I'd want revenge if I were in your shoes. I would want to shoot the bastards who did this. That's one thing I liked about the military. I got to fire a weapon. It was a great way to let off steam."

"I don't need all that negative energy. This fish is really outstanding."

Tricia eyed her. "Seriously? You're going to try and change the conversation like that?"

"I need to dig out my recipe for key lime pie. I think that's going to be my contribution to Christmas dinner."

Tricia's eyebrows went up. "Okay, I won't ask again."

"I started the day with dirty denture water all over my legs. Then I spent three hours sitting in a waiting room with the Faux News channel. When I asked them to change the channel or turn it off, the receptionist told me it was tuned to Fox for the patients and the doctors—not me. But they did invite me to wait outside. So right now, I'm just too tired to be angry. My plan is to go to bed early after I give thanks that I'm not in that business anymore. I'm not even sure if I can make it through dessert."

"I made flan. Do it for me."

"I'll push myself." Sonny dabbed her lips with a paper napkin. "Only for you." She forced a beatific smile to cover any lingering anxiety over the less-than-ideal day she had just suffered through. But Sonny feared it would be a long time before the daydreams of taking revenge on Charlotte's attacker could be laid to rest.

Chapter 16

CRUKINSHANK SURVEILLANCE

Tuesday, December 23, 2008 – 7:02 p.m.

Milo had often been told that he had his father's patience. The older Purdie was a Vietnam vet who worked as a mechanic during the week and hunted every other weekend. Both job and hobby required a considerable amount of forbearance. Milo often accompanied his father into the Everglades to hunt game and had witnessed his father's legendary patience in action. Purdie Senior had passed away nearly three years ago in an accident involving a hydraulic lift at work. As much as he idolized his father, Milo considered patience not only his greatest asset but his birthright. It was, he thought, an excellent measure of his character. In fact, in his first interview with Mr. Winslow, when asked what he thought was his best quality, Milo didn't hesitate. "Patience," he said. It never occurred to Milo that part of the reason for his vast supply of patience might be linked to his inability to process information. It generally took Milo a while to arrive at a conclusion, and sometimes he didn't arrive at all, but just kept wondering, like a flywheel that never engages.

But following his sins of the year before, Milo was determined to cultivate more of his father's traits. Gus Purdie was a ladies' man in the sense that women liked to flirt with him. But he never had eyes for anyone but Priss. He had come home from boot camp and married her before his first tour in Nam. And when he came home from the war and settled down in Naples, he took to her and his three sons with absolute devotion. But it was his relationship with Priss that Milo was focused on of late. Gus brought her flowers and new appliances, took her hunting and camping. Milo had tried to emulate this role but always ended up short. He attributed this failure to a lack of confidence. His father was sure of himself and humble at the same time. Milo had no problem getting girls, it was keeping them that proved difficult. At one point in his less-than-glorious past, Milo was so convinced of his virility, he had actually made two adult films. Now that he was using his father as a moral yardstick, he realized that had been a poor choice.

Now he was faced with the dilemma of how to handle the situation in 408. Rather than running to Mr. Winslow with suspicions about the booth, Milo had decided to conduct his own surveillance and see what, if anything, was happening. His gut told him something hinky was afoot. But he couldn't take suspicions to his employer. Winslow would want proof. When Milo had some evidence, then he would go to his employer and lay it out for him in a professional manner. Milo wondered if he should use a manila folder or a brown envelope. Either way, he resolved to type up his findings on his mother's computer. Until then, he had his camera, a new pair of infrared binoculars, a pocket-sized tape recorder, and patience.

Milo was in 410, the vacant booth next door to 408. He had a fairly clear shot of the interior of Grace's storefront, but couldn't see much past that. When he arrived from the loading dock outside, the only lights in the building were the light blue emergency bulbs similar to the lights found on the stairs in a darkened cinema.

It was 7:02 according to the faint glow of his wristwatch. He snapped on a mini Maglite flashlight and secured it in his mouth, so he could make an official entry in his notebook.

12/23/08 — 7:02 and the store appears to be closed. No movement. He wrote slowly, sounding out each word. With the same attention to detail, Milo panned his beam of light around the enclosure. It somehow seemed smaller at night, he thought. The milk crate he had planted there earlier worked as a seat. Milo sat and waited, listening to the sounds of the Crab at night. Crickets whirred without pause, and occasionally he heard a car from Vanderbilt Beach Road pass by. But mostly the place was eerily quiet. Milo's stomach began to growl around seven fifteen, reminding him that in his haste to begin the surveillance operation, he had forgotten to eat something for dinner. He thought about the vending machines at the end of the aisle. A candy bar would make his stakeout more comfortable. Since the machines were only accessible through the back entrance at this hour, Milo had to leave through the loading dock, travel the length of the building, and go in the side entrance. Although it meant leaving his self-appointed post for a few minutes, Milo decided the risk was worth it.

Climbing down the short concrete wall, he landed beside his cart. He cranked it up and sped to his next stop. Holding the light between his teeth, he juggled the ring of keys attached to his belt until he found the one he was looking for. The machine was turned off for the night, so he had to fish around behind it to find the plug. It hummed to life and Milo licked his lips. "Hmm, chips or Snickers?" He finally decided on the candy bar, unplugged the machine, and headed back to his position.

Anticipating his return, Milo had left the outside door of the unit unlocked. He heard voices even before he reached the handle and froze. Shoving the last four inches of the chocolate bar into his mouth, Milo carefully opened the latch to avoid making any sound. He had one foot in his stakeout location unit when he heard the first few bars of a popular hip-hop tune and recognized the ring tone of his cell phone. Moving quickly, he stepped back outside, but the movement caused him to lose his balance. As he slipped off the concrete dock and into the side of his golf cart, his elbow gouged a hole in the canvas top, and the camera slipped out of his pocket and skittered across the concrete dock. When Milo finally connected with the ground, he froze, listening and alert.

The voices were gone, but he heard the sound of a car engine as it faded away. He had to fudge his next entry, but at least there was more evidence that something fishy was happening in 408.

Heard voices, women's, but couldn't see who they belonged to. Car left 7:43. I don't have a good feeling.

Chapter 17

AGENTS WINNIE AND PELL GET INTO THE CHRISTMAS SPIRIT

Wednesday, December 24, 2008 – 9:00 a.m.

Agents Winnie and Pell started the day in fine form. Following a two-mile run on the beach, they showered and had a 350-calorie breakfast. As they rolled down Tamiami Trail, with two lattes in the cup holders between them, Winnie read the fax report they received the night before.

"Paige Chesley was arrested last week for selling marijuana to a minor. The arresting officer also discovered an assortment of pharmaceutical drugs in her glove compartment. The search was found to be illegal and therefore inadmissible as evidence. Some of the pills, however, matched the batch numbers of the stolen shipment, which in turn put Paige Chesley on the agency's radar. Meanwhile, her husband came up with the cash to liberate Paige on the marijuana charge, which still stands. She is now out on bail awaiting her day in court. As far as the agency can tell, Paige is expendable in the mob's drug chain or her backers would not only have sprung her but paid for her legal defense as well. That is, even if they are aware of her bust, which is unclear at this point. There is a good possibility they don't know that the pharmaceuticals were found, since they were not admitted into evidence. And we, meaning you and me, don't have much authority here."

"Can we interview her?" Pell asked.

"Only about the weed."

Pell was the first one out of the car. She collected her blazer from the backseat and, once on, rolled her shoulders, taking a moment to relish the fit. Winnie was already halfway up the flagstone walk in front of the suspect's house. She turned and did a double take.

"That's not regulation." She pointed to the recently added Christmas pin on her partner's lapel.

"Relax. It's Christmas, Agent Winnie."

"Is that what you were doing in the mall last night? Buying froufrou jewelry?"

Tucking her chin, Pell examined her pin and then pulled a tiny gold chain. The Christmas tree lit up. Pell smiled with childlike satisfaction.

"Ooh, pretty," Winnie mocked. "Maybe we can sing carols after we interrogate the suspect."

"Why are you so cynical?" Pell seemed genuinely offended. She pressed the doorbell and abruptly turned her back to Winnie.

"I'm sorry. The estrogen fairy paid me a visit this morning."

Pell peeked into one of the windows beside the door and rang the bell again. "I'm going to have to start marking your visits from the fairy in my calendar, so I can be better prepared for your moodiness."

"I said I was sorry. I can't help it. One minute I'm ready to cry, the next I want to pistol-whip someone."

"Thanks for the heads-up. Have you ever thought about taking something?"

"Pell, do you really want a medicated partner? I need my edge. It's not like this every day, just once a month."

"I'm going to go around back. Wait here in case she comes to the door. And for the record," Pell said, walking backward, "you're bitchy more than once a month."

Winnie's reflective lenses made it impossible for her partner to know that she was in weepy mode at that very moment. She pounded the door a bit too zealously with her balled fist and was shaking it out when the phone in her blazer began to vibrate.

"Yes?"

"Hey, it's me."

"Yes, your name came up on caller ID. What do you want? Did you find the suspect?"

"Yeah, and it's not pretty."

Winnie was already moving around the side of the house. "Dead?"

"More like dead drunk."

Winnie snapped her phone closed. The sound of her shoes on the brick deck around Paige Chesley's pool was muffled by the noise from the filtration system. A determined robotic sweeper scavenged the bottom of the pool in search of debris.

Paige Chesley lay sprawled on her back in a lounge chair. Her mouth was open as she slept, and a large black cat groomed the unconscious woman's hair. The feline had already teased Paige's brown mane into a gourd-shaped coif and was busy licking the other side into submission.

"How long do you think she's been out here?" Pell asked.

"Long enough for Muffy there to give her that pretty new do."

"Think we should get the cat off?"

Winnie cocked her head and folded her arms across her chest. "Actually, I'd kinda like to see where Vidal Kitty is going with this. Aren't you curious about what it's going to look like when the cat finishes?"

Pell picked up a tumbler from the glass table beside Mrs. Chesley's chair and sniffed the contents. Her head snapped back. "Oh, yeah. This woman is toasted."

"Ya think?" Winnie drew out her cell phone, took aim, and snapped a photo of the inebriated woman.

"That's real professional."

"Look, you have your tree pin and I have this." Winnie turned the phone around so her partner could see the photo.

"We need to question her, Winnie. I think we should get her inside and sober her up."

"You don't sober people up. You wait for the alcohol to leave their system."

"What about a cold shower and coffee?"

"You've never been drunk, have you, Pell?"

Pell visibly deflated.

Not wanting another squabble, Winnie walked over and tugged on the chain of her partner's lapel pin. The Christmas tree lit up and Pell smiled.

"Let's get her in the house." Winnie shoved her arms under Paige's back and looped them through hers, then lifted her torso. "C'mon, get her legs. Mr. Kitty there is going to have one hell of a hairball anytime now."

Pell did as she was told. "She must have on suntan oil. Her legs are really slippery."

"I know, I know. Let's just get her in the house." Winnie waddled backward toward the slider. "Put her down for a second, I need to catch my breath. I'm gonna have to put my end down, so I can open this." Winnie bumped against the back door. "You might as well put your end down, too."

Paige Chesley took the moment of stillness to unleash a torrent of her partially digested breakfast. Winnie had just enough time to clear the threshold of the back door before the eruption. Pell's upper lip curled in disgust. Paige moaned and managed to open her eyes only to have them roll back in her head.

"Do you think we should call nine-one-one?" Pell found a hose and turned it on. She began to spray the bricks around Paige's head.

"They'd just pump her stomach, and she already did that. I'd rather stay with her and get something useful. It's not as though we have a whole lot to go on."

Pell sprayed the soles of her shoes. "You don't think she needs medical attention?"

"No. I think she's numbing her pain with booze. The woman lives in a house like this but sells drugs. And where's her husband? I'd get my drunk on too if I were in her shoes." Winnie slipped the belt of Paige's bathrobe from around her waist and secured it under her arms. "I think I can drag her the rest of the way. Go ahead and see if there is a shower on this floor."

Once again Pell obeyed. Winnie knew her partner would object, so she waited until Pell left before retying the robe sash around Paige's ankles. The body was easier to drag backward, and Winnie was able to get her into the kitchen before Pell returned.

"There's only a sink and toilet down here. We're going to have to get her upstairs." Glancing at the woman, she asked, "What's this?"

"Trust me. I've moved bodies before and it's much easier this way. Watch."

Winnie drew the bathrobe tie over her shoulder and proceeded to pull the limp body with ease across the terrazzo-tile floor. Paige's silky negligee was bunched up around her neck, but neither agent seemed to notice.

"Oh, that is much better. Can I try?"

Winnie gladly handed over the terry-cloth towline. "I'm going up to find a rope or something, so we can get her up these stairs."

"Good idea." Pell headed to the bottom of Mrs. Chesley's ornate staircase.

Agent Winnie returned with a purple pashmina scarf, which she quickly secured around one ankle, and then fastened the robe tie around the other.

"You think that's strong enough?"

"Well, we'll see." Winnie started up the stairs with her leg in tow.

A third of the way up, Pell lost her balance. The two agents stood frozen as Paige Chesley's head bounced down the steps, her slack body coming to rest on the bottom stair.

"Don't worry, she'll never know the difference between that and her hangover," Winnie said to calm her partner.

After no small struggle, the FLABI agents finally got their suspect safely to the top landing. They paused to catch their breath, and this time noticed Paige's nightgown was off her body and clinging to the gourd-shaped mass of hair in a Victoria's Secret turban. Winnie bent over and squinted.

"Is that a thong?"

Pell nodded knowingly. "It is now."

"Let's get her in the shower."

Paige Chesley came to under a stream of chilly water. Her makeup from the day before began to melt. She opened bleary eyes and allowed her head to drop back against the tiled wall, muttering obscenities all the way.

"She looks like a cast member from one of those *Night of the Living Dead* movies." Winnie took aim and snapped another photo.

"I never watched those movies," Pell noted.

"Wait! Did she just say…" Winnie squatted and listened. "*Beetlejuice*. She just said *Beetlejuice*."

"Now I did see that movie," Pell nodded knowingly. "Remember that scene in the end with him in the waiting room?"

"Pell, I need you to focus. Why don't you go down and get a pot of coffee going. I'll stay here and make sure she doesn't drown."

Chapter 18

CHARLOTTE
IS
DISCHARGED

Wednesday, December 24, 2008 – 9:50 a.m.

Bethany found her younger sister dressed and sitting on the edge of her hospital bed. The white bandage around her head was concealed under a lightweight knit cap. Instead of appearing injured, Charlotte actually looked rather stylish. As Bethany approached, she noticed her sister was cradling a genuine stuffed armadillo. "That's kind of gross. I'm surprised they let you have that in here." Bethany cast a disparaging look at the authentic nine-banded variety of armadillo in Charlotte's lap. "How long have you been waiting?"

"She doesn't like you either," Charlotte noted matter-of-factly.

"Who?"

"Marsha." Charlotte thrust the armadillo toward her sister and shook it as though Bethany was completely daft.

Bethany recalled her mother's words that morning when she had been recruited to pick Charlotte up from the hospital and bring her home. "Don't engage your sister. It will be your ruination if you do." Bethany sighed. She had two small children and was only beginning to learn how to deal with them. She considered her daughter under similar circumstances and how she would head off a tantrum. "I apologize, Charlotte."

Charlotte stroked the rigid animal, but did not look up.

"And I apologize to Marsha also." This got Charlotte's attention. "Why don't we get her a blanket, so she doesn't get cold? I checked the temperature this morning and it was barely seventy degrees. We don't want Marsha to get sick this close to Christmas."

Charlotte's face was unreadable when she finally looked up. Bethany took this as an affirmative and headed to the nurses' station. When she returned, Bethany carried a blanket from the maternity ward two floors down. She offered it to Charlotte, who promptly swaddled Marsha the armadillo like a newborn child. The discharge nurse appeared in the doorway with a wheelchair, and the trio moved down the corridor to the elevator.

Bethany was in the midst of a very unpleasant divorce. Long suspecting her husband of extramarital activities, Bethany had hired a private investigator to make the case. A series of torrid photos confirmed her suspicions, and Bethany wasted no time walking out the door of their million-dollar home in California and driving her Lexus SUV across the country to Florida, while divorce proceedings got under way. As a type-A personality, stress had always been a part of Bethany's life. Still, with Christmas a day away, she dared to hope for a respite from the tension, but as the elevator doors closed Bethany was realizing why she had been sent to collect her sister. Her parents, too, were hoping for some respite, and she was the unfortunate sacrifice that made it possible.

The descent was going swimmingly until the elevator they were on stopped, and another patient in a wheelchair, pushed by her husband, boarded. The young woman held a tiny bundle in her pink blanket. She smiled rapturously at the child in her arms and then knowingly at Charlotte. When the new mother noticed the scaly black tail protruding from Charlotte's blanket, she gasped and looked away.

Even as the elevator filled, the youngest Delaney looked straight ahead and never once blinked. Bethany closed her eyes all the way and visualized the bottle of merlot waiting for her in her parents' refrigerator.

"Wait here and I'll get the Lexus." Bethany was anxious to distance herself from the spectacle her sister was causing and hurried out to the parking lot.

"Didn't Mom tell you not to engage me?" Charlotte asked, as the Lexus pulled out of the circular drive behind Naples Memorial Hospital.

"I'm taking you home. Then I'm going to take one of your sedatives with a wine chaser and watch my soaps the rest of the afternoon."

"You should get some pointers from Sonny. She knows how to deal with me." Charlotte was uncharacteristically smug.

Bethany looked straight ahead.

"I'd like to stop by the mall and do some Christmas shopping."

"You're kidding! Tell me you're kidding."

"I'm not kidding."

"Char, I don't have the stomach for the public humiliation that you seem to revel in. I can't do it!"

"If you leave your attitude in the car, I'll leave Marsha."

Bethany seemed to consider the proposition.

"And would you take me to the Highlands so I can pick up a check? The McDonalds owe me for last week. They called and said I could come by anytime."

"I'll wait here." Bethany found a spot not far from the Highland Terrace's main entrance and parked. Once her sister was through the sliding doors, Bethany dialed their home number. Not surprisingly, the answering machine picked up.

"Mom, it's me. Don't worry, everything is under control. I have Char and she wants to go shopping. She said she feels up to it, so I'll have her home as soon as she finishes. Call me if you need anything while we're out."

Minutes later, Charlotte emerged from the building with two elderly people in tow. Despite their advanced age, the couple moved quickly. Bethany was instantly on high alert when she noticed the woman carrying her pocketbook. She rolled down her window, hoping this was not an ambush.

"This is Edgar and Alva. I told them we were going to the mall, and they want to come along. I told them they'd have to ask you first."

"I just need to pick up a little something for my great-granddaughter," Alva piped up, winking at her husband.

"And I have to keep an eye on her." Edgar's smile was disarming.

"I have to pick up my kids at one o'clock." Bethany knew her excuse sounded lame, but it was true.

"Good, that gives us a couple of hours!" Charlotte held the door for her comrades and helped Alva buckle her seat belt.

Chapter 19

TESS DECIDES ON HECTOR'S CHRISTMAS GIFT

Wednesday, December 24, 2008 – 10:01 a.m.

"Where'd you go yesterday?" Tess climbed into the Audi beside Hector and fastened her belt. She had taken her first dose of the Parkinson's medication that morning, along with a drop of diazepam under the tongue, and so far hadn't noticed any side effects except for feeling very relaxed.

"What do you mean?"

Tess slowly cranked her head around. "I called you yesterday morning, and you didn't answer. Where'd you go? Is that a difficult question?"

"No. I, uh, just felt like going to breakfast."

"See, that wasn't so hard, was it?" Tess gave him a light slap on the cheek. "You seem a little nervous. Did you sleep all right last night?"

"No. Actually, I was up and down all night. Something I ate, maybe."

"Well, we have a short day today, so you can get home and take care of yourself. I just need you to drop me at Carm's. I gotta get her magazine back to her." Tess patted her bag.

"Carmen's? We're going to Carmen Bustamante's right now?" Hector was doing his utmost to keep the fear out of his voice, no mean feat with Smiling Tess Fontana reading his every movement.

"No, we're going to stop in and have daiquiris with Carmen Miranda. Why don't you pull the car over and I'll drive? On second thought, why don't I take you to your place and I'll do this alone? I can drive myself."

Hector pulled into traffic and had to swerve to avoid hitting an oncoming car. It blew its horn and the driver yelled something as they passed.

"Okay. You know what? You nearly creamed that guy. Pull the effing car over. I'm driving."

"I got it. I just didn't see the guy. That's all. I got it."

"Hector, I started taking my meds this morning and you are not helping things."

"I'm sorry. Let's just get everything done and I'll go home and sleep it off."

"Fine, you motherless dirtbag." Several minutes of empty air time filled the space between them. Feeling remorse over her outburst, Tess searched for a line of conversation. "Hey, do you think you'll be up to going to the party tomorrow night?"

Hector shrugged as he guided the car onto Gulf View Boulevard.

"I think you should, 'cause I got you something I know you're gonna like."

"I didn't know I was invited," Hector mumbled, still smarting from her tirade.

She leaned over and pinched his cheek. "Of course you're invited. You're my date. Carmen is expecting you."

He found a parking spot in the shade, knowing Tess would notice the effort. "I'll run the magazine up to her. You wait right here." He had to dig deep to find a convincing smile.

Tess handed him the *Reader's Digest* from her purse and returned his smile.

"I got you something you're gonna like, too." Hector slipped his sunglasses down and winked.

Hector wasn't out of the car a minute before Tess recognized the sound of his cell phone ringing. Unbuckling her belt, she felt around his seat and found it in the floorboard. She stared at it, trying to figure out how to answer it. "Hello?" She remembered he flipped it open to talk.

"Hi!" came a perky woman's voice on the other end. "Hector?"

"Uh…no. Hector stepped out for a second. Can I take a message?"

"Is this his mother?"

Tess felt her nostrils inflate as a white-hot heat blossomed in her gut. "Yeah, this is Hector's mother. Who am I speaking with?"

The young woman tittered like a schoolgirl. "This is Christie. I wanted to confirm his…massage appointment." Another irritating titter. "I took the early shift, so I'll get off around five and be at his place by seven-ish?"

"Sure, honey. I'll make sure he gets the message." Tess seethed, but managed to control the urge to smash the phone on the dashboard.

"Bye," the young woman's voice said before she clicked off.

"I'm the mother of all mothers." Tess snapped the phone closed. As an afterthought, Tess opened the device again and with little effort found her way into Hector's call history. She would bet this girl knew Hector. Tess hit redial and waited.

A man answered, "Cheetah Club, this is Al."

"Hey, Al, I'm looking for Christie. Is she around?"

"She's about to take the stage. You want to try back in about twenty minutes?"

"Sure, Al. I'll do that. Happy holidays, my friend."

"Happy holidays to you, too."

Tess gritted her teeth and considered the situation. Hector was a free agent. He did not know that his Christmas gift was a ring or that Tess was already planning a spring wedding. They had never even discussed fidelity. It was Tess who had assumed he wasn't seeing anyone but her.

She felt her fuse burning and knew she likely had seconds before she blew. With a round of expletives locked and loaded, she decided to go ahead and check Hector's contact list. There were no surprises, but then he wouldn't be stupid enough to actually put her in his contact list. As an afterthought, Tess worked her way into Hector's recent calls. The heat from her anger turned to ice when she recognized Carmen Bustamante's cell number. He might have had breakfast out yesterday, but he'd had it with Carmen. And she had called him back within the hour—twice. It only meant one thing. Smiling Tess Fontana knew she had been tagged.

At that moment, Hector reappeared. He was smiling and his stride was definitely brasher. The *goomba* had brass. Tess struggled to control her shaking hands, the shaking caused by fury, not Parkinson's. Keeping her eyes trained on the man as he headed across the circular driveway toward the Audi, using her thumb and index finger, Tess felt for the latch on the glove box. She opened it and felt her revolver in her hand. *Not here. Not like this. Not today*, she thought, and withdrew. Then she casually dropped the phone to the floor where he could easily retrieve it.

Tess watched him as he approached the car, his tight black pants, and the way his shirt opened to reveal the mat of black hair she loved to run her fingers through. Knowing he was wearing T-Rex cologne made her breath catch. And that swagger; she loved Hector's strut, the way he carried all that cocksure confidence. Tess was simultaneously filled with loathing and lust. By the time he slipped into the driver's seat, she was ready to jump in his lap.

Hector seemed to sense her appetite. He turned to kiss her and was surprised at her response. She grabbed a handful of his hair and pressed her lips to his. He closed his eyes and pictured Christie. "Whoa! Did you miss me?" He blinked when she released him.

"Let's go shopping, baby." Tess's mind was already grinding out possibilities for her future, and none of them included Hector.

Chapter 20

PAIGE CHESLEY WISHES SHE WAS DEAD

Wednesday, December 24, 2008 – 10:14 a.m.

"Paige? Paige?" Pell was losing patience. "Paige, I know you can hear me. I'm not gonna stop talking till you answer some questions."

"Paige? I'm her partner and can assure you she means it. She'll talk till your ears bleed."

"Okay, okay, okay." Paige's speech was still slurred, but after an hour of cold water, hot coffee, and cajoling, she was coming around. "I'll say whatever you want, do whatever you want. What do you want?"

Agent Winnie had dressed the accused in a clean, dry bathrobe and wrapped her hairdo from hell in a large white towel, which was now draped across her shoulders. Winnie had also removed the worst of yesterday's makeup from Paige's face with a warm washcloth. She had nearly been vomited on again for her trouble.

Pell pulled a chair up to Chesley's, so their knees were nearly touching. Paige's head lolled back, and she shut her eyes tight as though she was about to be sick again. But instead of heaving, she began to weep. "What do you want?" she sobbed.

"Paige, we just want to talk about the drugs you had in your glove box."

"This isn't about the house?"

Pell's eyes narrowed and she looked to Winnie to see if she was equally confused.

"The bank is foreclosing on us. We haven't been able to make our payments in over a year."

"We're not interested in evicting you, Paige. We just want you to tell us about last week's bust."

"I don't know. I don't think that's such a good idea. My lawyer told me not to talk to anyone."

"That's great advice," Pell approved.

"It is?"

"Yes. Any lawyer worth his or her fee would tell you that."

"Court-appointed," Paige interrupted. "I had to have a court-appointed one because we don't have two nickels to rub together."

"Okay, you're being honest with me. I'll be honest with you. If you want to call your lawyer right now, I'll get you the phone but…" Pell paused, giving Chesley a moment to grab the lifeline of hope. "You should also know that we are in a position to help you, maybe even save your life."

"Save my life? Are you kidding me? Save my life from what? Look around. My kitchen looks like a bomb went off, my husband left me two days ago and took our kids to his mother's place, and I'm expecting a knock on the door anytime from the sheriff tossing me to the curb. I've sold all my jewelry, my IRA is gone. What's left for me to save?"

Winnie patted Pell's shoulder much the same way a professional wrestler tags her partner when she is anxious for a shot at the opposition. Pell stood and turned the chair over to Winnie.

"I'm Agent Winnie."

Paige screwed up her face. "I don't care if you're Santa Claus, everything has already been taken. There's nothing left for you to save. You might as well go on home and let me do my time. The sheriff already told me I'm going to jail."

"You do have that pretty new hairstyle." Winnie leaned back and folded her arms across her chest.

Paige's hand went to her hair, and the grimace returned. "What the hell happened to my hair?"

"Your cat is quite the stylist."

"I don't have a cat."

"Paige, are you aware that you were in possession of a stolen pharmaceuticals? Those drugs were on their way to a veterans' hospital in Key West. All we want to know is how you got them."

"No. No, that can't be right. I had some nickel bags and a couple of pills from someone's grandfather. The old guy died, so he didn't need the pills anymore."

"So you weren't aware of where the drugs came from?"

Paige pulled her robe tight and buried her face in her hands. "I keep thinking things can't get any worse...and yet they do." She headed back toward the path of wretchedness, snuffling and working herself into yet another crying spell.

Winnie's hand went to the suspect's knee. "Listen, Paige. We think the mob is involved, and if we're right, you're gonna have a lot more trouble than you've ever imagined. Just hear me out. If you will agree to cooperate with our investigation, we'll make sure you do as little time as possible. Considering this is your first offense and you had less than five ounces on hand, there is a good chance that you might not even spend a day in jail."

Chesley seemed to consider the proposition for several seconds. She swallowed the last of her coffee, put the mug down with purpose, and finally brought her eyes to meet Winnie's. "What do you want me to do?"

"Let's start with where you got the drugs." Pell had been waiting to ask the question. She grabbed another chair and drew it near.

"From a kid on my son's soccer team. His name is Jose."

"How old is this Jose?"

"Maybe fifteen or sixteen. I know he doesn't have his license yet, because I've seen him in the driver education class when I come to pick up my son after school."

"So your supplier is a sixteen-year-old?"

Paige turned to Winnie and nodded.

"How did you two end up together?" Winnie, sensing they were on a roll, continued to press Paige.

"Not long after Darren—he's my husband…soon to be ex-husband—lost his job, Jose came up to me on the soccer field. He said, *You're Scott's Mom, right?* I said yeah. He said he'd seen me on the sidelines before. We just started talking. I don't know why, but I started telling him about Darren and the house. When we were getting ready to leave, Jose took me aside and handed me a joint."

"When did all this start?"

Paige shrugged, "Maybe late August, early September. The next time I saw Jose, he said he could help me get my hands on some cash. Of course I listened. We've been taking money from Darren's folks. I've been going to the food pantry. We cashed out the IRA. There was nothing left. And it isn't like there are jobs in town that pay two hundred thousand a year. You're lucky if you can land something for maybe ten an hour. I don't mind working, but I still have to pick up my youngest from school…"

The fact that her youngest had been taken away from her hit Paige anew like a punch to the solar plexus. She doubled over and hid her face in her hands.

Pell got up and prepared a fresh pot of coffee. Winnie, who was always uncomfortable around crying, unless she had caused it, motioned her partner outside.

"I have a bad feeling about leaving her like this. If they find out she's talking, they could come for her anytime. She's an easy target. That's what I'd do. Make her disappear before she ends up in court."

"She should be on suicide watch," Pell continued. "And it's Christmas. No one should be alone. The chief is not going to approve money for us to put her up."

Winnie took her phone out and deleted the earlier photo. "I don't trust Shoat to protect her."

"And taking her into custody would really piss him off."

Winnie began to smile. "Yes, it would."

The wailing inside grew louder.

Without further discussion, the agents went back inside. Each poured a fresh cup of coffee and then took their seats in front of the suspect.

"Paige, unless you have some objection, we'd like you to come with us." Pell made the offer, hoping the chief would back her up.

"We'll help you pack, get you out of here. You shouldn't be here by yourself."

"What if my family comes home?"

"I'll go to the neighbors on either side and leave a card. We'll make sure they know how to find you," Agent Pell assured her.

"Why don't you tell me where I can find a suitcase," Winnie said, "and I'll help you pack a few things."

"What about my hair?"

Winnie recalled seeing a pair of scissors in the knife caddie. Yanking them free, she headed toward Paige.

Pell quickly stepped between them. "I'm sure she meant that figuratively."

Chapter 21

SONNY'S DHARMA

Wednesday, December 24, 2008 – 10:30 a.m.

Sonny had worked as a software editor, a salesperson, and a private-duty caregiver. In between these short-lived careers, she was a barista, a gift-wrap specialist, and a secret shopper. These jobs had all been part of a greater search for Sonny's true calling. That calling finally came the first time she set foot on a yoga mat. By the time the hour-long class ended, Sonny knew what she was born to do.

As she parked her Subaru outside Highland Terrace, Sonny was filled with the memories of the last client she had cared for. She scrolled down to Tricia's phone number on her cell phone and hit the call button.

"Hello?"

"Remind me again why I'm doing this?"

Tricia chuckled. "Because your sister needs help right now, and you're able to deliver."

"How did my class go?"

"Your sub is pulling in a crowd. It's a good thing you hired her when you did."

"How many?"

"Sonny, you're trying to engage me in a conversation to postpone the inevitable. Go get the old guy, take him to get a haircut, and we'll talk when you get back to the studio."

"Are you trying to get rid of me?" Sonny held the phone up and stared at it. "Hello?"

She slipped the cell into the pocket of her freshly pressed khaki pants, and took a purposeful yoga breath. After her last client, she had gathered up all her scrubs and donated them to charity. Hopefully, Mr. Phillips would not cough, sneeze, spit, or otherwise expose her to his bodily fluids.

He answered the door to his unit just as she was reaching for the bell. Tall, with a full head of white hair, Mr. Phillips beamed happily and swept his arm inward as an invitation to Sonny. "I'm Dean, and you must be Sondra." Dean clapped his hands. Come in. I just need to get my sweater, and I'm ready and raring to go." Lean and long-legged, Dean headed toward his bedroom.

From her position in the entryway, Sonny spotted Mr. Phillip's Christmas tree, trimmed in Victorian splendor. The smell of balsam filled the condo and underneath the branches was an assortment of gift-wrapped packages. Her eyes continue to scan the room, taking in the red and white carnation flower arrangement, tactfully hung mistletoe, nativity scene, and wall of unwrapped boxes.

"I'm all ready for Christmas." Dean reappeared, drawing a gray sweater over one arm.

"You must have a huge family or a lot of friends," Sonny commented, gesturing to the unwrapped packages.

"Oh, those aren't Christmas presents." He picked up a small brown box and eyed the label. "This is an electric peeler. I got it for…oh, heck, I don't remember why I got it. Must have been a good price. And this here"—Dean picked up another box from his collection—"I think this is the magic bullet blender. This is good for smoothies. You just put your fruit in and mash the button. After ten seconds, you pop off the lid and voila. There's a fresh smoothie, and you can drink it right out of the blender. It's also dishwasher safe."

"You must watch a lot of late-night TV."

"Yep. Ever since Marge, my wife, died, I have a hard time sleeping. Seems like I always end up with the TV on. I can't go back to sleep till I've bought something. That's the worst kind of insomnia. Could you use a George Foreman Grill? I've got a dozen of them, and they're just taking up space."

"Wow," was all Sonny could say.

"Yeah, and the UPS gal just dropped off a Pilates machine. I don't know where I'm going to put it yet. I'm not even sure I can use it."

"If you have a spare bedroom, you could set up a gym," Sonny ventured.

"My spare bedroom doesn't have room for one more thing. Come here, I'll show ya."

Sonny followed her host through the condo, past a collection of Hummels, family portraits, and half a dozen authentic samurai swords proudly displayed in his living room. He opened the door and Sonny was mortified to see the room was stacked to the ceiling with unopened boxes.

"I've got them overflowing in the kitchen, too."

Sonny sometimes wondered who would buy the products pitched on late-night TV: the Magic Bullet Blender, the Wonder Clothe, the Lint Man, and the Never Needs Sharpening knife assortment. Turning her attention back to Dean, she realized the senior was single-handedly keeping the economy afloat. "I'm sorry about your wife. How long has Marge been gone?"

Dean wagged his head bitterly. "Almost two years. She broke her hip, then got pneumonia in the hospital. She was gone in less than two weeks."

"Do you have children?" Sonny had a destination in mind for her line of questioning.

"I have two daughters. They live in California, so they don't get out here very often. And I've got one granddaughter in Tampa. She's in school. Studying to be a veterinarian like her granddad."

"Is she coming down for the holidays?"

"She said she might come over tomorrow evening if she has time. And she might bring her fiancé to meet me. That's why I need a haircut."

"Well then, we better get going." A wave of kindness washed over Sonny. There was enough distance between her last client, Conrad Furfir, and this moment to make her soft. For one brief minute, she contemplated giving her phone number to Dean Phillips for future haircuts and errands. Then Sonny recounted all the reasons she had left the caregiving profession—the bodily fluids, the odors, the physical strain. Sonny never had a desire to marry a man. After caring for her last employer nearly three years, she knew she had made the right decision. She punched the down button for the elevator and tried to picture what Tricia would look like when she was eighty.

Chapter 22

MILO AIMS TO GET TO THE BOTTOM OF THINGS

Wednesday, December 24, 2008 – 11:30 a.m.

Milo deftly whipped his golf cart up to the loading dock where he had parked the night before. Drumming his fingertips against the steering wheel, he listened to the exchange on the walkie-talkie.

"Roy, I need you to change the light bulb at the front desk sometime before you go home. Or you can just drop me off a hundred-watt bulb, and I'll do it myself."

Milo collected the walkie-talkie from the passenger seat and considered what he was going to say. He had to sound convincing.

"Hey, Mr. Winslow, I ate something that disagreed with me last night. I'm going to be in the head for a few."

"All right, Milo. I think we can manage for a while without you. You take your time. Hope you feel better."

He locked the walkie-talkie in his glove compartment, looked at his watch, and went into what he liked to call ninja mode.

Milo closed his eyes in an effort to ratchet up his other senses. He took several short breaths like a boxer entering the ring, summoning his powers of observation and readiness. "Steel your nerves boy," Milo's father would say every time he drew a bead on his prey. These were the words Purdie Junior heard every time he entered the ninja mode. It was the place of stillness and supreme focus. He could hear the tiniest noise. His skin tingled at the slightest change in wind direction. Milo was at the peak of alertness. He exhaled slowly before opening his eyes. Milo Purdie was ready to get down to business.

Scanning his surroundings, Milo saw nothing out of the ordinary. The loading docks were active, and customers moved between the wings at both ends of the building. He climbed out from behind the wheel, popped his wide-brimmed hat into place, and made his way to the rear of the golf cart. From the caddie well, he removed a shoe box, tucked it under his arm, and headed to the loading dock outside 409.

Inside the empty storefront, he squatted over the box and removed the lid. Two palm-sized listening devices were nestled in packing peanuts. Milo had paid a visit to the Security Shack on his break earlier that morning. Located in booth eighty-seven, the store featured all manner of spy equipment, and self-defense items that didn't require a permit, along with home security systems that could be monitored remotely. The store carried some surprisingly cutting-edge apparatus.

After explaining a beautifully concocted story about how he suspected one of the retailers was selling sexually explicit items to underage shoppers, the store proprietor, Festus Hummer, had picked out several items he felt would be perfect for gathering enough information to build a solid case.

"This is how you do it," Festus explained, as he produced a box cutter from his back pocket. He carefully opened each of the two listening devices. "I'm going to put a strip of double-sided foam tape on the bottom of each one. I'll go ahead and put in the SIM cards, too. Then all you have to do is peel this top strip and stick it someplace close to the counter. Don't get it too close to the phone or the register. The phone can screw up the signal, and the register can drown out the sound. Maybe put it on a wall nearby. I've even put them on the top of a wall clock. No one can see it, and it's usually located behind the counter. When you've got it in place, dial the number on the back side. You can listen in to whatever is going on in a twenty-foot radius. The monitoring is in real time, so be ready with your recorder. Shoot, if I didn't have to be here to man the store, I'd help you out."

"I appreciate that, Festus. I'm thinking I can manage it."

Festus looked disappointed.

"But if I need backup, you'd be the first man I'd call," Milo assured him.

"When I worked as a private investigator, I could go undercover forty-eight hours straight with nothing but a thermos of coffee and a cooler with a couple of sandwiches. Used to pee in paper cups. Those were the days." Hummer sighed forlornly. "Then I lost my license. How was I supposed to know there was an FBI stakeout in progress? One little mistake and they pulled my license."

"I thought you lost your license for smoking," Milo scowled.

"And that too. I thought an ounce was legal."

"It is, just not in the state of Florida."

"Yeah, I'm clear on that now, Milo."

It was Milo's turn to sigh heavily. "Is there anything I need to know about this thing?" He held up a package containing his new Bionic Ear.

"Now, that is what you're gonna use if you want to follow the person. Once the customer leaves the store, he or she will be out of range of the surveillance bug. So you just clip the earpiece on your hat or plug it into your recorder and aim the mic here at the subject. It's good for about twenty feet again, so it's a good idea to have a visual on 'em. Milo, are you sure you don't need any video equipment? Don't you want photos? I mean, if you're going to gather evidence for Winslow it would be good to have photos."

"If I don't get what I need by the end of the week, I'll be back for the video equipment. I got a camera on my cell phone, too." Milo pointed to the cell phone clipped on his belt in between his clip-on mace and clip-on Palm Pilot.

Festus pointed his index finger at Milo's midsection and grunted. "You look like some kind of spaceman, like you got a command center around your middle. Where the heck do you put your walkie-talkie? One more thing on your belt and you're liable to lose your pants."

Milo bit his lip and did a quick scan of the shop. "I got it." He retrieved the walkie-talkie from a shelf across the room and, following Festus's advice, clipped it onto his pants pocket. He felt like a real cop.

"Here!" Festus thrust an empty shoe box at Milo. "Put everything in here. It won't attract attention."

After a generous discount on the items over and above his employee discount, Milo spent all his purple Stone Crab money plus fifty dollars of his own government-minted money. With a quick glance in either direction, Milo left the store, shoe box in hand.

The next step required a little more thought. Milo planned to do some reconnoitering before he placed the bugs. But in the event he found a good location, he wanted to have the bugs ready to plant. From where he stood, he could see Grace's storefront. He assumed she was in the shop, likely behind the counter. When he entered, there was no sign of the pretty Asian girl. The cash register was unattended.

"Grace?"

"Hey, Milo."

The security guard turned to find Cole Delaney from across the aisle.

"Hope I didn't scare you."

"No, Cole. I was just stopping in to see if Grace had any more of those purses like the one I got for my mom."

"Well, she stepped out to use the restroom, so I told her I would keep an eye on the place till she got back."

"Yep. That's how things work around here. We're a team at the Crab." Milo put his free hand on his hip, thinking it would be nice to have a gun there, or at least a billy club. The company allowed him to carry mace, but until a few days ago, Milo opted not to. He had blinded himself a year earlier when he accidentally wiped his eyes with a handkerchief coated in bug repellent. The recollection of the pain, paired with self-inflicted blindness, was enough to make Milo steer clear of all aerosols, including hairspray. Lately he realized that he needed something to defend himself in the event he happened to encounter an uncooperative perp. He prayed that if he ever had to use it, he would remember to point the spray away from his face.

"Well, since you're here, I've got a couple from Minnesota interested in an armadillo. Would you mind taking over? Grace'll be back any second."

Milo nodded, "Sure."

"I tell you what, Milo, armadillos sell like hotcakes."

Milo considered what Cole had said and wondered how long it would take him to learn taxidermy. Before he could slip all the way into his day dream of making millions by selling stuffed armadillos, Milo remembered why he was there. He set the shoe box on the counter and removed one of the bugs.

There was, in fact, a clock on the wall behind the cash register. Milo scanned the room for something to stand on. Grabbing the bar stool Grace kept behind the counter, Milo peeled the double-sided tape off, climbed up, and quickly planted the device out of sight.

"Hello," Grace called softly.

Milo nearly lost his balance, but recovered and got down without incident. "I happened to look up and saw that your clock had stopped, so I just replaced the batteries."

"Oh, I didn't notice. Thank you, Milo."

He returned the stool to its place and squared his shoulders. "Well, you're welcome."

Grace's smile wavered and Milo realized he was making her uncomfortable.

"Um, do you happen to have any more of those purses like the one from yesterday?"

"I don't right now. But I'm expecting a shipment later today. Maybe you can stop by tomorrow."

"All right, I'll do that. I suppose I should get back to work." Milo touched two fingers to his forehead and saluted. "I'll see you tomorrow, Grace."

"Milo," Grace called after him. She held the shoe box up. "Are these yours?" She read the side of the box and looked confused. "Ballet slippers?"

"I carry my supplies in here." He took the box and shook it. "Like batteries." Milo made haste back to his golf cart, anxious to test the new equipment. The faux white leather squeaked when he slid onto the bench seat. Smiling at his incredible cleverness, Milo fished his cell phone out of his pocket. The moment of excitement ended abruptly when he realized he had forgotten to write down the number on the back of the bug. As he pulled away and headed down the aisle, Milo was already forming a new plan. The oversight made him more determined than ever to get to the bottom of things. In the meantime, he needed a corn dog, maybe two.

Chapter 23

WINNIE AND PELL SEARCH FOR JOSE

Wednesday, December 24, 2008 – 11:50 a.m.

"Sea Breeze?" Winnie ducked into the passenger seat. "Sounds more like a convalescent home."

"I'm just hoping we can make a little headway with what's left of the day. Everybody is already in holiday mode. Makes it difficult to get anything done."

The agents pulled out of the hotel parking lot and into the heavier-than-normal, last-minute shopping traffic on Highway 41, secure in the knowledge that Paige was safe in Pell's hotel room reading magazines.

Pell asked, "What would you be doing if we were home right now?"

"I'd be watching the clock at the shop, tapping my fingers on the keyboard, just fidgeting. Then when five o'clock rolled around, I'd make a beeline for the door, and head over to my brother's house. We go caroling every year on Christmas Eve. It's a family tradition."

"I've heard you sing, and you should be glad you have a regular job."

Winnie retorted, "What would you be doing, your Ladyship? What does someone with a chronic case of Pollyanna complex do to celebrate?"

Pell slowed for a light and turned to her partner. "She reminds herself that her partner is more acerbic than usual because she is hormonal. Then she'd wonder what you were going to do for Christmas Eve."

Winnie nodded scornfully. "It sucks that we're here away from our families. But at least I'm with my partner. I think we should consider making a reservation for lunch tomorrow. Just because we're on a case doesn't mean we have to skip Christmas, right? Light's green."

"Yeah. I think it would be good to get Paige out, too. She was real depressed when we left."

Winnie asked, "Can you imagine? Losing your house, your family, and then facing jail time. I'm sure a change of scenery won't hurt."

Pell gestured to the GPS on the dashboard. "Would you turn that so I can see it? Thanks. It wouldn't surprise me if she slept the rest of the day. But one way out is if she can help us with the case. If we can find this Jose, kid, we'll probably be able to move up to the next rung on the gang's ladder."

"Not if. When. We'll find him. I think you turn right up at the next light. And I'm thinking if we can get a hold of a yearbook and take it back for Paige, she'll be able to recognize the kid. We might get lucky. Who knows? Maybe we can bust him tonight."

"Winnie? It's Christmas Eve. Do you really want to wreck a family's Christmas? And what if we have to babysit him, too?" Pell turned in a slow, wide arc and flinched when the horn of the car behind her blew. "You'd think they'd be more patient, with all the elderly and tourists around here."

Winnie turned. "Pell, the driver behind you is at least a hundred and fifty. Have you tried the long pedal on the right?"

"There it is." Pell took her time pulling into Sea Breeze High School's driveway, forcing the cranky senior to nearly scrape the side of their rental car as she peeled around the agents, and gesturing with a crooked but effective middle finger.

"I'm driving back to the motel," Winnie noted informatively.

"Did you like high school?"

Winnie replied, "I had no use for high school. What about you? I'll bet you were into every sport."

"Actually, I lettered in track, tennis, basketball, and soccer. I was also on the debate team and——"

"Why am I not surprised?" Winnie interrupted.

"Well, what did you do in high school?"

"I studied. I think that's what you're supposed to do."

The two walked briskly toward the front of the building, trotted up the steps, and headed for the main entrance.

"Looks pretty dark. I don't think it's open," Pell stated.

"Let me try around back, see if anyone is in one of the offices or something."

Pell tugged at the door to verify her assumption, then watched as Agent Winnie jogged down the sidewalk and disappeared around the side of the building. She pressed her face to the glass door. Cupping her hands by her eyes, she scanned the hallway. There was no movement or sound inside the building. Behind her, the cord from the bare flagpole made a *plinking* sound in the breeze. Pell felt her phone vibrate and automatically flipped it open.

"This is Agent Pell."

"Hey, I found a window back here. It's halfway open. I just need a hand to get up and inside."

"I'll be there in a second." It was Pell's turn to jog around the building. She spotted her partner halfway down the length of the structure.

"Just give me a boost and I'll climb in."

"Winnie, how about we call the principal and see if he or she will just come and open the door?"

Winnie's face began to harden. "How about you give me a boost and let's get this done."

"No. You just want to break in there and do it the hard way."

"Pell, I'd be happy to do it your way——"

"But?"

"But this is how it will play out. You'll have to call the sheriff's office. His plucky but cosmetically challenged secretary will keep you engaged on the phone for half an hour as payment for getting you the number. Then you'll dial the principal. But he or she won't pick up because he or she is headed north to enjoy a little cold weather and the big city. So we waste an hour standing around here. Meanwhile, Shoat gets word we're here, and he drives over so he can sniff the lead we got!" Winnie's voice grew louder as she spoke, until the final word in her diatribe, *got*, came out of her mouth, leaving her red faced and panting, her lips speckled with flecks of spittle. She eyed Pell speculatively. "Stop judging me."

Wordlessly, Pell bent and clasped her hands together, making a stirrup for her partner's foot.

In one fleet movement, Winnie launched herself up to the window and grabbed the sill. "I'll find the library and see if they have the yearbooks." She drew herself through the opening. "Then I'll…" Winnie's body suddenly went limp—hanging half in and half out of the window, her legs splayed against the wall.

The tall blonde agent tugged the hem of her partner's pants. "Winnie? Hey. Are you okay? C'mon, quit screwing around."

An explosion sounded several feet away, causing Pell to draw her firearm. Before it cleared her holster, a short brown man in a gray uniform appeared. His legs churned as he charged toward her. His weapon of choice, a baseball bat, was locked and loaded over one shoulder. As the little man ran at her like a cannonball, Pell took a wide shooter's stance and leveled the barrel on his nose. The man slipped, dropped the bat, and scrambled to his feet. Before the agent had time to re-holster and pull out her badge, the man was up and running again, this time in the opposite direction. As he tried to put as much ground between them as possible, Pell took up pursuit.

She caught his collar as he reached for the door that the agents had missed in their earlier reconnaissance mission.

"*Lo siento,*" the wiry man begged, as Pell easily pressed him against a cinderblock wall and cuffed his slight wrists.

"*Donde esta, mi amiga?*" Pell spun the man around and flipped out her badge. "*Yo soy policia.*" She read the name embroidered on his shirt. "*Ramon, donde esta la mujer pele negra?*"

Ramon swallowed. Overpowered and reduced to submission, he became contrite. "She is in the locker room. I'm sorry."

"Take me to her, Ramon."

Agent Winnie's torso was still limp when they reached her.

"Ramon, I'm going to take off the cuffs and you're going to help me get her in here. Okay."

Ramon nodded, his eyes still downcast.

"What are you doing here?" Pell slipped the key in and slid the metal bracelets off the man's wrists.

"I work here," he said softly, as his hands dropped to his sides.

"Maintenance?"

"*Si.*"

"It's Christmas Eve." Pell shook her head. "I can't believe they have you working Christmas Eve. Get one of those wrestling mats and drag it over here." As Pell pointed, she noticed a makeshift bed in a far corner of the room. Beside the cot, clippings from a pine tree were stacked beside a duffel bag and a handful of books.

Ramon caught her eye as he slid the blue padding under the window. He looked away, focusing on the *gringa* who was now moaning, clearly uncomfortable but still unconscious.

"She lifts weights, so she's gonna be pretty heavy. I'm gonna lift her legs and we'll both try to keep her from slamming down, okay?"

Ramon turned out to be surprisingly strong despite his size. Winnie landed with a gentle thump and a groan.

"Winnie?" Pell lightly slapped one cheek and then the other. "Officer Winnie? Ramon, do have some ammonia you could pour on a paper towel or something?"

The man darted to a cleaning cart. He poured ammonia on a paper towel and tentatively reached across the inert body, handing it to Pell.

One whiff of the powerful odor caused Winnie's head to snap back. "Betty? What the hell? What's going on?"

Ramon leaned over and looked down, bringing his hands to his knees. "I hit you with the bat. *Lo siento.*"

"Oh," Winnie noted matter-of-factly, before her eyes closed again.

In the distance, the sound of a wailing siren could be heard.

"I'll bet that's Shoat." Pell rocked back on her heels. "Did you call the police, Ramon?"

"*Si.* I thought the *gringa* was trying to break in."

"She was." Pell sighed and scratched her head. "This is exactly what wasn't supposed to happen. Okay, here's what we're going to do. Ramon, would you drag *mi amiga* out the back door? I'm going to get our car. You sit tight with her till I get back. Can I trust you to do that?"

Ramon nodded sheepishly. "*La puerta frente esta a la izquierda,*" he said, and pointed over his shoulder to the front door.

Pell stood. She brushed her knees and then headed briskly for the front door. "*Gracias.*"

Sheriff Shoat The Younger was the first to respond to the call of a possible B and E at the school. He pulled into Sea Breeze High School's lot, badly scraping the already scarred undercarriage of his car. In the not-so-distant past, he had played football for the Titans, Sea Breeze's arch rival. For that reason, he couldn't help feeling a little game-day antagonism. Exiting his vehicle, Shoat panned the grounds, nodding dubiously.

A dangerous looking gray shark appeared on the sign in front of the school, its teeth bared for attack. Troy was a fisherman and knew this type of shark was not one that lived in local waters. He wasn't sure if it was an actual species at all. This was the school of the affluent. They were the only high school in town with their own golf team. Yet somehow, they couldn't figure out what kind of sharks swam right off their beach. The sight of the sign always made him scoff. Today was no exception.

He straightened his hat and started toward the side of the building. Shoat stopped short when he notice tire tracks in the otherwise immaculate Bermudagrass lawn.

"Hey, Sheila," Troy said into the mic on his shoulder. "Is there another car in the area? I might need backup."

"Roger that, Chief."

The young policeman pressed his back hard against the side brick wall of the administration building, drew his weapon, and readied himself for a classic shooter's stance. Then, with the speed of a viper—or so he liked to believe— Troy chanced a quick look down the back side of the building. There was no sign of villainy; even so, he thought it prudent to keep his weapon handy.

Ramon watched the man in the uniform slide around the far side of the building, and then signaled that the coast was clear for the Ford Taurus to make its escape. Pell closed her eyes as she gently guided the big sedan over the curb. Something underneath scraped, and she prayed the rental service wouldn't notice the damage. In the backseat, Winnie grunted.

Pell rolled down the passenger window and said, "Get in, Ramon."

The little man shook his head.

"I'm not gonna arrest you. C'mon."

Reluctantly, he climbed in beside the driver.

"Put your belt on, Ramon." Pell hit her turn signal, and with her trademark judiciousness, she pulled into traffic.

Chapter 24

KARMA, THE GIFT THAT KEEPS ON GIVING

Wednesday, December 24, 2008 – 1:15 p.m.

In the time it took to get from the mall to Highland Terrace, Mr. Phillips fell into a peaceful slumber. Against her better judgment, Sonny had allowed him to finish his ice cream cone in her freshly Armor-alled and vacuumed car. But the first scoop of chocolate almond along with his recumbent position and the angle of the sun, proved to be the ideal setting for sleep.

Inevitably, the remaining scoop of mint chocolate-chip ice cream began to melt. But even in sleep, Phillips managed to keep the cone aloft. From the corner of her eye, Sonny noticed the green orb dripping on his sweater. There seemed little point in pulling over or waking him, so she continued on her mission. With the massive complex looming large over the palm trees, Sonny turned onto Highland Avenue and headed toward the building's entrance. The instant her front tires touched the brick pavers of the circular driveway, the ice cream was ejected, leaving its waffle cone base and landing squarely between Mr. Phillips's thighs.

Sonny later reasoned that it was her hair-trigger reflexes that caused her to reach for the ice cream. It was at the unfortunate moment that Mr. Phillips woke to discover an empty cone and a woman's hand between his legs. Both parties yelped, and Sonny had to swerve to keep from driving into the fountain.

"I was trying to get the ice cream." Sonny held up the dripping brown blob before launching it out her passenger's open window.

"Well, it would have been okay. I wouldn't have minded. Marge, my wife, used to say I made her frisky."

"Be that as it may, Mr. Phillips, I'm spoken for."

"A fellow can dream." He tossed the empty cone out the window.

Dutifully, Sonny parked and came around to the passenger side to lend assistance if it was needed. Phillips declined and pulled himself out of the car.

They rode the elevator up in silence. When it finally bobbed and came to rest on his floor, the door opened to reveal a short, squat woman flanked by an enormous darker-skinned woman in scrubs.

"Howdy, neighbor," Phillips sang out as he stepped into the hall. The smallish woman grunted. Her aide didn't even give him the courtesy of acknowledging his presence.

"Nice neighbors," Sonny reflected out loud.

"Yeah. They pretty much stick to themselves. It gets noisy over there sometimes, when they're out on the balcony, but I don't say a word."

"Mr. Phillips, do they bother you? I'd be happy to talk to whoever is in charge here and let her or him know."

"No, honey. That's okay. I'd rather not have the hassle." Phillips took out the key to his unit and aimed for the lock. After several misses, he turned to his escort. "They're just over there playing cards. No crime in that."

"Is it bad enough that you'd want to move?" Sonny deftly turned the key and pushed open the door to the unit.

"Not at my age. No more moving except into the ground. No, I can tolerate the noise. But…" He stopped to reconsider.

"But what? If they aren't being good neighbors, someone needs to be notified."

"Well, I went over the other night. I heard Sinatra and lots of laughing. I figured they were having a Christmas party. So I got together some goodies over here and paid them a visit. But they were all very jumpy, and that big one practically threw me out the door."

Sonny considered this for a moment, and then asked, "I don't suppose they were close to Anita Lemoyne?"

"The short chubby one isn't, but one of her cronies started hanging around Anita in the dining room. I don't know how long they've been acquainted, but Anita didn't seem very interested in pursuing a friendship, if you know what I mean."

"No. I don't know what you mean." Without thinking, Sonny drew her right foot into the side of her left leg above the knee. Whenever she got nervous, Sonny responded by going into a convenient yoga posture. Vrksasana, the one-legged tree pose, seemed like the thing to do at the moment.

"The woman, Chubby's friend, kept going over to Anita's table when they were in the dining room. Of course Anita was friendly to her, but you could just tell the other lady wasn't her cup of tea."

Sonny continued deeper into her posture, pressing her palms together in the middle of her chest and then raising her hands overhead to create a triangle. "Chubby's friend?"

"Yes." Mr. Phillips watched curiously, cocking his head to one side as Sonny sprouted imaginary branches. "Do you mind if I ask what you're doing?"

"Not at all. This is Vrksasana, the tree pose," Sonny noted absentmindedly. "Sounds like Chubby and her friends aren't people you want to socialize with anyway."

"Well then, she shouldn't have sold me the Viagra."

Sonny reversed her tree by switching legs. As she reached her fingertips overhead, something occurred to her. "Chubby sold you Viagra?"

"Her name's not really Chubby. I just call her that because I don't like her anymore or her Jolly Green Giant."

"Where on earth did she get the Viagra? That's not over the counter, you need a prescription. Is she married?"

"No. There are no men over there, just Chubby and her friends." Mr. Phillips became more animated as he explained. "That's why I thought they sold me the pills. I thought they were looking for a little action. And I'll admit I was somewhat intimidated by the thought of having to satisfy all of them."

"Okay," Sonny interrupted. "I don't need to hear that part. But I'm curious about the pills. By the way, what is Chubby's real name?"

"Carmen Bustamante. But I don't know the big girl's name. She makes me nervous. You know what I mean?"

"Did you talk to the police, Mr. Phillips?"

"No. It's kind of embarrassing. I'd hate for my daughters to find out I spent two grand on pecker pills."

Sonny nodded. "I understand. That's a lot of money."

"Speaking of which, how much do I owe you for today?"

"No charge. Today was a gift from Charlotte. She just asked me to fill in for her until she was able to drive again."

Behind his thick, black-rimmed glasses Mr. Phillips's eyes welled up. "You tell her merry Christmas. And I'm looking forward to having her back real soon." Something occurred to the elderly gentleman. He held up a bony finger. "You wait right here."

Mr. Phillips returned with two boxes, which he extended toward Sonny. "These are for you and your sister." As he spoke, his eyes grew large and round. "You can cook an entire meal in this thing. Breakfast, lunch, or dinner, all in less than five minutes. Just imagine."

It was readily apparent to Sonny that her charge was reliving the excitement of his original purchase. Star-struck and filled with wonder, Phillips was overly animated, as though he was pitching the product.

"You can make those fancy sandwiches like you get in a restaurant. You can make quesadillas, you can even put in a piece of Spam with tater tots and a few peas or corn and you practically have a whole meal. The Abracadabra even makes dessert."

Sonny left the Phillips residence cheerful, a box tucked under each arm. She approached her car, wearing a beatific smile, anxious to personally deliver Charlotte's gift to her.

As she reached for the driver's side door, Sonny's knees suddenly grew weak. The boxes tumbled from her hands. In the seat where Mr. Phillips had been sitting minutes earlier was a large dark circle. Memories of large dark circles flooded back to her. A sofa, a bed, the leather seat of a Mercedes. Sonny lurched forward, clapping her palms against the roof of the Outback. "No," she wailed plaintively. There was no way urine would ever come out of her upholstery. She wasn't even sure she would be able to drive the car knowing what was riding in the seat beside her. (This only added to her Vata imbalance.)

With the desperation of a woman on the edge, she hit number one on her speed dial. "Help!" Sonny gasped.

"Sonny?"

"Yes," she answered weakly.

"Honey? Are you hurt?"

"No."

"Are you in danger?"

"No."

"Has there been an accident?"

"No."

"Has someone died?"

"No."

"All right. What's the matter, then?"

"He peed in my car," Sonny managed with great effort.

Tricia sighed loudly. "Honey, pee in your car does not cross the threshold for what I consider a tragedy."

"It's horrible. I can smell it. I haven't even opened the door and I can smell it."

"First of all, you'll get through this. No one is shooting at you, no one is dying, so get your ass in the car and roll down the window."

"I don't think I can."

"You know if he dumped in your car, I'd be more concerned, but this isn't so bad."

"It's not your car!"

"So what do you want me to do?"

"Come get me."

"What about your car?"

"I'll call Triple A."

"I want you to listen to me and listen closely. Are you listening?" Tricia's tone was firm and unyielding.

"Yes."

"First, grab one of those antibacterial wipes you have everywhere and hold it over your nose. Second, get your ass in the car and roll down the windows, all of them. Then drive over to the studio and we'll switch wheels. Do you think you can do that?" There was a long pause. "Are you actually crying?"

Chapter 25

THE BRIDGE CLUB'S MERCH

Wednesday, December 24, 2008 – 1:20 p.m.

Smiling Tess Fontana crossed her arms on the deck railing and leaned forward to catch the sunlight. From her perch on the balcony of Carmen's condo, she had a glorious view of the Gulf and the pool below. White-capped women bobbed in the water like eggs being boiled. There were very few men in the pool, or in the complex for that matter. She thought of Hector. He was certainly going to have a shorter life expectancy.

The new medicine was making Tess feel slow and lethargic. Her energy level flagged by the hour, and she felt depression closing in on her. The only bright spot in her day was the thought of plugging her boyfriend. She was already looking forward to seeing the look on his face when he realized she had turned the tables on him. She blew a stream of smoke straight up and ground the butt of her cigarette in the ashtray Carmen kept on the patio.

Inside, the Jersey girls were working an assembly line. From a box of pink-colored tablets, Flobo meticulously poured and counted out pills on a pharmacist tray. Using a car oil funnel she had commandeered from her mechanic, she poured them into a three-inch-by-three-inch baggie. The packet moved next to Connie, who eyed and pinched the Barbie-sized baggie, sealing it tight.

Carmen took the product and nudged it into the lining of a waiting handbag. The purse was then passed to Muscia, who packed it in a nondescript brown box. The bottom of the box contained a solid inch of generic ground coffee to protect the product from being detected by drug-sniffing dogs. Three boxes were stacked neatly by the front door awaiting their next stop in the supply line.

"How's Hector?" Flobo called, without looking up from her task. "I haven't seen him around lately. You get a new a piece of ass?"

"No. I think Hector will be my last. I don't think I have the energy to break in a new one. He's probably out Christmas shopping," Tess noted nonchalantly. She pretended to examine her paint-chipped fingernails. The response seemed to satisfy Flobo.

"Carm?" Flobo continued. "Are you going out tonight? Is Ralph Junior coming over?"

"Would you shaddup and count," Carmen looked up long enough to glower.

"How 'bout one of those rolls? You have any left from the other night?"

Connie sealed the packet she was working on and passed it to Carmen. Then Carmen Bustamante turned her tiny black eyes on Flobo. "Tell you what, Flo. When we finish here, I will personally go to Delaurentis's and get you all the rolls you can eat. But right now we got work to do. We have a time limit. And you see all those boxes?" Carmen pointed to the remaining stack. "We really need to get everything packaged, so it's not lying around here in case we have visitors—if you know what I mean. Besides which, we've got to be completely prepped for the day after Christmas. Because when we get paid for this merch, you'll be able to buy Delaurentis's and eat rolls morning, noon, and night. So can you focus just a while longer?"

"All right, Carm. I meant no disrespect."

"Yeah, not to mention you'll get your greasy fingers on the pills and the stuff here," Connie noted, as she sealed a pack of carefully blended pills which, when taken together, produced an impressive and long-lasting high.

Tess strolled in and took a seat at the bar. She fingered the petals of a silk flower arrangement. "Do we have any pickups today, anything I can help with?"

"No," Carmen said flatly, without the courtesy of making eye contact.

"Jose needs oxy." Flobo squinted as she measured the pills for the next cocktail mix. "Yo, Muscia. Can you get my glasses outta my pocketbook? Yeah, he said one of his crew has gone off the grid, but orders are piling up. I told him he could make a buy tonight, but he said he'd wait till the twenty-sixth and get everything all at once. It's just as well, everything should be ready when we open for business in the new place."

Muscia, who had been listening to the conversation, appeared in the open bar area between the kitchen and living room. "Do we need to get involved with this missing person?" Like Carmen, she too avoided eye contact with Tess.

Carmen shrugged, "Probably one of his junkie friends. You know how they are. You can't depend on 'em when they're straight, never mind when they're strung out all over the place."

"You want me to drive my car?" Flobo asked.

Connie said, "No. We'll use my car. It's bigger."

Carmen nodded in approval. "Yeah, I'd like to get it done in one trip and Connie's Caddy should be able to accommodate the whole load."

"Do you mind if I drive?" Flobo asked.

"Yes, I mind. It's my car. I'm driving. And you just made me lose count."

"I'm not going if she drives," Flobo announced.

"I'm right here, Flo. And if you want to drive so bad, nobody's stopping you from following in your car."

Carmen watched the two volley words between packages.

As if appealing to a judge, Flobo turned to Carmen. "She's got the cataracts."

"I got it in one eye, and I'm still here."

This last statement struck Carmen as particularly amusing, and she began to chuckle. Her porcine eyes grew smaller as her cackle became merrier. "You two just take my car and Muscia will drive. Problem solved."

"Carm, you want to have drinks later?" Tess came around the table where she could face Bustamante and take a measure of the boss's frame of mind. Not that Carmen was an easy one to gauge. But after nearly six decades of friendship, Tess was able to spot one or two of her soon-to-be-ex-friend's tells. Behind her hooded black eyes, Carmen revealed no emotion. Rather, it was the effort she put into making eye contact with someone who already had a price on his head that broadcasted her plan.

Carmen the Nose Bustamante only looked human. Inside, she was cold and robotic. Although Tess never knew Carmen to have a conscience, she was deathly afraid of getting caught and doing time. Consequently, the grandmother of three was not only savvy in her business dealings but cautious nearly to the point of paranoia. Tess knew Carmen always had escape plans and was not above throwing her friends or family members, including her son, under the bus to save herself.

"Not tonight." Carmen looked up. Her eyes locked onto Tess like a guided missile and bore into her as though Tess had already taken the bullet.

Tess did not flinch. There was no doubt that the hit was in. Carmen was talking to a ghost. "I'll drop your gift off tomorrow." Tess exhaled quietly and made ready to leave. She knew she was Hector's top priority and Carmen was doing her part to make the target available.

"That'll be nice." Carmen did not break the gaze.

"Yeah, I think you'll like it." Tess nodded, smiled, and headed for the door. She had her confirmation. Now she needed a plan. "Merry Christmas, everyone."

Chapter 26

MILO GETS GRACE TO TALK

Wednesday, December 24, 2008 – 4:55 p.m.

With dusk fast approaching, Elizabeth pulled up behind Milo's golf cart and parked her silver Highlander. She came up to the loading dock using the stairs and stuck her head in the back door of 411. Leaning in, she looked around, noticing the changes that had occurred since she had been there earlier in the day. "Hey, are you about ready to call it a day?"

Hearing his wife's voice, Cole was smiling before he turned around. "I sold all but two of the 'dillos." Cole was referring to his vast assortment of stuffed armadillos. Since the start of his taxidermy career five years earlier, he had amassed dozens of the beady-eyed creatures. They filled his locker-sized freezer and appeared on his doorstep with regularity several times a week. Having grown up in southwest Florida, Cole had friends from every walk of life. One, in particular, had unlimited access to dead animals. An old high school flame had become a sanitation worker specializing in road kill removal. Sally's route took her from one end of the county to the other. She was always on the lookout for "quality kill," which she deposited outside Cole's front door. Sanitation Sally had an uncanny ability for spotting fresh and barely blemished cadavers. And her recovery skills were unmatched, as she carefully shoveled fur, feathers, and scales from the pavement all day, every day.

Elizabeth had encouraged her husband's hobby until word got out that he needed carcasses to practice on. After that, he rarely experienced a shortage of armadillos, raccoons, and opossums. And Elizabeth used the garage door for her entrance and egress for fear of what she might have to step over if she used the front door. Lately, she hoped her husband would find a way to move the base of his operation to the flea market so that she could reclaim the front stoop and decorate it with flowers.

"Nothing much left to get rid of. Someone even wanted the big rattler."

"Want me to help you close up?"

Cole came to the lip of the loading dock and knelt. "I want to know if you got me my Christmas present."

"Cole, honey, I've had it in the closet since April, but I did get you a little something you didn't ask for."

"Hey, Mrs.——," Milo broke off. "Hey, Elizabeth. Hey, Cole."

"Hey yourself, Milo. You all set for Christmas?"

Milo blushed. "Is there such a thing?"

"You have big plans?"

"No. Just me and my mom. What about you all?"

"Our three girls are all coming over, and our grandkids."

"Sounds like a good time. Well, I won't keep you all. I've got to finish my rounds. I still need to get a few things on my list before everything closes." The security guard tipped his hat and headed toward the nearby stairs.

Out of sight, Milo hurried down the aisle to where Grace was sliding her wire gate at the front of the store closed.

"Grace! Wait!" Milo had intended to sound strong and self-assured, but somehow he heard desperation in his voice.

The dark-haired girl flinched and turned. She appeared relieved when she saw it was Milo. "Yes, Mr. Purdie?"

"Hey, Grace. I just wanted to talk to you. Do you have a minute?"

"I suppose a minute is all right," she said in her soft, lilting dialect.

"Let's step inside. I'd prefer to speak in private if that's okay."

"Yes, of course. Please come in, Mr. Purdie."

"First of all, call me Milo. Second, I know something is going on here."

Grace's eyes grew large. "Please don't arrest me."

"Whoa. I'm not going to arrest you. I don't even have handcuffs. Well, actually I have some at home—never mind. The point I'm trying to make here is I have a gut feeling that those women who come in here after hours are up to something. I can't prove it. Help me out here, Grace."

The young woman closed her eyes. Her chin dropped toward her chest. "I am so ashamed, Mr. Purdie."

"Milo."

Grace looked up with tortured eyes. "I came here on a school visa. But I knew before I left my homeland that I could not live in fear and without basic freedom. When the plane took off, I knew I would never see my homeland again. I am afraid, but now I cannot go back to my country." She pressed her lips tight as though she could hold back more words. "We should go now."

Milo realized his mouth had fallen open while she was talking. He closed it while considering how to play his cards. "Let me take you to dinner. We can talk this over."

She stopped suddenly. "Mr. Purdie, the clock continues to tick. We must leave."

"Why? What's gonna happen? What's the big hurry?"

"They are coming. They told me to be out by six." She slipped by Milo and positioned herself outside the gate.

"Or what?" Milo followed her, aware that he was quickly losing control of the situation he had come to handle. "I'm doing my best to try and help you," he pleaded.

"I cannot afford to ask." Gripping the rolling gate, she began to pull.

Milo placed his hand above hers to stop the gate from moving. "Just let me do one thing."

She looked skeptical, but her resolve fell away when she saw the determination on the man's face. After a second, Grace nodded.

"I'll be in and out in less than a minute." He pressed his palms together.

She gave a slight nod and Milo brushed past her. He located the stool he had used earlier and climbed up without effort. In a flash he had the phone number on the bug written down in his notebook.

"What did you do?" Grace asked when he reappeared.

Milo pulled the wire gate closed and stood back.

Grace stepped between him and the gate, the lock still in her hand.

Milo was thinking of his father when he said, "I'm going to get enough evidence to get them busted. You don't have to do anything. When we have something concrete, I'll just take it to the police. And hopefully, that will take care of your worries. This is my country, and I won't let you live in fear." Milo planted his fists on his hips and stood a little taller. "No, m'am, not on my watch."

"Thank you, Mr. Purdie—Milo."

Milo nodded sharply. He squared his shoulders and turned to face her. "I'm just doing my job. Now, may I take you to your car?" He could easily see himself dating this woman. He would take her to the Italian restaurant on Pine Ridge, and they would sip cappuccino after dinner. There would be walks on the beach, stopping every few feet to gaze into each other's eyes before a meaningful kiss. Even if they didn't end up marrying, Milo wouldn't mind spending a night or two or three with Grace.

"Also part of your job?"

Grace could not see the slight upturn of Milo's lips as he escorted her out to the golf cart. He drove to the rear of the parking lot, where the last few merchants were preparing to leave, and helped her into a well-used Honda Civic.

She looked up before pulling away as Milo patted the top of her car. "I still want to take you to dinner."

Chapter 27

THE DROP

Wednesday, December 24, 2008 — 6:10 p.m.

The women had waited until the security guard pulled out. Then they had waited in the adjoining marina parking lot another ten minutes to make sure he was gone for good. The Cadillac cut its lights before pulling to a stop in front of the loading dock.

"Wait here." Muscia stepped out first and scanned the alley between the buildings. Christmas Eve—it was not likely anyone would be around. But Muscia wasn't paid to play the odds; she was paid to be certain. A possum made its way down the center of the asphalt, blindly pausing to sniff before hurrying on to the next odor, always searching, always on the move. The creature vanished in the darkness of a cement overhang. Muscia watched stoically before concluding that is was safe to move the merchandise. She slipped on a pair of latex gloves which she had handy in a pocket of her scrubs.

As ordered, Grace had left the outer gate unlocked. The padlock dangled from the mesh, so Muscia slid the gate wide enough to pull the metal door behind it and slip inside the booth. She clicked on a mini Maglite that hung from a cord around her neck. It took seconds to locate a lamp near the cash register. She had been to the location twice, but this was the first time she'd been inside in the dark. Muscia took her time roaming the area with her beam of light until she was comfortable that the space was secure.

Muscia went to the lip of the loading dock. "All clear."

The passenger and rear door of the Caddy opened. Connie and Flobo stepped out as Muscia hit the trunk release with her key fob. The bigger, younger woman hopped back to the ground and began removing boxes from the trunk while the other two carried boxes between them. Connie moved easily up the three steps to the dock while Flobo had to use the rail and stop halfway to catch her breath.

"It's not this one, is it?" Flobo pointed to the door at the top of the steps, 410.

"No." Muscia slid a box up on the dock. "Next one, four-oh-eight."

"This one is unlocked. Someone forgot to lock up when they left." Flo continued pointing to the door.

Muscia shrugged and reached for the next box. "You lock it." Her baritone command left no room for question.

Flobo handed her boxes to Connie, who was none too pleased with the chore. With great care, she hooked the metal pin through the door latch and squeezed the lock tight. "Wouldn't want any bad guys getting in," she said, and couldn't resist a chuckle ending in a convulsive snort.

"We're nearly done here, no thanks to you." Connie was already up the steps with another load.

"It's freakin' cold out," Flobo commented, and rubbed her palms together.

"It's winter. Whadda ya think?" Connie reminded her.

"I think it's freakin' Florida. It ain't s'posed to get cold this far south."

"And yet here we are, in Florida, and it's nearly forty."

Flobo waddled back to the open car door and wrangled another box free. "Well, it's killing my arthritis."

"You heard about those 'ritis boys, right?" Connie asked.

"What?"

"Arthur is the worst."

"I don't get it." Flobo grunted and strained against her own body weight.

"Arthuritis, he's the worst. Now you get it?"

"That's stupid."

"Why don't we get Muscia to stop at Dunkin' Donuts on the way home and we'll get a hot chocolate?"

The trio set the boxes on the cement outside the booth until all eight were accounted for. Then Muscia easily jumped the four feet back onto the dock and took each box in turn inside the booth. She placed them in stacks of two in an area that had been cleared behind the cash register. When she finished the task, Muscia returned the boutique to its original darkness before locking up. She lit on the ground like a gymnast and silently slipped off the gloves before getting back behind the wheel.

"Okay, we good?" Flobo asked.

"Good."

"Good."

"All right, I'm dialing. Hey, boss, you're on speaker. I'm just calling to let you know we're done."

Carmen's voice was so clear it sounded like she was in the car with them. "Make the calls."

Chapter 28

CHRISTMAS EVE, FLABI STYLE

Wednesday, December 24, 2008 — 6:23 p.m.

Agents Winnie and Pell, Ramon, and Paige Chesley sat around the coffee table in Pell's room.

Winnie scowled at her partner, then plucked a card from Pell's spread. Pell's face remained expressionless, even though the Old Maid had just been liberated from her hand.

"I am not having fun," Winnie growled, even before she saw the card.

Pell sighed. "That's the bump on your head talking."

"*Lo siento*." Ramon stared intently at his hand, still intimidated by the angry agent.

A perfect three-inch-by-three-inch patch of hair had been shaved from the back of Agent Winnie's head where an emergency room nurse had taken four stitches to close the gash caused by the blow from Ramon's bat.

Pell said, "Look. We're kind of trapped here until after Christmas and things get active again."

"Yeah, I get that. But why does he have to be here?" Winnie jutted her chin in Ramon's direction.

"That's a rather snarky tone to take on Christmas Eve, don't you think?"

"I got a bald patch, and the right side of my body is black and blue. I'm allowed to be snarky. In fact, I'm supposed to be snarky. What the hell does snarky mean, anyway?" Winnie tossed her cards on the table. "I bet that's snarky, too!"

"It means to take a tone of nagging or sarcasm," Paige Chesley said. She had a new haircut, which not only repaired the damage done by the mystery feline, but also changed her appearance and lent her an air of confidence. She hadn't cried in hours and was becoming more personable the more distance she put between her last drink and the present moment.

"I'm sorry," Winnie said with great effort.

"I am also sorry." Ramon put his cards down and opened his arms to embrace the *gringa*.

"Don't touch me or I'll turn you into a fuckin' piñata. Wait, was that still too snarky?"

"No. That was flat-out sarcastic, Agent Winnie." Paige Chesley was growing increasingly bold without the alcohol and drugs in her system.

"We're in a holding pattern right now. Ramon is here until we can make sure Shoat doesn't pick up a scent of what is going on. And I owe him one 'cause he helped me get you out of there today. I wouldn't have been able to get you fixed up if he hadn't been there."

"He caused this," Winnie said, angrily pointing to the back of her head. "Ow," she winced, and immediately launched into a stream of invective that caused everyone present to blanch.

When the tirade came to an end, Pell got up and filled a glass with tap water. She picked up a pill bottle and held them out to her partner. "It's time for another. Every four hours you can take one as needed for pain."

"I go now," Ramon said softly.

Pell returned to her seat and turned to the slight man. "You're free to go, Ramon. We're not holding you. You understand that, don't you? I just want you to know that if you choose to stay, you're welcome. This little sofa pulls out into a bed and you can spend the night. I'm sure it is more comfortable than the floor, but it is your decision whether to stay or not. I'll be happy to drive you back to the school."

Three pairs of eyes focused on Ramon, who shifted uncomfortably as he appeared to consider his options.

"He attacked an agent. He should be behind bars."

"He thought you were breaking in. He was just protecting the school. And you know damn well we can't hand him over to Shoat without putting him on our trail. What's it gonna be?"

"How long are we supposed to keep him?" Winnie snarled, enjoying the effect it had on Ramon.

Paige watched the banter the way one watches a tennis match, turning left and right between volleys. Ramon continued to study the ground with fevered deliberation.

"I can take him back after lunch tomorrow. Shoat will think he went some-where for Christmas, if he even bothers to follow up, and I'm not sure he's smart enough to be curious."

"I have a question?" Ramon's voice was soft as though he dreaded drawing any attention to himself. "Who sleeps in that bed?"

"Me," Pell answered. "I'm in this room and Agent Winnie is next door. She'll be bunking with Paige."

Paige Chesley piped up. "Do I have a say in this?" Her cell phone began to ring and vibrate, demanding attention. She studied the caller ID. "It's Jose."

Pell nodded, "Put it on speaker and answer it."

"Hello?"

"Hey, Mrs. Chesley, this is Jose. Are you okay?" The teen at the other end sounded genuinely concerned.

"Yes, Jose. Thank you for asking."

"I'm glad. I haven't heard from you all week and was a little worried."

"Yeah, I had a touch of the flu. But I'm all right now."

"That's good. I'm just calling to let you know we're supposed to make a pick up on the twenty-sixth."

Paige watched Pell for her next cue. Pell nodded.

"I'll be there. Just give me the time and place."

"We're scheduled to be there between six forty-five and seven p.m. The place closes at six, and they want to make sure everyone is gone. And we have a new place. Do you know where the Stone Crab Flea Market is?"

"Yeah. I've been there once or twice."

"Well, go around back to booth four-oh-eight. The girl behind the counter will give you a black leather handbag."

"A purse?"

"A black leather handbag—that's what I was told. She'll hand you this purse, it's got your specific order in it. The merch is hidden in a panel on the bottom."

"Do I pay her?"

"Yes. Bring the envelope you've been using. Then we go to a new system. Once you get rid of your inventory, take the purse back with the cash in the same panel. You hand it to the salesperson and tell her you'd like a refund. She'll hand you the cash for your cut. Easy, right?"

Pell indicated that Paige should cover the mouthpiece. "Ask him if he'll be there."

"Are you there?"

"Yes, Jose, I'm here. Am I going to see you?"

"Maybe. It depends on whether I can unload what I have now. So, maybe. Why do you ask?" The voice at the other end sounded the slightest bit cagey.

"I just wanted to wish you a merry Christmas."

"Oh, okay. Thanks, Mrs. Chesley. You have a good holiday, too."

The whole conversation lasted less than five minutes. The young man was polite. Anyone listening would never consider that a crime was in the offing.

"Good-bye, Jose."

"Bye, Mrs. Chesley."

Paige Chesley folded her cell phone and wearily looked up at the agents. "Now what?"

"I think I will stay," Ramon announced definitely, his bony chest puffed to its fullest.

Winnie's eyebrows furrowed in a dark line as she turned to him. "Shut up, you turd wagon."

Pell cupped her hand in her chin and paced. "Jose obviously knows what you look like."

"Yes."

"So there is no way one of us can fool him?" Pell brainstormed. "Do the higher-ups know what you look like?" Pell pressed on, clearly following a line of logic.

"No."

"Presumably the people up the chain of command know what Jose looks like."

"Yeah. He has said things to make me believe he interfaces with them from time to time. I'm not a hundred percent sure, but the way he talks they've at least met."

Pell nodded sagely. "All right. I think we need to take Jose out of the picture. He's not the one we want anyway."

Winnie leaned forward, resting her forearms on her thighs. "If we arrest him, we'll have to put him in a holding cell and he might talk to Shoat."

Pell picked up the thought and continued. "Then we'll have to do it in such a way that he can't notify Shoat or the people who are pulling the strings. We'll have to move on him when he pulls out of the flea market."

"Why not let it play out with Chesley and the kid? We'll stand back until they come out. Pick her up and get the kid whenever. It's not like he's going anywhere. We want the kingfish, right?"

"I don't know," Pell said thoughtfully. "Maybe we should call for backup."

"This is what my tax dollars are paying for?" Paige crossed her arms and arched one eyebrow.

Winnie felt around the back of her head. "How long do you think it will take for my hair to grow back?"

"Why? Are you planning on entering a beauty contest in the near future?" Pell made no effort to disguise her incredulity. "Can you please just try to stay focused? We need a plan and there isn't much time to put it together."

The scolding caused Ramon to snigger and Winnie, in turn, trained her eyes on him the way a Florida panther appraises a domesticated goat. His brown eyes grew large, his Adam's apple bobbed nervously. The fear seemed to arouse Winnie.

Pell stepped between them, knowing that her partner's way of dealing with stress was generally some form of violence, and this time Ramon didn't have a bat to protect himself.

Chapter 29

TESS'S FIRST LOVE

Wednesday, December 24, 2008 – 6:58 p.m.

Smiling Tess Fontana tugged the collar of her jacket tight and crossed her arms over her chest; the temperature had gone down with the sun. It had not exactly been the kind of day she had expected to have this close to Christmas. There were no smiles for the people she passed en route to her unit. There was no plan to attend the candlelight ceremony at Our Lady of Perpetual Prayer. There was neither eggnog nor mistletoe. Instead, Tess had spent the first part of the afternoon feeling the weight of being snubbed by her best friend, the same best friend who had put a hit out on her. It didn't take long for Tess to come to the conclusion that Carmen Bustamante was just following her true nature. She was as cold as any reptile and governed by the same tiny prehistoric brain. Carmen was completely in character; it was Tess who had been mistaken when she thought Carmen would never turn on her. How many times had she seen Carmen shake the hand or kiss the cheek of a soon-to-be-departed *friend?* Ironically, it was usually one of Tess's bullets that sent them on their way into the next life. Knowing this did not take the sting out.

If that wasn't enough, there was the last four hours she had spent on her balcony contemplating what to do with Hector. Earlier in the week she had envisioned sitting across the table from Hector, a candle burning between them. She imagined him handing her a gift, something in a small box with tasteful wrapping paper and a delicate bow. Instead, she was home alone, huddled in a velour jacket she had intended to gift to Connie for Christmas. And by now Hector was playing hide the sausage with some young stripper from the East Coast. Within the span of a single day, she had been betrayed by the two people she had considered to be her closest friends.

"Screw this," she snarled. She ground her cigarette on the glass tabletop because the ashtray was overflowing and blew out a final breath of smoke. Leaning her head back against the lounge chair, Tess realized the only way to protect herself was to follow her true nature. Below, she heard voices coming from the pool deck. Beyond that, the waves tumbled ashore. It was a night like any other. Quiet reflection time was over; Tess got to her feet and went inside.

After decades of dedicated service and loyalty, Carmen the Nose Bustamante was kicking her to the curb. Hector already had someone new in his bed. But both Carmen and Hector had made two serious miscalculations. They overestimated themselves and underestimated Tess.

She hadn't reached the top of her profession by having regrets and guilt. No, Smiling Tess Fontana had practiced and honed her natural talent. She took pride in her work and was well respected by her peers. At the end of the day, she came home to her first love, the sleek wood finish, rubber butt, and blue metal barrel of her favorite rifle. Wearing the white cotton gloves she kept for handling her tools, Tess lifted the weapon and embraced it. She sighted down the barrel imagining Carmen's face. Her finger released the trigger. Tess closed her eyes, realizing she couldn't shoot Carmen or Hector. She did not want the blood of either on her hands. There would have to be some other way to make them pay.

Chapter 30

MILO'S CHRISTMAS CAROLERS

Wednesday, December 24, 2008 – 8:29 p.m.

Milo's recollection of being locked in while the women carried out their activities was dutifully reported in his notebook—minus a few details. He did not mention the part about forgetting to bring the lock on the empty unit in with him while he was on surveillance, or how he saw the feet under that door shortly after the women arrived. Nor did he give any details about the feeling the realization caused when he heard the actual click of the metal lock slipping into place, effectively sealing him in the unit. He also left out the fact that he had been forced by necessity to call his mother, and to slide his own master key under the one-sixteenth-inch opening at the bottom of the door so she could get him out. His report, however, did include a well-documented account of the women next door. He had video footage of the top of Muscia's head, along with the scraping sound of boxes being moved. He had their complete conversation, which conveniently started after he was locked in. In an effort to keep his story fresh, he had written down everything while waiting thirty-five minutes for his mother to arrive.

Upon returning home, Milo walked his dog, Boomer, before shedding his uniform and heading into the shower. The shower, typical of the kind found in mobile and manufactured homes, came as a solid piece and could be installed in minutes with a little caulk and elbow grease. Milo liked it because it had a built-in soap dish, an acrylic towel rack, and a high-gloss finish that resisted mold.

He stepped over Boomer, who lay sprawled across the shower mat, joyfully chewing an early Christmas gift, a rawhide bone flavored with ham. The sliding glass doors quickly fogged and steam boiled from the enclosure. But after the day he'd had Milo needed a hot shower. He pressed his palms against the plastic walls and bowed his head so that the water cascaded over his neck and shoulders. Then, in an effort to forget the worst part of his day, Milo tried to recall the best part of his day.

Edwin Winslow had paid Roy, the maintenance man, his regular day rate to wear a Santa suit and allow children to ask him for their heart's desires while the parents took photos and generally looked on with more pride than the child deserved. The gesture was good marketing; providing a Santa served to warm the shoppers into spending more in order to prolong and deepen the holiday experience. It was good for Roy, too. Sitting most of the day made him forget he only had one leg. Milo closed his eyes and smiled. Every time Roy put one child down he had sworn it was the last time he'd do a favor for Edwin. Then the next kid would run into his arms and it would start all over.

Ideally, Milo would have stayed in the shower longer, but he was in fact anxious to wrap his mother's Christmas gifts and watch *A Charlie Brown Christmas*. Wrapped in a maroon bathrobe, he towel dried his hair and returned to the living room.

The living room was actually a multifunctional room with a sofa, recliner, weight equipment, and entertainment system. The walls were decorated with vintage record albums, army recruitment posters, and a stuffed boar head he had inherited from his father's collection. The two racks of deer antlers had gone to his brothers, and his mother had kept the twenty-five-pound bass which had been a wedding gift from Milo's father. Milo used one of the boar's tusks to hang his Crukinshank hat on. The keys for his pickup truck hung from the other tusk.

Not until Milo sat back on the brown leatherette sofa did he notice the remains of his dinner. He had left the Salisbury steak TV dinner on the coffee table to cool off before going into the shower. Now all that remained was a mangled piece of the plastic tray and the broccoli florets, which were untouched. "This isn't funny." Milo stared at the culprit, who chewed with great gusto on his ham-flavored bone. Fortunately, the assortment of spy apparatus atop the coffee table was still intact.

Milo collected the pieces of chewed plastic and broccoli florets, and tossed the debris in the garbage. Searching the freezer compartment, Milo found a stack of pot pies, no doubt from one of his mother's visits. He grabbed the top box, tore it open, and popped the pie in the microwave. "This one is mine," he said, glancing down at the pit bill. "I buy you a Christmas present and you eat my dinner."

The stout-chested animal suddenly dropped the bone and stood. He drew up beside Milo's bare leg and leaned against him.

"I'm sorry, too. I'm a little on edge. It's just this girl. Yeah, I know girls are nothing but trouble. But this one is slammin' hot. She looks like..." Boomer looked up with more disinterest than usual, then trotted back to his treat.

The microwave beeped and Milo brought his second attempt at dinner to the coffee table. Generally, he liked to watch a sports channel while he ate, but tonight, Milo was eager to number each piece of evidence, starting with the video footage. He slipped the flash card into his laptop and watched the upload bar turn green.

He jumped when a knock came at the door. Scowling, Milo looked over at Boomer. The big dog didn't move but chewed in rapt delight, his powerful jaws working over the bone, spurred by the intoxicating flavor of ham. Milo knew before he looked through the peephole there was no danger or Boomer would have been on his feet before the knock even sounded.

Indeed, Milo observed six stocking-capped children eying the peephole and recognized the brood as a neighbor's children. The family lived three units down. Besides their own offspring, they took in foster children as well, so there was an endless supply of little ones spilling out of the dirt yard and into the road, where they played soccer and football depending on the season. Several times a year the girls would sell him boxes of cookies. Milo's mother finally informed him that they were not, in fact, Girl Scouts. "Honey, you can get these at Publix for half the price," Priss Purdie had explained. "Those girls are probably trying to make some cash for who knows what. But I'll tell you this, if you want to help those children, buy a couple of boxes of condoms and leave 'em on the doorstep."

Milo opened the door a crack, leaving the chain in place. "Hey."

"Hey, Mr. Milo," a tall girl said. "We're caroling. Do you have a favorite Christmas carol we can sing for you?"

"Yeah, hold on." Milo closed the door and slipped off the chain. "Do you all know 'Silent Night'?"

"Sure," a little boy missing his front teeth spoke up. "Si-uh-lent Night," he belted out the first few words in a nasal, high-pitched voice. The others jumped in and caught up. After one verse they all stopped, smiled, and blinked in the cold night air.

"That's it?" Milo asked with lifted eyebrows.

"Si-uh-lent Night," the small, ambitious boy started again. The oldest girl nudged her brother and everyone's hands came out of the ratty coat pockets, palms up. The little boy was still singing after Milo handed each child a dollar bill. He closed the door and chained it, but the boy kept singing. After the fifth time around, Milo cracked the door, threw out a fiver, and allowed Boomer to poke his snout out in order to reinforce his determination that the concert was officially over. One of the hooligans snatched up the bill, as the other siblings scrambled down the stairs and swarmed toward the next victim's house.

"Dang," Milo shook his head. "I'm gonna start answering the door with my gun handy." He shuffled back to the sofa and discovered an empty pot pie bowl. "Boomer!" he yelled, then snatched the bone from between the dog's front paws and threw it across the room. The rawhide bone left a dent in the opposite wall. A split second later, Boomer skidded over to retrieve his new toy, tossing it in the air and snagging it between his massive jaws.

Armed with a beer and a package of stale crackers, Milo reviewed the video. No matter how hard he tried, three women unloading boxes at a loading dock simply did not cross the threshold of illegal activity. He sighed and collapsed into the sofa. From out of nowhere, Boomer leaped up beside him and rolled onto his back, paws in the air, belly up.

"Does this feel good?" Milo vigorously scratched the dog's underside. "How about this?" He scratched vigorously under Boomer's chin. "I know what you like, don't I?" He pressed his cheek against the canine's head as he continued to rub with the greatest affection.

Milo was so focused on pleasing the pit bull that he did not hear Boomer begin to retch. Without warning, a warm gush of Salisbury steak and pot pie liquid suddenly appeared in his lap. Boomer smacked his lips and blinked, looking more surprised than Milo.

"This is why you shouldn't eat people food," Milo scolded, as he gingerly got to his feet while holding the hem of the bathrobe to contain the liquid TV dinners. He carefully withdrew one arm and then the other from the terry cloth sleeves before allowing the bathrobe to fall in a heap on the floor.

When he reemerged from the shower, Milo returned to the scene of the crime to discover that the remaining saltines were gone, along with the bathrobe. "Boomer," he called, and trained his ear. He discovered the dog in the laundry room, gnawing his bone with renewed voracity. Beside him lay a chewed maroon terry cloth sash.

Boomer with someone's shirt and shoe

Chapter 31

TESS MEETS HECTOR'S GIRLFRIEND

Wednesday, December 24, 2008 – 10:52 p.m.

Smiling Tess Fontana was not smiling as she sat in the parking lot of the Pier Hotel and Tennis Club across the street from Hector's condo. Her Audi was safely concealed between a pair of SUVs. It was highly unlikely that Hector would think to look for her car tonight, which made her mission that much easier. He had called around seven p.m. to inform her that his stomach problem had escalated and he now feared his intestines were hosting a bug of some sort. He apologized about the timing, but thought it wise to stay away in order to avoid exposing her. Tess had gamely played along with the dimwit. The entire conversation had lasted less than a minute. Tess had hung up shaking her head in disgust.

She leaned forward and stared at the door of his condo, desperately wanting to be on the other side of this issue, but she wasn't sure what exactly the other side would look like. For as long as she could remember, Tess had known her own parameters. It was not as though there was much room for advancement or invention. She was given a target, she took care of it. The end. Her mind wandered down the roads she might have taken, roads which would have led her far from where she was at this moment in time. What if she would have kept her window dressing job at Macys? What if she had never met the army sharpshooter? Both those critical crossroads had seemed like small choices at the time. Yet they had led to this inexorable conclusion. She wondered if the sharpshooter's body had ever been found. She'd just rolled him under a log. Tess looked down at her hands, folded and resting in her lap. The right one trembled ever so slightly, but she knew with time it would get worse. She hadn't taken her medicine since the discovery of the plot against her. Keeping her wits about her was more important than a little trembling. Then she reasoned the shake was likely due to the temperature. It was forty-seven degrees when she left her condo, probably colder now.

But this cold was nothing compared to New Jersey in the winter. She snorted at the thought of her home. There was nothing there for her anymore. And she had never been very keen on the eastern coast of Florida. Twice she had visited the area. The first time left her with a bad taste in her mouth, the second time, a worse taste. The heat was as extreme as Jersey winters were cold, but southeastern Florida had the added duress of heavy traffic, foreigners, and crime. While she had no experience with Arizona, Tess thought it might make for a good place to retire. The climate was nice enough, but then, any climate is generally an improvement on New Jersey's brutal winters. And there was always Italy if she decided to put some real distance between her future and her past.

Someone pulled into the parking lot across the street, and a couple in formal attire exited the vehicle. She watched them take the elevator and disappear into one of the units on the top floor. Hector's building was a lot like Hector himself, past its prime. The structure had been built in the early seventies and its age showed. Efforts to keep the complex up-to-date were impossible as there were only three stories, a fact which dated the construction to a time when builders were not allowed to build any higher. The materials used in the façade also heralded back to the days when limestone was popular. It had likely been white when first installed, but over the years, the color had changed. It was a mottled orange where the copper-tainted ground water hit it twice a week when the sprinklers came on. The rest of the ornamental rock varied in shades of gray. But it did have a nostalgic charm to it.

Tess was envisioning the building on the day of its completion when the door to Hector's condo suddenly opened. It was three a.m., and Tess was stoked on the heat of her anger. Her instincts were as sharp as they'd ever been, and she felt her body moving like a fine-tuned machine. She was not just a mechanic; she was Smiling Tess Fontana, the Mechanic.

Exiting her car, Tess moved stealthily toward her target. Since she wore black, the night swallowed her into itself.

As soon as the young woman boarded the elevator, Tess started up the stairs at the opposite end of the condo. She chanced a look over the second-story railing and saw the woman's head as she walked toward the parking lot.

Tess was nearly to Hector's door when she was surprised by the *ding* of the elevator. It was too late to turn around and reach the far stairs, so she hurried past Hector's door and pressed herself against the limestone wall around the corner of the building, hoping no one would head in her direction. She waited several seconds and finally heard the elevator door open, followed by one set of footsteps. It sounded like a lone individual and Tess thought the footsteps were moving away from her.

She took her hand out of her pocket, ready to abort if need be. But the footsteps stopped suddenly. She ventured a quick look around the corner and was taken aback by the sight of Hector's girlfriend.

The young woman sensed her presence and smiled. "Merry Christmas," she said softly, and Tess knew she'd been spotted.

"Merry Christmas," Tess answered in kind. She came out of hiding, intending to retreat to the stairs and call it a night. As she drew near, she saw the young woman had a large handbag propped on her knee and was fumbling through the contents.

"There they are." She held up a ring of car keys. "Hey, I know you." The girl grinned and aimed her index finger at Tess.

Tess stopped abruptly, again caught off guard. "I don't think we've met." She stroked the weapon in her pocket for reassurance.

"I'm Christie." The younger woman extended her hand toward Tess. "And you're Mrs. Rinaldi. Hector has told me all about you."

"A pleasure to meet you Christie." Rinaldi was Hector's last name, and Tess was curious as to why Hector would have bothered to mention her in the first place, and second, why he would discuss her with his girlfriend.

"He has a photo of you two on his dresser." Suddenly, Christie's eyebrows dipped ever so slightly. "Is everything alright?"

"Everything is fine," Tess lied. "I've been out with a friend from college catching up."

"Oh, well, Hector is asleep. But I can wake him. I know he'd want to get up if he knew you were out here." She nodded apologetically. "Golly, I thought nursing homes were pretty strict. My grandmother lives in one on the other coast and they try to have everyone in bed by eight. By the way, how is your irritable bowel issue?" Christie was genuinely concerned with the well-being of the older woman.

Tess deflated ever so slightly when it occurred to her that Hector had obviously introduced her as his mother.

The younger woman reached out and took hold of her elbow. "You don't look well. Let's get you inside. You probably need to get to the toilet, right?"

"No, Christie. I'm just a little chilled. Listen, it's late. I'll give Hector a call tomorrow. Would you mind walking me to my car?" With each word, Tess felt her blood cool. She hadn't intended to hurt the girl. But survival trumped intention.

"Sure." Christie offered her arm.

Reluctantly, Tess assumed her role as Hector's mother and wrapped her fingers around Christie's cloaked forearm. "I really appreciate this."

"No problem, Mrs. Rinaldi. We're going to be spending a lot of time together, but I'll let Hector tell you all about it."

"Oh?" Tess pretended to hobble.

Christie nodded, and blinked back tears. "Yep." She slipped the glove off her left hand and wiggled her ring finger, as if Tess needed any help spotting at least two carats of diamonds.

"Well, let me be the first to congratulate you...*dear*." She added the last word for effect. "Have you set a date?"

"Not yet. I wasn't expecting it. You know a girl always hopes, but I honestly didn't know anything until a few hours ago."

"Well, I know you'll be a beautiful bride." Tess stepped ahead of Christie into the elevator.

The subterfuge continued all the way to the parking lot, when Christie paused to ask, "Where are you parked?"

"Oh, I'm across the street. That's my Audi over there."

"Golly, you had to walk a long way. I always park here in front."

"Christie, honey, how long have you all been seeing each other?"

"It'll be three years this month, actually." Christie was clearly crestfallen that her beau hadn't mentioned her to his mother. "He told me that you were anxious to meet me, and we would try to get to your nursing facility before the big day."

Tess clenched her jaw, her shoulders grew tight.

"We're almost there," Christie comforted, misreading hostility for fatigue.

As they approached the Audi, Tess slowed. "Honey, would you mind getting my blanket out of the trunk? It's so cold I believe I'll throw it over my legs on the way home."

"Sure. Do you think Hector will be mad that he didn't get to introduce us?"

Tess clicked her key fob and the trunk sprang open. "No. I'm sure he won't mind that we've met."

Christie bent over the open compartment and leaned in. "I don't see a bl——"

The butt of Tess's gun came down hard on the blonde's skull, making a wicked crack. Christie froze in place as though her body was considering what it should do next. Tess watched in horror as the girl turned slowly and blinked.

"Ow!" Christie swayed. Her body finally decided to collapse.

Backing away just far enough behind her victim, Tess drove her foot into the girl's backside and shoved her into the car a second before Christie fell unconscious.

The young woman's legs dangled over the fender, but there was enough weight from her torso already inside the trunk that Tess was able to wrestle the body in completely. Although this was not part of her original plan, Tess felt a wave of calm restore her confidence.

Working quickly, she opened the briefcase she kept in the backseat and removed a roll of duct tape. Less than a minute passed before she had the stripper securely bound and gagged. She got behind the wheel and cranked the car. "Uff." Tess shivered and turned the heat as high as it would go. While she waited for the temperature to get comfortable, Tess popped the glove compartment and exchanged the thirty-eight for her .22 Ruger. With practiced skill she screwed the silencer into place and slipped the weapon between the seats.

The drive out to the Everglades was uncomplicated. There were no cars on the road at that hour of the morning. Even so, Tess opted to take Tamiami Trail rather than go through the toll plaza on I-75 and risk having her car recorded on the surveillance video.

Hector had always been the one to scout out dump sites. It was his responsibility to research remote areas, decide where they could easily dispose of a body, and where nature was most efficient and would hasten the decomposition process by converting the remains into unidentifiable piles of animal waste. She had to admit, Hector excelled at this aspect of his job. But there was a time early in her career when the young mechanic had to find her own dump sites. New Jersey's geological features included the Pine Barrens, where winters and foraging animals could make a corpse vanish in less than two weeks. She had dumped a few in the East River using the old cement-the-feet-in-a-tub trick, but that was in the days when every button man between the Bronx and Philly was using the East River to dispose of vics. She imagined a vast underwater wise-guy cemetery, heads bobbing eerily from the riverbed. But the waterway was notorious for being polluted, so there was little chance the living would venture below the surface. She remembered two instances where she had dumped stiffs in rival territory to throw the scent off her trail. For a while she favored dumpsters behind Chinese restaurants. Then Newark became a sentimental favorite. There was generally more than enough crime to keep the cops there busy, so her stiffs ended up in the landfill following a brief sojourn in a dumpster behind a meat-packing facility. During business hours, Tess frequented the store. "No one cuts a pig like the boys in Newark," she would tell the butcher, as she pointed to the thick center cut chops in the display case.

"Those were the days," she murmured as she pressed on into the darkness. She still wasn't certain about her destination. This part of Florida was not as easy as New Jersey. There were no Chinese restaurants out this far, and no meat packers. Her headlights cut the immediate darkness. To her left was a canal, but she didn't know how deep it was. Foliage and wetland lined the right side of the road. But that wasn't an option. She had to get rid of the stripper deep in the Everglades, where the odds were that the body would never be recovered.

To the best of her knowledge, Anita Lemoyne was the first of her hits to be discovered. And right now, Tess was determined that she would be the last. She remembered passing a place called Shark Valley on her last excursion to Miami. To the best of her recollection there was a green sign and a stretch of roadway that headed straight into the tropical wilderness. Tess turned on the radio. A preset station was playing "Silent Night." She sang along to keep exhaustion from creeping up.

The problem with being a mechanic in south Florida was the miles you had to put on your car, she thought, as she glanced down at the odometer. It wasn't the driving so much as the increased possibility of bodily fluids, skin, and other evidence ending up in her vehicle. On the other hand, she reasoned, nature was much more efficient down here. At that moment, Tess spotted one of the numerous tacky billboards advertising airboat rides. A disproportionately large alligator appeared to leap from the brackish water, jaws agape, tail churning close to the terrified airboat passengers. She shuddered and set the cruise control to fifty miles per hour as she guided the vehicle dead east. Aside from her headlights, the night was darker than a cave at midnight, and she wondered what someone would do if he or she broke down.

Forty minutes passed before the sign to Shark Valley finally appeared in the distance. Tess flipped on her high beams and slowed as she approached the unpaved road. She eased the Audi onto the uneven surface and crept forward, uncertain of what lay ahead. A large, dark shape loped across the road in front of her and Tess slammed on the brakes. The body in the trunk shifted in response and Tess felt it connect with the panel separating the trunk from the passenger compartment. The shape slipped into the darkness, and Tess wondered if she'd actually seen anything. Her hands began to tremble. She suspected it was the shock, not the disease that had caused it. "Oh, boy." She breathed and planted both palms against the steering wheel.

It was after four a.m., when Smiling Tess finally spotted a promising site. There was a small opening in the foliage off to the right side, and she could just make out the water which she took to be part of the swamp. "Finally," she growled, and set her teeth, determined to finish this part of the job. She crept forward and suddenly felt the familiar sensation. But instead of her hand, it was her right foot that began to tremble. Tess overcompensated and accidentally pressed the accelerator instead of the brake. The Audi lunged forward, heading down the embankment. In the next instant, Tess felt a powerful explosion against her chest and face as the car came to an abrupt halt. The thrust and violence of the movement left her stunned and unable to move. Somewhere in the distance, she heard a bump, and everything went black.

Chapter 32

WHEN GOOD GIFTS GO BAD, OR, HOW NOT TO USE A NETI POT

Thursday, December 25, 2008 – Noon

Sonny pulled into her parents' driveway in Tricia's jeep. Noting the digital clock on the dashboard, she turned off the engine and paused to inspect the house her parents called home. There were no carcass-carrying garbage bags or animal corpses on the front porch—a refreshing change, she thought happily.

The house was tastefully decorated with strings of white icicle lights. An evergreen wreath with a traditional red bow hung on the front door. In painfully sharp contrast to the Christmas display was Elizabeth's collection of yard gnomes. The Germanic horde had begun a decade earlier when a local garden supply center went out of business. The first two gnomes brought back memories of *The Sound of Music*, and Elizabeth had snatched them up by their pointy red hats and bought them, along with a new hose, the one item Cole had asked her to look for. The dimple-cheeked Karl and Adolph were made of plaster and had long since turned to dust, disappearing into the garden. In the ensuing decade, Elizabeth had become obsessed with the little statues, and at last count, there were over a hundred wee folk throughout the yard. Hurricane Charlotte the year before had claimed most of her collection; a few had been retrieved from neighbor's trees and roofs, but this inspired Elizabeth to restock. One had only to look behind a tree or under a fern to find a lederhosen-clad woodcutter or farmer. They sported all manner of yard implements or vegetables. Their polyresin pink lips beamed with pride. Despite the protests of her daughters (with the exception of Charlotte), the wee folk refugees had a new homeland and were actively colonizing the Delaney yard.

With her arms full of gifts wrapped in newspaper comics, Sonny came up the front walkway. Elizabeth's latest gnome, Rodrick, stood at the front door lifting a lantern as though to light the way. A tiny faux evergreen had been added to the scene, as though Rodrick was tending a Christmas tree. And in March he would no doubt be tending a faux basket of eggs for Easter. Sonny cocked her head. Rodrick looked very similar to Adolph, and she realized he was probably the third generation of gnome to live at the Delaney house. The gnomes, however, were better than the roadkill left by Sanitation Sally and her father's other comrades. Using her elbow, Sonny pressed down the door handle and butted the door open.

She was immediately assaulted by the sound of Jimmy Stewart. "Look here, Mr. Potter," boomed the inimitable voice of George Bailey through the house. Sonny knelt in front of the Christmas tree and arranged her gifts as Stewart continued to scold old man Potter from the media room in the rear of the house.

She came around the corner into the kitchen and found her mother handing plates to Charlotte. "Merry Christmas!" Sonny shouted.

"Merry Christmas!" they shouted in a duet, but neither one looked up.

"Why is the TV on so loud?"

Charlotte hustled past her carrying her load. "So they can hear it."

Sonny scowled and headed to the family room. She found Mr. Phillips laying claim to her father's La-Z-Boy and an older couple occupying the sofa. All three were mesmerized by the colorized Christmas classic.

Sonny recognized the glassy-eyed gaze. Her nieces and nephew got the same look when they were under the spell of the LED screen. And the look was as good as a nap for keeping them occupied and out of trouble.

Mud Pie, the family dog, eyed her from his crate. His tail did not wag, nor did he appear to be happy to see her. Sonny knew this expression; it was more of a hypnotic stare. She quickly forced her eyes away. Making eye contact with the little canine would only cause him to turn on his beguiling charm, which in turn would result in her opening the cage door. And once freed, Mud Pie would begin his rampage—biting ankles, lunging into the refrigerator every time the door opened, and circling the dining room table waiting for scraps to fall in the floor. Everyone was safer with the five-pound Chihuahua mix behind bars.

Returning to the kitchen, Sonny bent over the stove beside her mother and peered in at the ham with its brown sugar glaze.

"I got a turkey too, for the McDonalds. Edgar and Alva are Jewish." Elizabeth eased the door closed. She closed her eyes and inhaled the fragrance of Christmas dinner.

"I didn't know we were having company."

"Well, honey, I didn't either. They're your sister's friends."

"Charlotte's?"

"Of course."

"You know that's Mr. Phillips?"

"Yes, I know that's Mr. Phillips."

"And you know he peed in my car yesterday?"

"No. Actually I wasn't aware of that. Somehow it didn't make the local news. But in his defense, I've come close to having to change my underwear after riding in the car with you."

"That's hysterical!" Sonny shouted blandly. "Do you even care that he's sitting on Dad's recliner at this very moment?"

Elizabeth paused and pressed her index finger to the corner of her mouth. "But he's not on my nice Italian leather sofa, right?"

"That would be correct."

"Okay, then." She handed her middle daughter a pile of silverware. "Take these in to the dining room and give Char a hand setting the table. Please," she shouted politely.

"You're actually willing to sacrifice Dad's chair and quite possibly a dining room chair?"

"Go." Elizabeth pointed to the archway separating the kitchen from the dining room. And though she was a good five inches shorter than Sonny, she still maintained her parental authority.

Pouting, Sonny began to lay out the forks and knives.

"You're doing it wrong." Charlotte came along behind her and made the necessary changes to meet the proper standards for good etiquette.

Sonny handed her the bundle of utensils. She went to the window and stood looking out.

"Bethany's running late!" Elizabeth yelled. She put three trivets down the center of the table and appraised her work. The tablecloth, a red and green plaid, was decorated with live evergreen cuttings and pine-scented candles.

"She's here." Sonny watched as the Dodge Caravan pulled into the driveway. The passenger door slid open while the vehicle was still rolling. Eight-year-old Eliot shot out of the backseat and sprinted toward the house. His older sister, Bette, caught up and was the first to reach the front door. Bringing up the rear was six-year-old Vanna.

"Grandma!" they shouted in various pitches according to their ages, and charged in Elizabeth's direction.

"Uh-uh." Their grandmother shook her head and pointed to the front door. "Go help your mother, then hugs."

Bette ignored her and wrapped her arms around her grandmother, burying her head in Elizabeth's shoulder. At ten, she was tall and wiry like her grandfather.

The TV suddenly became quiet and Cole strolled into the room wearing his red and green Christmas flip-flops, an early gift from his wife. "I had to turn down the TV, I think my ears were about to start bleeding. Well, look who is here." He draped an arm over each of the older grandchildren. "Let's go see if we can help your mother." As he drew even with Elizabeth, he extended a cushion from one of the lawn chairs. "Is that what you wanted?"

Elizabeth put the cushion in the chair at the head of the table. "Make sure Mr. Phillips sits there," she directed Charlotte. "Go ahead and call your friends to the table. I don't want the turkey to dry out." She turned to her middle daughter. "Where's Tricia? You told her noon?"

Charlotte stopped in her tracks and stood completely still.

"Char? Is there something you might want to add to this conversation?"

"No."

"Turn around, Charlotte Delaney, and look me in the eye."

On her best days, Charlotte Delaney's behavior could be characterized as odd. Today was one of those days. While both conditions were manageable, together they became a genuine challenge, more for her family than her doctors. Not only was Charlotte unable to lie, she did not know how to dissemble, nor did she understand the concept of even the smallest white lie. This in turn opened the door for her family to exploit Charlotte's childlike honesty. In the wrong hands this same frankness had proven dangerous. Every member of the household had learned early on not to ask Charlotte for her honest opinion about anything, because they were likely to get it.

Charlotte turned to face her mother.

"Where is Tricia?" Elizabeth asked, as though she had just injected her daughter with truth serum, which in essence she had simply by asking for the truth.

"I asked her to pick up some presents for my friends on her way over." Charlotte's face remained expressionless; even her eyes appeared to blink mechanically, as though they were being operated remotely.

Sonny's shoulder's sagged. "Today? You asked her to shop for you today? You realize, of course, everything is closed, right?"

"Not everything." Charlotte turned on her heel and, holding her arms rigidly by her sides, she hurried in the direction of the TV room to collect her guests.

Sonny felt the first tingle of a meltdown. After growing up in a household with Charlotte, no one was surprised when Sonny began having anxiety attacks, least of all Sonny herself. Over the years, she had learned to launch herself into a yoga pose and stay there until peace was restored. Though the behavior invited more than a few stares, it was better than waiting out the rapid heartbeat and dizziness.

"At least she's getting along with your sister."

"Tricia gets along with everybody."

"Charlotte doesn't. She's a tough nut, but she really seems to trust Tricia."

"I don't know if it's trust so much as manipulation. Char uses people, Mom."

"She's not well," Elizabeth defended. "For Pete's sake, she's suffered a major head trauma this week."

"Please! Head injury or not, she uses people."

Elizabeth considered daughter number two's point. "That's true. Still, she can't drive for at least a month."

"Well then, why didn't you and Dad get whatever she wanted?"

"Hello? I've been cooking since six a.m. You think that cornbread, gravy, and all the other traditional stuff fixed itself?"

Sonny appraised her mother. "I'd be willing to wager a paycheck that you ordered everything at Fresh Market and picked it up this morning. And they don't open till eight."

"I did not." Elizabeth seemed genuinely offended.

Eyes narrowed, Sonny headed for the garbage can to search for boxes, bags, and other incriminating evidence.

"All right!" Elizabeth stomped in her red espadrilles. "I did, however, make the dessert."

"Mom?" Sonny had her foot on the pedal that lifted the garbage can's lid.

"Fine, I got a pumpkin pie and a pecan pie at a bake sale last night at the clubhouse. Are you pleased with yourself?"

"Okay, that explains your whereabouts. So why didn't Char ask Dad to take her shopping?"

"He was busy, too."

"Yeah, busy in his house of horrors back there, skinning something."

Elizabeth paused again to visualize what Sonny suggested. "Yes, that's true, but he also had to pick up Charlotte's company. It all happened very unexpectedly. Besides, you have more to worry about with Bethany."

"Have you told her?"

"No. But she won't mind. Well, I don't think she'll mind." Elizabeth placed two fists on her hips and glared. "It's Christmas—lighten up."

Sonny held up her hands. "Hey, I'm not the one who has potty mouth. Let's just hope everyone has his or her hearing aids turned down low."

"At least she gets along with Tricia."

"Again, Tricia gets along with everybody. In fact, she loves me enough to hang around my family. And I'm going to nominate her for sainthood."

"She gets my vote," Elizabeth raised her hand. "We're not that unique, honey. You like to think we are, but let me tell you, you've never lived with carneys." Elizabeth's eyebrows rose and her face grew serious as she faced off with her daughter. "Just remember that when you think it can't get any weirder. Yeah. My mother rode a motorcycle in an iron mesh ball. That's weird. My father—"

"Your weird childhood does not mean you have a monopoly on weirdness."

Elizabeth answered Sonny with a shrug of her shoulders. "Go ahead, then."

"Go ahead, what?"

"Bust a move." Elizabeth waved her hand. "Get it out of your system. I know you're dying to break out in a tree or something."

Sonny considered the invitation. "I'm okay. Tricia will be here any time." She patted the Purell hand sanitizer packets in her pocket and swallowed. Sonny felt as if she was losing contact with the earth under her feet. Her Pitta constitution was unsteady at best and her less-dominant dosha, Vata, left her feeling light-headed and confused. Five minutes in Hero might help, but she was not about to give her mother the satisfaction.

"If this is the worst thing that happens to you today, you'll be fine." Elizabeth tried to be encouraging. "C'mon, it's Christmas."

As the Delaneys and their guests began assembling around the dining table, Tricia pulled up in Sonny's Subaru. She hurried toward the house, carrying a laundry basket full of neatly wrapped packages. Sonny went to help.

Returning to the table, they took their seats as Elizabeth made the introductions.

"Mr. and Mrs. McDonald, this is Tricia. Tricia, this is Mr. Phillips." She gestured to the man seated at the far end of the table.

Mr. Phillips smiled politely. "Merry Christmas."

Sonny turned to Tricia to remind her of the man's infraction the day before, but stopped abruptly when a dinner roll bounced off her head. Offended, she looked across the table and discovered that her mother holding the bread basket and giving her a look of warning. Before anyone else could see Elizabeth's dark side she passed the basket to Charlotte.

"Please pass the butter," Elizabeth said, sounding remarkably like Scarlett O'Hara in *Gone with the Wind*.

And without further ado, Christmas dinner at the Delaneys' got under way.

Sonny piled salad and green beans on her plate. She'd already decided to have turkey instead of ham. In the background, traditional music played, lending a serene joy to the occasion.

"Granddad, would you pass me the gravy?" Six-year-old Vanna knelt in her chair and pointed.

"Sit your ass down in the chair, honey bunny," Bethany said, gesturing with her butter knife for the little girl to behave.

The next moment seemed to play out in slow motion. Sonny looked up in time to see the ceramic container filled with turkey gravy moving from hand to hand toward her youngest niece. It took her a second to realize that something was wrong, very wrong. And then the meltdown started.

"That's the neti pot I bought you for your birthday! You were supposed to use it to help with your allergies—not for gravy!" Sonny's face burned with betrayal as she faced her mother.

"Honey," Elizabeth attempted to soothe her daughter.

But Sonny was already rising to her feet. Her napkin fell to the floor as she stormed out of the dining room, leaving an unholy energy in her wake. Elizabeth was right behind her.

"What's a neti pot?" Vanna poured the yellow gravy till it puddled on her mashed potatoes. She daintily dipped her turkey leg into the liquid.

"Yogis use it to clean their nasal passages," Tricia explained, and demonstrated by holding the gravy boat up to one nostril while tilting her head to the side.

"That's gross," Vanna noted self-righteously as she licked gravy from her drumstick.

Chapter 33

BABE IN THE WOODS

Thursday, December 25, 2008 — 1:00 p.m.

Tess woke to the sound of her own voice. She was moaning. Her chest felt as though someone was kneeling on her, and a strange smell filled her nostrils. She opened her eyes and tried to move her arms, but discovered that they were pinned down. A huge pillow materialized in front of her face, and she realized the airbag in her Audi had somehow deployed. The frames of her glasses were broken in half and dangling from her nose. Tess squinted and refocused. "The fuck?" she asked out loud.

What the hell was going on, and where the hell was she? Her head felt like she'd been drinking all night. As she leaned back against the headrest, she recalled the events of the night before. Feeling along the door, Tess found the handle and opened the vehicle, but was still pinioned behind the airbag. She felt lower and located the seat adjustment, and moved herself back far enough to slip free of the Audi.

She dropped to her knees outside the car, unable to stand, not from any specific pain but more the result of disorientation. Tess realized she was somewhere in the damn Florida swamp. The nose of the Audi appeared to be sipping the mucky, dark water, but all four tires were still on dry land. Then she recalled the body in the trunk.

Turning, she discovered the trunk lid was open. The shock of it strengthened her enough to get to her feet. She staggered to the rear of the vehicle and looked in. Empty.

"Son of a..." Tess knew she had to pull it together. She'd avoided the penal system her entire life and wasn't about to slip up at this late date.

There were footprints, presumably Christie's. They led away from the Audi, away from the edge of the water, and disappeared into the foliage on the other side of the dirt road. She'd apparently gone straight into the Everglades. Tess stood at the edge of the undergrowth and focused. The bush was not just thick, it was impossibly dense. Christie wouldn't be moving very quickly. It might have been dark outside when she made her escape, and the temperature had been in the mid-forties. All this would make travel very slow, if not impossible. Tess looked at her watch and figured it was time to get moving either way.

From her glove compartment Smiling Tess removed her pistol, returned to the driver's side and shot the airbag. It deflated, and she was able to roll it into a manageable ball, so that she could reach the steering wheel. Repairing the Audi was out of the question. Hunting Christie into the wilderness of the Everglades was out of the question. Her only order of business was to get back to the condo and regroup. The one thing she had on her side now was time. It was Christmas Day and things would be closed. If Christie managed to get out of the Everglades, she faced a minimum ten-mile hike to reach the nearest asphalt leading back to civilization. And if the young woman took that route, there was a good chance Tess would spot her.

She got behind the wheel, closed her eyes, and fervently rubbed the Saint Christopher medal hanging from her rearview mirror. The engine started. Tess put the car in reverse and pressed down on the accelerator. The Audi's rear tires spun and then caught. It lurched backward and Tess slammed on the brakes. Putting the vehicle in park, she went to check the damage to the front end. A thick black limb was lodged in the grill. She tried to pull it free, but it was wedged in, and there wasn't time to muscle it out. Hands on hips, Tess studied the situation, and after a second, took out her pistol and shot the branch. She slipped in a fresh clip each time she ran out of bullets until only a shredded stump remained protruding from the grill. The Audi looked like it had just lit up an exploding cigar and the baffles on her silencer were fried.

Tess was moving in the direction of the driver's side when the ringing in her ears subsided. She stopped suddenly and frowned. That's when she heard the unmistakable sound of a cell phone ringing in her trunk. She found it in Christie's purse, which had managed to slip under the carpet in the space where the spare tire was anchored. It continued to chirp as Tess tried to figure out how it worked. When the musical ring tone stopped, Tess realized the device slid open, revealing a miniature keyboard. A text scrolled over the screen, "You get home okay?" Tess recognized Hector's cell phone number. Her brain locked on to a single ray of light that marked the next step she would take. With great difficulty, she texted back one word, *yes*, and hit the send button. She watched as the word vanished from the screen. Then Smiling Tess Fontana climbed behind the steering wheel and began the long drive back to Naples.

Likely as not, there would be little traffic out today. The problem would be parking the Audi in the Highland Terrace garage with all the surveillance cameras and security. Hector had just established that he was clueless about Christie. She imagined he was wondering where she was, so he could make the hit. The Audi would reveal her position.

As she headed back down the limestone-gravel road, Tess found herself thinking through her escape. She hadn't done this mental exercise in a while, probably decades, not since her first hit, in fact. Back then she was still getting used to her new line of employment, which was a good deal easier than dressing mannequins in Macy's. Tess planned for every eventuality. Back in the day, she was the only hit woman from the eastern seaboard all the way to the West Coast. She heard through the grapevine that there was a female hitter in Frisco, a Korean who preferred poison, wore nothing but silk, and loved the opera. *They called her Madame something,* Tess thought, and tried to conjure the name but it wouldn't come. *Madame what?* Tess lit a smoke and inhaled vigorously.

She had always been curious about Madame whatever. The cops had never caught her, and Tess suspected it was for the same reason that she had never appeared on their radar. Triggering people was traditionally a man's job; women didn't do this kind of thing. Of course, today there were probably more women in her line of work. One thing was for certain: after tomorrow, there would be one less button woman in the field.

In the early days, she had kept a pair of suitcases packed, stashed under her bed, handles out. One bag held cash, the other clothes and toiletries. It had taken her a few years to figure out that the cash needed to be in an offshore account. But the other suitcase was still under her bed—handle out—only now it also had a fake passport, credit cards, and a false ID.

Tess envisioned life in Italy, the motherland. She already knew how to speak a little Italian, mostly expletives and pillow talk, but she could learn the language. Unfortunately, she would have to sacrifice her condo, and that was where most of her cash was. There was an account in the Cayman Islands, but there was barely a hundred thousand in it. She didn't know how far that would get her, but Tess was certain she had to get out of the country.

She turned on the radio and sang along with Bing Crosby's version of "White Christmas."

Chapter 34

A VERY MILO CHRISTMAS

Thursday, December 25, 2008 – 1:10 p.m.

Dottie's was doing a brisk business by the time Milo and his mother finished lunch. They had arrived early in anticipation of a large crowd for the Christmas special: all-you-could-eat turkey with dressing and mashed potatoes with gravy. Priss remembered to bring baggies and Tupperware. Her purse bulged with leftovers. There was easily enough for another three meals. Milo had forgotten to bring anything but his appetite. He left with a full stomach and a gravy stain on his only tie.

"That'll come out with a squirt or two of Shout," Priss advised her son as she slipped on her seat belt. Predictably, the next part of her routine involved examining her hair and makeup in the rearview mirror.

Milo slipped a small box from the inside pocket of his suit jacket. The jacket had been on sale at Goodwill, and white went with just about everything, so

Milo handed over the ten-dollar bill without hesitation; it was a good investment. Since Milo hardly ever wore dress clothes, he had always wondered what the inside pocket was good for. "I got you something."

Priss acted shocked, but she was partial to high drama. She even cupped her hand over her mouth as though the box contained the Hope diamond. "Oh, honey. You know I wish you wouldn't spend your hard-earned money on me." Even as she was uttering this selfless sentiment, Priss was tearing at the wrapping paper as though she were dying and it contained some lifesaving antidote. "I need a gun to get into this." The petite woman finally ripped the cardboard to reveal a delicate gold ankle bracelet nestled in the cotton.

Milo realized he would not be able to salvage the box, much less the gold wrapping paper. "My friend gave me a real good deal. It's an ankle bracelet."

"I know that. Milo, it's just beautiful. I swear, I don't know why you're not already married with five children, the way you treat women."

Milo wondered that himself as he crossed his arms and beamed. He was the youngest of three boys. And with his father's passing, he was also the closest male relative to Priss.

"I got you something, too." She popped the trunk and gestured with her thumb. "It's back there. I didn't want anyone to see it and try to break into the car."

Milo lifted a long rectangular package from the compartment. It was wrapped in a page from the colored Sunday comics. His mother would not buy a whole roll of paper just to wrap one package.

Priss waggled her index finger at Milo. "I want you to open it when you get home. It isn't the kind of thing you open in a public parking lot."

Milo grinned. He knew it was a weapon of some sort.

"Ling is coming over around six for Chinese take-out. You wanna drop by?"

Ling was actually Ling Ling Woo, the manicurist at Priss's Casa de Beaute hair salon. Named after the giant panda that had been gifted from China to Japan, Ling seemed oblivious to the similarities she shared with her namesake. Like the giant panda in the Tokyo zoo, Ling was stout, round, and roly-poly. She often dressed in black and white clothing. Ling Ling also shared with her captive twin an affinity for bamboo shoots. That they were ordering Chinese food came as no surprise.

Milo shook his head. "I've already got plans."

"Well, here. At least take a baggie." Priss rifled through her purse for one with turkey and mashed potatoes together. "I'll give you one of these little gravy containers, too. No, take two. That'll tide you over awhile." Priss pressed the purloined lunch on her son. "You can have Christmas again tomorrow. And maybe the day after that, too. Or you can freeze it. I'm sure it'll taste good as long as it doesn't get freezer burn. And don't leave it out where that damn dog can get at it."

Boomer did not greet Milo when he opened the front door of his modular home. In fact, Boomer was nowhere in sight, a very bad sign. As soon as Milo stepped into the unit he realized why Boomer had made himself scarce. A yellow puddle spread across the kitchen linoleum and both swivel chairs at the bistro table had been shredded. The white leatherette lay in strips over the remaining foam cushions.

At first, Milo had tried to put an end to the dog's bad behavior, but with patience and determination the dog had worn him down. He wasn't hiding; Boomer was probably fast asleep, full of upholstery stuffing and faux leather, and content. Milo put his keys and turkey dinner on the letter table, took off his good jacket and tie, and went to work cleaning the mess. He was an expert by now, had the cleanup procedure down to five minutes which included running a mop over the floor. He took the waste outside and returned to find the compact beast with the baggie of turkey clamped between his massive jaws.

"No," Milo said sternly. The dog trainer on TV said the tone of the owner's voice had to be authoritative. Milo believed there was no room for doubt in his command until Boomer turned and ran toward the master bedroom. "No! I said no! No, Boomer."

With the mop still in his hand, Milo chased after his dog. Boomer scooted under the bed and Milo got down on his stomach. He glared as the determined pit bull ate his turkey dinner. Milo tried to prod the food away using the mop handle, but the dog remained focused on his mission, allowing himself to be jostled and poked as he blissfully ate his fill, baggie and all.

Realizing the futility of his efforts, Milo surrendered, leaving the mop protruding from under his bed. "You're a bad dog. A very bad dog."

In the last few months, Boomer had become increasingly difficult to handle. He had been banned from two pet supply stores, the dog obedience school had asked him to leave after only one class, and Milo had begun to dread coming home for fear of what he might find. The dog's destructive behavior was escalating and he was at a loss for what to do about it. Actually, Milo suspected Boomer's conduct had something to do with the fact that he hadn't been neutered.

But Milo had paid a breeder two hundred and fifty dollars for the pup and had every intention of making Boomer a stud. He had seen Boomer's parents and had the distinct honor of first pick of the litter. Boomer had official papers showing he had descended from a long lineage of show dogs.

Milo figured he could charge a hundred-dollar stud fee for what Boomer did naturally to the sofa, chairs, visitors, and anything he could get his paws on. He advertised Boomer's services in the *Naples Herald*, but had no takers, so he lowered the price to fifty. That ad ran a month with no response, and Milo dropped Boomer's fee to twenty-five with the promise that Boomer could do the job in one shot. To date, there had been no interest in Boomer as a sire for the next generation of quality pit bulls, so Milo was considering taking him to dog shows. People would be able to see in person what a truly great stud looked like. But unless he could work out Boomer's behavioral issues, there would be no shows. Milo was nearly to the point of not being able to take the powerful canine out at all, the way he pulled at the leash and snapped at anyone who got too close.

There was also the matter of a litter of freakishly ugly pups the next street over. Four weeks earlier, Milo had answered a knock at his front door and found an exceedingly hostile eyeball looking in his peephole. His first reaction had been to back away, but he recognized the face of the person standing on his front deck. The neighbor, a woman in her fifties, held a newborn pup out to Milo. Even though its eyes were not yet open the whining little animal looked familiar. A man waited at the bottom of the stairs holding a lead attached to a perfectly groomed lap dog. A pink bow held a tuft of hair on top of its head, but its eyes were somehow still covered. Milo assumed it was a female.

"Do you recognize this dog?" the woman seethed.

Milo looked from her husband to the woman. "Uh, no. But it shouldn't be too hard to find its owner. There's a mama dog around here someplace that's nursing, by the looks of the little fella," he offered.

"Bob, would you please explain the situation to this...young man," she practically spat. Bob climbed the stairs with the little dog in tow.

Milo noticed the teats at the same time he felt Boomer try to edge out of the front door. He discreetly pushed the door closed and did his best to ignore the beast scratching and yowling to get out.

"Mr. Purdie, I'm Bob Callahan, and this is my wife, Dee. And this," he beamed as the little dog stood on its hind legs watching its pup, "is Dame Pixie of Lancaster. You probably notice that she is a purebred."

"Really?" Milo tried to sound interested.

"Yes, really. Pixie is a shih tzu. We went to England to pick her from a litter sired by the Earl of Lancaster and Dame Lydia of Kent. She is the fifth generation of Lancaster champions. She cost somewhere in the ballpark of four thousand dollars—that, of course, includes airfare. Long story short, Pixie went into heat for the first time about three months ago." Mr. Callahan's facial expression flat-lined. He peeked over Milo's shoulder at the front door.

Milo swallowed. He recalled coming home from work and finding Boomer in the shed. Apparently he had escaped and been out all day. Milo now wondered if canine relations were illegal if both parties consented. There shouldn't be any problem since they were both purebreds.

"Mr. Purdie," Bob continued, "my wife and I expect you to pay for the damages."

"I suppose I could give you a couple of bucks for him." Milo gestured with his nose toward the puppy. The head on the little half breed was too large for the rest of its body, and any cuteness it might have had was lost on the freakishly massive jaw and classic shih tzu under bite. Milo grimaced. The pup looked more like a land piranha than a dog.

"Baxter isn't on the list of damages we're talking about. We'll be taking him and the other ones to the humane society as soon as they can be weaned. No, Mr. Purdie, I'm referring to the destruction to our home and our precious Pixie caused by your pit bull."

Milo frowned. "You all are the ones with the big fence?"

"Six-foot fence, to be exact." The sounds emanating from Milo's modular home were clearly making Bob anxious. He collected Pixie and clutched her to his chest.

Milo suspected Bob would sacrifice Dee to protect Dame Pixie if Boomer managed to escape.

"Well, Mr. Callahan, I don't mean any disrespect, but there is no way in hell Boomer could scale a six-foot fence. He's not very big."

"And tear through a lanai screen and knock a sliding glass door off the track. We have photos, Mr. Purdie."

Milo eyed the man. "You all took pictures of them doing it?"

Bob looked heavenward. "No. We took photos of the aftermath. We're not holding you responsible for the glass figurines that were broken in the scuffle. We think Dame Pixie probably did it trying to get away."

Milo looked down. "How much are we talking about here?"

"We've estimated our property damage at about sixty dollars, and the vet bill came to one ninety."

"How many puppies in the litter?"

"Just Baxter and two others...thank God," Bob said distastefully.

There was no doubt that Boomer was the daddy of the little half-breeds. From behind, Baxter was cute and looked like a classic, cuddly shih tzu. The problem was when Milo looked at the pup head on. Baxter was definitely a freak of nature, like the two-headed heifer Milo had seen at the 4-H club when he was little. Baxter looked like Boomer when he was coming. Going, he was undeniably Pixie's.

Milo wrote the Callahans a check for two hundred and fifty dollars.

"We still plan to breed Pixie one day. In the meantime, we would appreciate it if you could keep that beast of yours under control." Bob folded the check and slipped it in his breast pocket.

Milo realized if he didn't do something about Boomer's behavior, he would end up paying instead of collecting a stud fee for his prize pit bull.

Despite all the indicators that it was time, the twenty-five-year-old was not ready to have Boomer's jewels surgically removed.

His brooding lasted all of ten seconds. Remembering the Christmas gift from his mother, Milo sat with the package across his knees and hit the TV remote.

"All right!" When Milo pulled a new compound bow from the wrapping paper he was already imagining his next hunt. It was a thing of beauty, with a slick camo paint job, pulleys, and black grips. He had recently used one at a friend's house, but Milo never dreamed he'd ever have one of his own. He secured the string between his second and third finger while drawing a bead on an imaginary five-hundred-pound boar. He aimed at the TV, the buck head hanging over the TV, the dumbbells on the weight rack.

Milo was perspiring with possibilities when he returned from his bedroom wearing his favorite camo shorts and tank, and hunting boots. He had also taken a moment to swipe khaki war paint on his face. Milo spent the next ten minutes watching himself in the full-length mirror by his weight set, as he sighted on everything in range. Then it was time for his afternoon run.

As he was lacing up his running shoes, Milo paused to consider what Grace was doing today. In that moment he realized that Winslow had never said he couldn't carry a bow. And an arrow was just as deadly as a well-placed bullet, but unlike a gun, there was no sound. If he continued his surveillance, he would need something more than his audio/video equipment and can of mace. He would need real protection. Milo stroked his mustache and nodded.

Chapter 35

A BRIDGE CLUB CHRISTMAS

Thursday, December 25, 2008 – 1:15 p.m.

Muscia sat at the kitchen table. The lone chair at the bistro-sized table was considered hers and hers alone. Pieces of her thirty-eight were neatly arranged across a plastic placemat. The placemat had come from a dollar sale at a local tourist shop and featured a pair of sunburned tourists on the beach. She hated the placemat, but she hated trying to get gun oil out of the tablecloth even more.

Holiday music came from a small radio on the counter. The radio was used, maybe fifteen years old, but it worked, and it contained memories of her homeland that came to her whenever she tuned in to her reggae station.

It was Christmas, the best day of the year. Carmen had given Muscia a nice bonus to compensate her for having to work that day. But Muscia didn't mind working. She could clean her gun at home just as easily as at Carmen's condo; it made no difference to her so long as the gun was cared for.

Someone knocked and Muscia put everything down. She had to stoop down to look through the peephole. Ralphie was looking in. He hated to be called Ralphie, so that's how Muscia thought of him; a miniature of his father, a grown man trapped under his mother's thumb.

"Muscia, it's me. Open the freakin' door."

She sighed and unlocked the door.

Ralph Bustamante swept past her without another word. She knew he did not like her. The only reason she was there was because of Carmen. Muscia was also certain that Ralphie was powerless to do anything about her until Carmen was out of the picture.

Ralph Bustamante's eyes were even darker, smaller, and closer to his nose than his mother's. Like his mother, he had jowls instead of cheeks. When he smiled, his lips looked like a pair of hockey pucks.

"Here ya go, Ma. Merry Christmas." Ralph kissed his mother on the cheek before handing her a perfectly wrapped gift. "Hope you like it. April helped me pick it out."

"Hope you kept the receipt." Carmen made no secret of the fact that she detested her daughter-in-law.

"Ma, c'mon, it's Christmas. How about a little peace on earth, goodwill to all. At least April makes an effort."

"She's a lush."

"Why you gotta be like that?" Ralph sat on the love seat opposite his mother.

"I apologize," Carmen said. The act was uncharacteristically magnanimous. "She's your wife and that was disrespectful."

Ralph looked at her sideways and frowned. "Ma? You feelin' okay?"

"How are the kids?" Carmen continued.

"Doin' good. They're both smart kids. I got each of them a laptop."

"I'm impressed."

"Ah," he shrugged. "Somebody owed me a favor. You need one?"

The look Carmen answered him with served as a whipping.

"What do you want? I give those kids everything. They don't do without, believe me, Ma. Best schools, best clothes, best of everything. What else do you think they should have? And what are you doing for them? When was the last time you even called?"

"I call 'em on their birthdays, don't I?"

Ralph stood. "I'm not gonna spend my Christmas fighting with you."

"Sit down," Carmen barked. Then, in a more conciliatory tone, she said, "Please. Please sit down, Ralph. I apologize. The last two weeks have been very trying."

He returned to his seat. "What's goin' on, Ma?"

"I'm getting old."

Ralph had waited his entire life for this moment. The chink in his mother's armor had finally been revealed. He smiled inwardly; the feeling was intoxicating.

"Don't get any ideas."

"What?"

"I'm old, not stupid. I feel like having an espresso. You want one, Ralphie?"

Ralph knew this nickname was meant to put him in his place. But he had already glimpsed his future. His mother's jab was weak.

"Sure, Ma. I'll join you in a little espresso. You have any of those biscotti from that deli around the corner? That Delaurentis place?"

Muscia delivered the demitasse cups and biscotti on a silver tray, which she set on the coffee table between them.

Holding the tiny cup delicately between thumb and index finger, Ralph lifted his espresso and said, "*Buon Natale*, Ma."

"*Buon Natale e felice anno nuovo.* Your gift is under the tree. Muscia, would you bring him that red and gold package?"

Muscia seethed as she picked up the gift and handed it to Ralph. While she had no illusions about moving up into Carmen's position in the organization, Muscia felt she was far better qualified than Ralph. Since her expression was perpetually grave, Ralph did not notice her hostility.

"So," Carmen began.

Her son swept his hand over the pale peach sofa cushion. "Is this new?"

"*Stunad*. I bought this set when I moved in."

The corners of Muscia's lips turned up ever so slightly. Ralphie wasn't being promoted; he was getting a heads-up from his mother. She glanced back at him as she slipped into the kitchen. "*Stunad*," she whispered, adding another word to her Italian lexicon.

"So, you get in this morning?" Carmen sipped the oily black drink.

"No. I been here since last night."

"What, you got a *goomah* this side, too?"

Ralph snorted, "*Oobatz*! I can hardly handle the one in Lauderdale. You kiddin' me? I suppose you're going to tell me my father had a *comare* here and there."

Ralph chuckled. His mother did not. The conspiratorial grin on Ralph's face dissolved.

"So, how long you in town?"

"Long as it takes, Ma, long as it takes. I gotta work somethin' out with a guy in Venice."

"Like what? You cuttin' me out of some action?"

"Ma, please. You got the numbers here and this new thing. You just want a piece 'cause I got a piece. Let me do this." Ralph used his arms and hands as part of the conversation.

"Okay, I'm just curious."

"I got a little somethin' comin' in to the docks up there. A couple of boxes from Fidel."

"Oh," Carmen nodded. "Gotcha. So how are things going on your end?"

"I gotta tell ya, Ma, we're getting some heat over there."

"Feds?"

"Freakin' FLABI." Ralph pressed his palms to the sides of his head. "They just keep sniffin' around."

"Let 'em sniff."

"Easy for you to say. No one is gonna suspect you. Nice little old Italian mama, no one would think twice about you."

"I'm not nice," Carmen reminded him, and she seemed proud of her personal assessment.

"Can she hear us?" Ralph gestured in the direction of the kitchen.

"Doesn't matter if she can. She doesn't care, she doesn't know, whatever."

"How is your crew? Everyone good?"

"Yeah. You know that *cugine*, Hector?"

"Yeah. He's Aunt Tess's boy toy, right?"

"Well, I got him doing a piece of work for me."

Ralph shrugged. "Okay. What you do over here is your business."

"It's Tess."

Ralph blew out a gust of air. "Are you serious? She's my godmother, Ma. I can't believe you'd sanction this. Tess is like you're oldest friend. She's been cleanin' up after you since you started this. You can't whack her. That's—"

"She's sick, Ralph. Yeah, that's right. She's very ill."

"So you're solution is to ice the woman? Seriously, Ma?"

"How about this, she screwed up her last job."

"What happened?

"The vic died before Tess could whack her."

"The vic is dead, though, right? So what does it matter?"

"I pay for a whack so I expect a whack. Then the body turns up the next day."

"Okay. I see your point."

They sipped and reflected a moment, as though out of respect for the soon-to-be departed.

"So how is business on your end, Ma?"

"I hope you came prepared."

"Prepared for what?"

"I got a hamper full of dirty laundry."

"Like, how much are we talking about?"

"Five hundred large."

Ralph choked on his biscotti. He clapped a napkin over his mouth. "Five?" he sputtered, as a look of delight swept over his face.

Carmen nodded. "Five."

"Ma! You're a freakin' genius! I don't believe this!"

"Believe it. We got some serious laundry in there. And quite honestly, I'm not comfortable having it around."

"Well, Ma, you're gonna have to sit on it till I get back from Venice."

"Better be this week. Tomorrow we're going to collect for the last shipment, and I gotta tell ya, it's gonna be even bigger."

"And you thought retirement would be boring. I'll stop in sometime this week. And so you know, we got another delivery coming next week."

Carmen asked, "You got another truck?"

"I got another truck."

"I think you ought to wait."

"Wait? Wait for what?"

"I'm telling you to wait."

"Help me understand, Ma. I've got a sixteen-wheeler loaded with oxy, Vicodin, you name it—and you wanna wait? What for?" Ralph tested the water.

Carmen slowly got to her feet. Her hip was clearly bothering her, but she made her way around the table separating them and stood over her son. Several seconds passed as she stared down at him.

Muscia peered around the corner. Her weapon—cleaned, oiled, and reassembled—was in the pocket of her scrubs. She eased her hand into that pocket as she watched the pair with rapt attention.

Carmen leaned toward her son. "You ain't got the *stugatz*," the old woman snarled, and waited, daring her son to move, to blink, to challenge her. He remained motionless. "I do," Carmen said slowly, leaving no room for interpretation.

He felt the sting and humiliation of her words as though she had physically struck him across his cheek. He blinked in disbelief.

Finally, Ralph threw up his hands. "No big deal. We'll wait."

When she moved to back away, Ralph flinched, his hand lifted to protect himself.

"The matter is settled, *capiche?*" When Ralph remained silent, Carmen asked, "You have something to say?"

Ralph finally put his hands down and relaxed. "No. We'll wait. You let me know when you're ready."

The sound of the doorbell caused both of them to look away.

"Who is it?" Carmen called to Muscia.

Muscia, who had been watching the drama play out, was closer to the door than Carmen realized. Once again she peered through the peephole. "Constance and Florence."

Carmen rolled her eyes as she sank back into her seat. To Ralph, she said, "I don't know why she can't call 'em Connie and Flobo like everybody else." To Muscia, she said, "Let 'em in already."

"Aunt Connie and Flo?" Ralph asked innocently enough.

Carmen turned back to Ralph. "Shut up, you degenerate."

Ralph offered her upturned palms. "What? What I do?"

Flobo and Connie stood patiently outside the door. Each held a foil-covered plate.

Muscia unlocked the door and held it open.

"Merry Christmas," Flobo and Connie said in unison.

"Mmm," Muscia growled pleasantly to acknowledge their presence.

Flobo cocked her head. "Muscia? Do you ever smile? Let me rephrase that. Have you ever smiled? At any time in your life, do you remember smiling?"

"Merry Christmas," the Amazon mumbled, and turned toward the kitchen.

"Aren't you gonna take these?" Flobo held up her plate.

"No," was the dark reply.

"Ralphie," Flobo said loudly. "How the hell you been?" She set her plate on the table and headed out to the balcony where Ralph Junior was lighting up a cigarette.

"Aunt Flo." He held his arms open.

"Ralphie, you gotta give up the smokes. They'll kill ya. I'm serious."

"It's good to see you," Ralph said, as though he hadn't heard her.

"I didn't know you were going to be here." Connie joined them on the balcony.

He kissed her cheek. "Yeah, well, I had some business on this coast and decided to come here first and see Ma."

"April and the kids come?"

Ralph wagged his head. "I don't like having them around when I've gotta do business, ya know? Besides that, Muscia scares the shit out of everyone, including me. She's a big bastard."

Flobo nodded. "Yeah. And she's just as mean. But she'd kill for Carmen."

"Yeah, she is good protection," Connie added. "How are things going over on the other coast? Things moving along all right?"

Ralph shrugged and stroked his mustache. "We get our share, what do we care. How about you?"

Connie shook her head. "Yeah. It gets boring sometimes, but you can usually pick up a bingo game or some poker. And now they got those Vegas-style clubs where you throw away your money. I'm not complaining, though."

Flobo continued, "Yeah, look where we live. An old folks home for rich people. It's too cold out here. I'm going in."

"Tess been by yet?" Connie asked.

Ralph turned away, taking his gaze out over the balcony. "Not while I been here."

"Hey, Ralphie, I got your favorite, prosciutto and some nice provolone. Put that thing out and come in."

Ralph nodded. "You remember my father?"

Connie cocked her head thoughtfully and smiled. "Yeah, I remember your father."

Florida armadillo

Chapter 36

SONNY'S GIFT TO FLABI

Thursday, December 25, 2008 – 1:30 p.m.

When the Delaney crew, Tricia, and guests began filing into the living room to open presents, Sonny was already there. She was standing on one foot, her left. Her right leg extended ninety degrees behind while her arms stretched forward as though grasping for something just out of reach. She had held that position an impossibly long time, breathing steadily, eyes locked on a blinking Christmas tree light, a blue one. She knew she should be focusing on a red one to help her reduce the Vata imbalance, but blue was her favorite color, and she felt entitled on Christmas to watch the blue light.

"What's Aunt Sonny doing?" Eliot asked, as he passed en route to the mountain of gifts that waited at the base of the tree.

"That's Warrior Three," Tricia answered, figuring she was the only one besides Sonny who was familiar with the asana.

"Why is she doing that?"

"Because your Aunt Sonny is a yoga-holic." Bethany pushed down on Sonny's raised leg as though it was a lever that needed to be pumped. Sonny lunged forward, arms flailing. She stumbled and then caught herself. "Was that really necessary?"

Bethany rolled her eyes. "Why don't we declare all family holidays yoga free? That way, you can deal with your issues at home and we won't have to watch."

"At least she didn't run over to the sink and start washing her hands," Elizabeth noted helpfully.

"I'm not dealing with an issue. I'm trying to ground myself. I've got a lot of Vata going on."

"What's Vata?" Eliot asked his mother.

Bethany's eyes grew large and she reflexively clapped her hands over the little boy's ear. "Don't listen," she snapped at her daughters, whose ears she couldn't reach.

"It's just a kind of energy," Tricia answered. "It just means she's feeling light-headed, and spacey. Is that about right?" She looked over at her partner.

"Oh, hell, I'm like that all the time," Elizabeth chirped. "It's called menopause."

Sonny grimaced. "I wasn't doing it because I was stressed, and it's not menopause. I'm not even forty." She was increasingly aware that her frustration over not being able to avenge Charlotte was the major contributing factor in her Vata imbalance. But that was more information than her family needed right now.

Cole said, "Lizbeth, I don't know if your behavior exactly qualifies you to lecture."

"Why not? I'm an expert on energy. Hell, I'm this close"—she held up her index finger and thumb as though she were going to pinch something—"to being able to ignite something."

"You're having a hot flash right now, aren't you?" Cole stated the question.

"As a matter of fact, I am having a private summer as we speak." Elizabeth Delaney stood, turned, and walked out the front door. The temperature outside was unseasonably cold, with a high of forty-five degrees. Everyone in the living room turned to stare out the bay window, and watched as Elizabeth tore off her sweater and began unbuttoning the shirt underneath. Cole rapped his knuckles against the window and shook his head, mouthing the word *no*.

"Homeowners association has already given us one warning. Seems the retirees in the gym don't appreciate having a woman strip down to her bra while she's working out on the treadmill. I should add it was a woman who didn't much like her husband staring at another female." Cole cleared his throat.

"Is that what we have to look forward to?" Bethany asked.

"There are things you can take, like black cohosh or soy supplements," Sonny offered.

The front door opened and closed. A cool and collected Elizabeth joined her family. She covered Mr. Phillips, who was already asleep in Cole's recliner, with a decorative throw. Then Elizabeth Delaney alighted daintily on the sofa beside her husband and cuddled under his outstretched arm.

"So, who's gonna start?"

"Me!" Eliot raised his hand.

His six-year-old sister held a package in her lap. It was wrapped in Dora the Explorer paper and topped off with a pink bow. The littlest Delaney sat patiently waiting her turn, a rare occurrence indeed.

"Look at mama's good girl. Let your sister go first," Bethany said, noting her daughter's unusually considerate behavior.

With all eyes upon her, the child instantly turned into the tiny animal they all recognized, tearing at the paper and ripping the box open with a ferocity reserved for wild creatures. Eyes wide, delirious with joy, Vanna freed a Barbie and held the toy aloft.

Sonny turned to her older sister, and whispered, "Are you kidding? I thought you were a feminist."

"I didn't get her that," Bethany retorted.

"It was on her Christmas list. Santa brought it," Elizabeth hissed.

Bethany swiveled to face her mother. Like a Wild West shootout, the two women fired off their most dangerous looks. Eyes smoldering, they glared at each other for a solid ten seconds. When the smoke cleared, it was Bethany who blinked and turned back to the tree.

"You go next, Eliot," Elizabeth prompted her grandson.

Bethany reached under the tree and read the tags till she found one for him. "And there had better not be a gun in there." Though she spoke under her breath, Bethany's tone was still menacing. "Please tell me that's not..." Bethany's shoulders sagged when her son held up a stuffed armadillo.

He ran to his grandfather and hugged him. "It's just like Aunt Charlotte's." Eliot held the stuffed creature over his head like a trophy.

Charlotte's eyes narrowed, as though she had been betrayed. Even though her collection of stuffed armadillos was well over twenty-five, she had yet to meet the armadillo she didn't like.

"Where are your husbands?" Mrs. McDonald asked, looking from girl to girl. The two elder Delaney sisters turned to their parents for instructions. Charlotte was still focused on her nephew's armadillo. Her gaze did not waver.

Elizabeth pointed to her youngest. "Charlotte is too smart for marriage. And we need her here. She will take care of us in our old age. Right, Char?"

Charlotte didn't take her eyes off Eliot's gift.

"Bethany," Elizabeth pointed to her eldest, "is divorced because her husband—"

Daughter number one raked her index finger across her throat and gestured to her children.

"Can I say *asshole?*" Elizabeth mouthed the words so there was no mistaking them.

Bethany nodded. "Yeah. I say that all the time. They're used to that one."

"Because her husband is a two-timing asshole."

"I didn't say you could say all that. Just asshole."

Vanna held her Barbie up and pretended the doll was talking. "Daddy's an asshole."

Mrs. McDonald brought her fingers to her lips as a wave of confusion washed over her.

"And one day, we hope, Tricia will marry our Sonny."

Sonny stood, and without a word entwined her arms so that her palms came to touch, and then crossed her legs in the same fashion, balancing on one foot.

"Garudasana, the eagle." Tricia nodded approvingly as she provided commentary.

"So, what are your folks doing today?" Elizabeth asked Tricia.

"They always go to my aunt's house in Miami. They don't like to spend the night, though, so they'll be home later."

Bethany walked a tall box over to her father. Cole's excitement quickly faded. "A Master Vac Professional Vacuum?"

"I thought you'd like it," Elizabeth defended her gift. "It's your own personal vacuum."

"Lizbeth, we have a nice Kenmore in the closet. Why on earth would I want my own vacuum?"

"Well, for one thing, it matches the Power Mop and Turbo Broom I got you for your birthday. And it's also made for men."

Cole's look went from disappointment to incredulity. "How do you know this is made for men? It looks like any other vacuum. And there is a woman in the picture on the box."

Elizabeth pointed an index finger, the nail painted Harlot Scarlet, at the offending appliance. "It's shiny, black, and ominous." She concluded by tapping the box and nodding authoritatively. "Can't you just see yourself using it in your hobby room? Rolling it back and forth, sucking up glass eyeballs and fur?"

"Oh, that's what this is about." He chuckled. "You don't want me using the one in the closet."

"Cole, you are the smartest man I know." Elizabeth pressed herself into him, flirting.

He nodded and rolled his eyes. "I was smart enough to land you."

"Boundaries, please," Bethany called, as she continued to excavate under the tree. She next picked up a gift and turned to Charlotte. "I can't imagine what this is."

Charlotte meticulously peeled away the tape, salvaging the wrapping paper for future use. She set the Mighty Grill on her lap and frowned.

Sonny's voice was strained as she held her pose. "It's from Mr. Phillips. He gave me one, too." She could see the man was still in turkey-induced tryptophan bliss, fast asleep and snoring lightly.

"Honey, your sister doesn't cook." Elizabeth turned to her youngest. "Why don't we give it to Goodwill?"

Charlotte hugged the box as though it was her sole possession. "I'm keeping it."

"And what the hell do you think you're gonna do with it?"

Charlotte quickly read the label. "I am going to make a grilled cheese sandwich in under a minute, and tasty hot dogs."

"Use a little judgment next time, please," Elizabeth told her middle child.

Charlotte pointed to three gift boxes shaped like Chinese take-out containers. "See who those are for."

Bethany made a production of reading the names on each gift tag. "Let's see, there's one for Mr. Phillips, Mr. McDonald, and this one is for Mrs. McDonald."

Mrs. McDonald, barely recovered from modern marital overload, held up a container of Metamucil. "Orange is my favorite."

Charlotte beamed.

Elizabeth scowled.

Bethany rolled her eyes.

Mr. Phillips's gift was lovingly placed beside him, where he would spot it when he woke.

Mr. McDonald pawed through his tissue paper and finally located his gift. He was already laughing when he held up a box containing an ear-wax removal kit. "Thank you, Charlotte. You shouldn't have."

Bethany turned to her younger sister. "Please tell me you didn't get me anything."

"I didn't. I made a list and Tricia got everything on it for me," Charlotte quipped.

"How about one for Grandma?" Elizabeth quivered with excitement. "Like that one there, with the pearl paper and blue bow."

Bethany's eyes narrowed as she gathered the package in her arms and opened the tag. "This looks like your writing," she said suspiciously, and probed the gift, trying to discern what it was. Her fingertips came to rest on a point at the very apex of the wrapped package. "Please tell me you didn't." Bethany handed the gift to Eliot, who shuttled it to his grandmother's waiting arms.

Elizabeth peeled away the paper to reveal a new gnome. She hugged the wee man and admired him.

"I know you must have run out of German names by now." Bethany wrinkled her nose disdainfully.

"Oh, no. I'm into the second and third generation. I'm starting all over."

From her statue-like position, Sonny began to unwind. "I just remembered something. I was supposed to call those agents yesterday," she noted out loud.

"Those FLABI girls?" Elizabeth asked.

"They're FLABI women, Mom. They told me I should call if I saw or heard something that might be suspicious. Excuse me." Sonny headed into the kitchen.

Bethany got to her feet and followed Sonny. Behind her were Tricia, Charlotte, and finally, Elizabeth.

"Excuse us," Elizabeth offered with an air of patrician etiquette she had learned from watching every episode of *Dallas*.

Chapter 37

A FLABI CHRISTMAS

Thursday, December 25, 2008 – 1:40 p.m.

Dressed in disparate outfits—from Ramon's gray janitor jumper and Paige Chesley's jeans and a sweatshirt, to the agents' usual khaki pants with white button-down shirts and navy blazers—the eccentric foursome climbed out of the Taurus.

Strands of Christmas lights framed each window and encircled the dessert case in Rita's Diner. Holiday music played from the three TVs over the counter as well as the mini jukeboxes at every table. Rita herself was dressed in a festive red crushed-velvet outfit.

"Merry Christmas." Rita welcomed the diners. "How is everyone this fine day?"

Paige Chesley was the first one through the door. Her eyes welled up when she saw the lights all winking at her at once. Pell put a hand on her shoulder and eased her forward so Ramon could get inside.

"We're doing okay. Glad you're open."

Rita stepped ahead of the group and counted out four menus without taking her attention from them. "Welcome to Rita's. I'm Rita." She pointed to her name tag. "We're open and we have two lunch specials. Four in your party?"

"Four," Pell confirmed. "Yeah, every restaurant we've been to is either closed or requires reservations."

"Well, we don't take reservations here. You're always welcome at Rita's. We serve breakfast all day—well, except for today. And we're open from seven to ten, seven days a week."

Rita seated them at a table in the rear of the diner. A surprising number of tables were full and the wait staff was busy taking orders and carrying trays of food. Everyone wore a Santa hat, along with black pants, white shirts, and black bow ties. They all appeared just as bubbly as their employer despite the fact that it was Christmas and they had to work.

"Can I start you off with something to drink?" Rita asked as she handed the last menu to Ramon.

"Okay, I just want you all to know that lunch is on me today, so get whatever you want," Pell stated magnanimously.

"Good, because me and the bean-eater here don't have a cent to our names. Nothing personal, Diego."

"My name is not Diego. It is Ramon," the man corrected for the umpteenth time that day.

"Hey, your English is getting better too, Raul." Paige's behavior was deteriorating by the minute.

"She's just doing that to be annoying," Pell explained.

"No. She is *estupido*." Ramon seemed convinced of this after listening to the woman for the last twenty-four hours.

Pell closed her menu and set it aside. "I'm getting the turkey dinner," she said to no one in particular. Then she turned to Ramon. "Actually, Paige is smart, but she's detoxing, so her mood is up and down because she has no control over it. The best way to handle an addiction is to go into rehab for a while. But in Paige's case, we don't have that luxury. The good news is, you get to go back to the high school after lunch, while Winnie and I have to put up with her a while longer."

The whole time Agent Pell was speaking, the man watched Chesley. When Pell finished, he leaned over and sniffed her. "Yes, but she smells better, not like...how you say?" He imitated someone throwing up.

"Vomit," Winnie offered. She was sitting on the other side of Chesley. "You're right. She does smell better today."

Paige's lower lip began to quiver and a fat tear rolled down one cheek. "I can't help it. You think this is fun for me?"

"My head is starting to pound. May I please have a pill?" Winnie rubbed her temples as she spoke.

Pell removed the bottle from her jacket and poured out one tablet. "You don't get another one till six." She reached across the table with the pill in the palm of her hand.

In a flash, Paige snatched the pill and tossed it into her mouth.

"Oh, no, you don't!" Winnie shot up from her chair, grabbed Chesley around the middle, and jerked her fist just below the woman's diaphragm. "Fuckin' junkie," she hissed in her ear.

The pill popped out of Chesley's mouth like a champagne cork and landed on Pell's bread plate. They all stared at it for a moment, along with the patrons at surrounding tables.

Then Pell picked it up and looked to her partner.

"No. Get me a fresh one." Winnie took her seat. "And you," she said to Paige, "don't you even think about it."

Ramon leaned toward Pell and covered his mouth as he whispered, "She is *estupido*."

"Screw you, Carlos." Chesney buried her face in the menu.

"Burrito." Pablo closed his menu.

"It's Christmas. You can't eat Mexican food on Christmas," Paige said indignantly.

"What do you think they eat in Mexico on Christmas Day?" Winnie fired back. "Turkey and dressing? Do you really think that?"

Pell hit the table with her fist. "Everyone shut up. It is Christmas. This is a day the world celebrates something good. It is a day when people are supposed to be kind to one another. It is a day when we have peace on earth. I know we don't have an ideal, traditional situation. But this is the best I could do for you all today. So unless you want to wait in the car—handcuffed and gagged—you'll be nice the rest of the day. Is that understood?" She glared at each of them.

Everyone at their table and the adjoining tables nodded obediently.

"I think that's your phone," Winnie said.

"Peace on earth, peace at this table." Pell eyeballed each of her companions as she unclipped her cell phone. "Pell speaking." Still listening to her caller, she covered the mouthpiece. "Order the turkey dinner for me. I'm going to take this outside."

A young man was placing a tray down beside the table when Pell returned. He set a plate of scrambled eggs in front of Winnie, a cup of soup and a dinner salad in front of Chesley, and a turkey dinner in front of Pell. A second turkey dinner was placed before Ramon, whose eyes were wide with possibility.

"What's up?" Winnie asked, as she liberally used the salt and pepper shakers.

"It was bizarre. One of those Delaney girls called. She said that we told her to call if she thought something was suspicious."

"And?" Winnie pressed.

"First of all, she said someone peed in her car so she forgot to call yesterday. Then she said the man who peed in her vehicle had bought a prescription drug from his next-door neighbor. Frankly, I'm more suspicious of this Delaney woman than the neighbor. She is a very peculiar person."

"Was it the mean one or her slightly saner sister?"

Pell turned to the other agent. "Hard to tell."

"Think we should check it out?"

"I do. Let's finish our traditional Christmas dinner. Good job, Ramon."

Chapter 38

VIRABHAD RASANA TWO - SEE THE WARRIOR, BE THE WARRIOR

Thursday, December 25, 2008 – 2:07 p.m.

The phone at Furfir Yoga and Tai Chi Center rang at 2:07 p.m. "Thank you for calling. We're closed until January second. You can find our class schedule at our Web site, Prana Qi dot com. See you next year." Sonny heard the message play, followed by the beep, and then the unmistakable sound of her mother's voice.

"Hey, are you there? I tried your condo and there was no answer. Helloooooo? Tricia? Sonny? Can you hear me?"

Tricia poked her head into the room where Sonny was rolling up new yoga mats.

"You want me to get that?"

"You don't have to bother. She'll just keep talking. How long will that thing record?"

Tricia shrugged. "I typically don't know the answer to questions like that."

"So after you all left, we had a family meeting and decided something has to be done. Bethany suggested an intervention and we all agreed."

"Now we should answer it" Sonny sprinted to the reception desk and grabbed up the receiver. "Mom?"

"I knew you were there. Nice of you to finally answer."

"I'm right in the middle of something." Sonny realized the machine was still on and recording their conversation. She pushed the button with an icon that looked like a bull horn. A second later she was sorry.

"So call me back when you're done."

Elizabeth was now on speakerphone.

"I can't now. What you said is scaring me. What intervention?"

"Oh, honey, you don't have to be afraid. The intervention is not for you. Actually, I was calling for Tricia. Is she there?"

"Wait, you have a family meeting without me and discuss an intervention. Now you want to talk to Tricia. I might remind you that I'm the sanest member of this family."

"You wouldn't get my vote."

"Hi, Elizabeth." Tricia shrugged in an effort to placate her partner, who was growing increasingly agitated. "What's up?"

"Hi, honey. Did you like your Waterpik?"

"I did," Tricia said enthusiastically. "I can't wait to try it tonight. It's supposed to be much better than dental floss."

Sonny turned her palms up and shook her head. "I knew I shouldn't have answered."

"I heard that. Go finish whatever it was you were doing and I'll call you later."

"I'm not going anywhere now. Not till I find out what's going on."

Elizabeth sighed, tsked, and sniffed. Sonny knew that all three sounds were accompanied by gestures and were part of an arsenal she used when she wanted to be dramatic. "Well, you know Mr. Phillips? Are you aware he has a shopping problem?"

"No. I had no idea. What kind of problem?" Tricia sat behind the desk and listened intently.

"Well, for example, he has a hard time sleeping at night and ends up watching those infomercials. He sees nothing wrong with buying everything being advertised."

"Mom, he's loaded and he's not hurting anyone. Plus, people like him keep the economy on an even keel."

"Are you still here?" Elizabeth asked a little too rudely.

"Fine. I'll go roll mats."

"Tricia?"

"I'm here. I'm listening."

"She's still there, isn't she?"

"Yes." Tricia grinned at Sonny.

"Honey, you weren't invited to the family meeting or the intervention discussion because you're having a vada imbalance."

"Vata." Sonny's mood was darkening. "It's pronounced Vata, with a *t*."

"Whatever. Tricia is generally the calm one. I just happen to think she's more balanced."

"You'd be right about that." Tricia playfully nudged Sonny.

Sonny pursed her lips, her nostrils flared, and the sitar music in the background suddenly sounded shrill and unbearable.

Tricia gestured with her arms, stretching them wide into a basic Warrior Two pose, and whispered, "See the warrior, be the warrior."

Sonny nodded and stepped into Virabhadrasana Two. The relief was instantaneous. She closed her eyes and sank deep into the posture, breathing with slow, rhythmic determination.

"She just busted a move, didn't she?" Elizabeth's voice was tinged with humor.

"A perfect Warrior Two. So, what about Mr. Phillips? Why is buying things a problem?"

"I think it became a problem when he started buying for the sake of buying. Not only has he dedicated his guest bedroom to storing these purchases, he has things like a sheepskin dog bed, but no dog. For some reason he felt compelled to part with three monthly payments of twenty-nine ninety-nine for an assortment of women's silk bathrobes, which I'm not proud to confess that I fell for, too. The model on TV made them look so comfortable."

"And he's widowed, so he really doesn't need these things." Tricia had gone into her military mode: serious, calm, and analytical.

"So you understand why we think you should go over there with Charlotte and have a talk with him."

"Me? You think I should go? I just met the guy." Tricia cocked her head at the phone and turned to Sonny for some logical answer.

"Actually, Char will do most of the talking. You'd be more of an interpreter. The voice of reason if Char wanders off message or gets antagonistic. Not to mention she needs someone to drive her."

"I don't get it." Now Sergeant Tricia was getting agitated.

"Me either," Sonny chimed in as she switched the pose to her left side. "Why don't you go?"

"Really? You know I'm an enabler. I've always been an enabler. I want people to be happy, whatever it takes. I'd end up telling him to buy anything he wants. Hell, I'd get on the phone with him and order two of whatever he's getting, one for me and one for him. In short, it would be counterproductive for me to go."

"Mom, this really doesn't involve us. Does he have any family?"

"Yes. He's got two daughters. But Charlotte said they don't speak. Neither one sent him a card for Christmas or even bothered to call."

"Did this behavior start shortly after his wife died?" Sonny came out of Warrior, rotated her wrist and ankles, and then came to hover over the phone with renewed interest.

"I'm going to say yes. Only because she hasn't been gone long, and this behavior is fairly recent."

"Classic Muladara block," Sonny said with certainty.

"What?" Elizabeth asked, clearly annoyed with her daughter.

"Hoarding is a symptom of a first chakra block. Unblock the chakra, no more need to buy everything he sees. Ergo, no more hoarding."

"Tricia, is she being serious?"

"Actually, yes. And she's right. You could spend a fortune with a shrink or a couple of sessions working on the first chakra. And he won't even have to leave his place. Sonny can—"

Sonny's face became a mask of horror. She waved her hands frantically and mouthed the words, "No, his place smells like pee."

"Good. I like that idea. It's much better than Charlotte's. She was going to steal his credit cards and cut them up. So it's settled. You and Sonny can pick up Charlotte anytime. What's your schedule look like today?"

Trapped between her partner's anger and pressure from Elizabeth, Tricia opted for the path of least resistance and walked away.

"Hellooooo?"

"I'll call you," Sonny felt her Vata rising. She was getting light-headed, definitely time to hang up; she needed both hands free for Utkatasana, chair pose.

Chapter 39

TESS RISES FROM THE ASHES

Thursday, December 25, 2008 — 2:13 p.m.

The return trip to Naples was faster with the advantage of daylight and asphalt. As Tess felt the traction of a paved road under her tires, she was surprised at how far she had actually ventured into the Everglades the night before. When she finally hit the city limits, Tess took the highway to her exit and headed west on the surface roads.

There was more traffic on Davis Boulevard than she had expected, and she managed to catch every red light, which afforded her the opportunity to utter a variety of Italian curses. Clenching her jaw, Tess forced her emotions into the background and focused on getting through the next few hours.

Minutes after leaving the highway, Tess was back in familiar territory. The westernmost edge of Tess's turf was bounded by Gulf View Boulevard. It also served as her street address. Despite being fantastically upscale, Gulf View Boulevard was a major misnomer to Tess's way of thinking. High-rise condos and multimillion-dollar mansions actually lined the Gulf, like a ten-mile wall, blocking any view of the ocean. Anyone driving on Gulf View may as well be in Idaho for the lack of scenery. Only those with deep pockets could afford to take in the view of the Gulf. Even more ridiculous was the width of the boulevard itself. With only two lanes, it would have qualified for a street in any other city. But like much of Naples, city planners took liberties, and those who could afford to live with an authentic Gulf view didn't mind the fantasy. For some, it was enough to have a Gulf View address, though they lived on the east side of the street and shared the view of the towering condos with every other tourist who passed by.

Tess happened to have a corner unit and could see the ocean from her bedroom. Unlike Hector, who lived on the east side of the street. His unit was bargain compared to hers, but he had to drive to the beach. Along with a view of the Gulf, the residents did not share the white sand beaches with common folk.

There had been a time when this address had been important to her, but today Tess was in self-preservation mode. She drove past Hector's condo slowly, like a tourist. From the street, she could see his unit clearly.

The shades were drawn; he was probably sleeping in. His prized Corvette was parked in its usual space, nothing was amiss. There were no black-and-whites, so Christie was likely wandering in the muck and Hector was not yet a suspect.

Tess took another pass in front of the building and then drove down a side street which intersected with an alley behind Hector's complex. As she pulled into the parking lot in the rear of her ex's building, Tess realized the adrenaline felt good. She hadn't eaten or had her usual two cups of coffee, but the spontaneity was giving her a rush.

The parking space she chose had a dumpster on one side and was partially covered by an untended palm in front. She buried the nose of the Audi in the palm and turned off the engine. While Tess allowed two minutes to tick by, she gathered her and Christie's belongings into a reusable shopping bag she kept for groceries. Using the spray cleaner she kept for her sunglasses, she wiped the steering wheel, driver's side door handle, and console to erase all evidence of her presence on the driver's seat of the vehicle.

Without a second glance, Tess walked away from her Audi and headed around the side of Hector's building. From the cover of a stairwell, she aimed Christie's key fob at the parking lot and began pressing the unlock symbol. It took three beeps for Tess to spot the car, a late-model navy blue minivan. It was not the kind of vehicle she expected a stripper to drive.

Christie had parked at the opposite end of the building, so Tess retraced her footsteps and approached the minivan from the other side. She was back on Gulf View in under a minute and heading home to her condo less than a mile north of Hector's.

Instead of heading into the circular drive, she turned into a sister complex across the street and pulled into guest parking. Tess entered her complex through the medical facility, waiting till the nurse at the reception area was looking away before she stepped through theautomatic doors and turned sharply toward the elevator. Surveillance did not exist in this no-man's-land.

The task of packing for the rest of her life was not as easy as pulling the suitcase from under her bed. Tess ended up filling an extra bag with her medication, every piece of potentially incriminating evidence, her tools of the trade, bank statements from the offshore account, and photos. In her well-organized mind, the process only took eighteen minutes. When she finished, she wheeled both suitcases to the door.

Turning back into her unit, Tess retrieved a knife from the kitchen and stabbed her bed pillow. Holding a framed photo of her with Hector, she slammed it on the edge of her bureau and then tossed it haphazardly toward the bed. The choreography of assault continued throughout her bedroom and ended finally at the suitcases, where she broke the heel from one of her pumps and left it behind the door.

Her phone rang unexpectedly and she jumped.

"If this is a telemarketer, hang up now. If this is one of my friends, you better leave me a message if you want I should call you back." The answering machine clicked off. The caller did not leave a message.

Tess looked at the caller ID. It was Hector's number. She did not pause to consider the unspoken message. Hector was taking care of business; he was checking to see if she was there. What he couldn't know was that Tess, too, was taking care of business. With an efficiency that reminded her of the old days, Tess slipped the blonde Anita Lemoyne wig over her pageboy and adjusted it in the mirror of her foyer. Then, using the butt of her handgun, she rapped the glass, shattering the mirror. She artfully tipped it off balance. Her condo now told the story of a violent abduction.

Tess took the service elevator to the basement and wheeled her baggage out the staff door at the rear of the garage. There was no surveillance here, and she was still flying under any radar. Only the staff used this door. Their shift had already started. No one was likely to leave via this door before three o'clock, when the next shift began. The heavy door closed behind her and locked. There was no going back now.

Although there was a sadness that accompanied her as she walked across the street, Tess knew better than to second-guess herself. There was no alternative. Besides, her plan was in motion and she was in her groove.

With great effort, she wrestled her bags into the minivan, turned on the ignition, and put more distance between herself and her recent past. Her plan was going surprisingly well. By the time she pulled into the Pier Hotel and Tennis Club, Tess was feeling forty years younger. At the registration desk, when informed that the only rooms left were street views, she even managed to act disappointed.

The man behind the desk acted equally remorseful as he handed her the key to room 207. "Enjoy your stay."

And if her confidence wasn't enough, Tess's luck was picking up. Leaving her suitcases in the doorway, she crossed the room and parted the sheers. Tess nodded approvingly. "That's what I'm talking about." Hector's unit was in perfect view. "Let's get this party started." Tess tossed her bags on the spare bed and went to work on the second part of her plan.

Chapter 40

CHRISTMAS WITH THE SHOATS

Thursday, December 25, 2008 – 2:40 p.m.

Troy was on his second cup of coffee. He handed the case file across the table to his father. Shoat Senior had been sheriff of Collier County until a stroke a year earlier had left him paralyzed on one side.

"What do you think, Daddy?"

Shoat scanned the first page and spotted so many grammar and spelling errors that he could hardly make sense of the order of events. He struggled to form words.

"I know, Daddy. And I don't have one lead. Not one damn thing to follow up on. Earl finished the autopsy. The victim had a heart attack. A heart attack is definitely the cause of death. After that, everything gets fuzzy. Her car ends up in the water with her in the backseat. That's a fact, but Earl believes she was dead before the car made it out of the parking lot. So it makes sense that she died in the backseat. But who would want to drive her way out to the Everglades to get rid of the body? Why not just call nine-one-one? Now, Earl has a bunch of tox screens out on her right now. And let's not forget someone cracked her driver's head. They busted her up good. I thought maybe the driver was in on it somehow, but I interviewed her." Shoat Junior shook his head. "She was just another casualty. Whoever did this might have thought they'd killed her. That would explain why they tried to hide the body."

"Family?" Shoat Senior struggled to express himself.

"Family seems more interested in what she left to each of 'em. I've seen the will and her three kids get everything. And before you ask, I checked. They all have alibis. This was someone from outside."

"Do more," Shoat struggled, and the two words took him too long. He sat back and closed his eyes.

"Daddy, I've interviewed her neighbors, her family, the staff where she lived, and the places she was known to frequent. The woman had no enemies. Well, except for a handful of biddies she was fighting with at the homeowners association. She was sweet as pie. Everyone loved and respected her." Troy shook his head wearily. "All we really have at the end of the day is a case of someone stealing a car with a dead body in it and then trashing the car. It could be that simple. Someone wanted the Rolls, whacked the driver, and took the car without realizing there was a body in the backseat. In that case, it's not murder. Might even be one of those gangs from across the alley. It wouldn't surprise me if they come over here to pick up some wheels and strip it in Miami. Imagine the look on the face of one of those gangbangers thinking they hit the mother lode, then he turns around and sees a body in the floor." Troy laughed heartily until he realized his father wasn't even a tiny bit amused.

"What about the drugs?"

Troy stared at his watch as his father spoke, as if timing the man. "The pharmacologicals?" he asked, before he had to endure his father's attempt at the difficult word.

"Pharma …pharma …" The elder Shoat struggled mightily with the word, unable to force the unmovable right side of his face to work properly.

"I don't think the two are connected. Just a coincidence. And you know those two women from FLABI are down here looking into the drugs. But they aren't gonna find anything. I'm betting one of those old guys got the pills from the other coast. Probably went to visit someone over there and got a hold of a Viagra or two. Hell, Daddy, I don't know how something like that turned up in the old folks home for rich people, but I'm telling you it's a fluke. We don't have that kind of thing going on down here.

Shoat Senior wagged his head. "No."

Troy's phone began to vibrate and he checked to see who the caller was before answering. "I gotta take this. It's the office."

As Shoat Senior thought back on the long road to his recovery, he realized his son was not only more frustrating than physical and speech therapy, but there was no end in sight as to when Troy might get smarter. *Motive*. He painstakingly wrote the word while Troy talked to someone from the station.

"Motive?" Troy read the note, narrowed his eyes, and considered this as he closed his cell phone and dropped it back in his breast pocket. "Hey, wasn't Mom's pecan pie awesome?"

The father pressed his lips together and gave his son the most withering look he could muster, given his paralysis. Then he sighed, exhausted from the futility of his effort.

"Mom? Can you get me another piece of that pie?" He yelled in the general direction of the kitchen where he could hear the water running. "Wait a second. You mean I should look at who would benefit from Lemoyne's death?"

Though it was a struggle, Shoat applauded, clapping one hand on his thigh.

"That call was from Sheila. She said we got a call about some woman who was visiting from Lauderdale. Apparently she's missing. I'll give it another twelve hours or so, see if she doesn't turn up on her own. Probably a domestic issue. But I will go back over to the Highlands and maybe interview the folks in the homeowners association and see what they have to say. Couldn't hurt, right? "

Shoat sat staring at his son, wishing he'd used condoms.

Chapter 41

LITTLE BLUE PILLS

Thursday, December 25, 2008 – 3:00 p.m.

"Was that the worst Christmas dinner ever?" Winnie pinched the bridge of her nose and shut her eyes as though exorcising the memory from her head.

Pell looked both ways before pulling out of the motel parking lot. "I think it might have been the worst one for Paige, but Ramon seemed to have enjoyed himself. I was kind of sorry to see him go."

Winnie looked at her sideways. "You're kidding, right?"

"Things will get better now. The witness is busy with a stack of gossip magazines. Ramon had his first turkey dinner and all is well with the world. We'll do this interview and still have time to pick up some eggnog and catch a Christmas movie."

"I think we should start with the man."

Winnie peeled off her sunglasses as they entered through the automatic doors. "Of course we should start with the man. Who else would we start with?"

"Are you in pain?"

"What? No! I'm not in pain."

Pell frowned, studying her watch. "You had that pill an hour ago. I'd have thought by now you'd be less cranky."

"That pill is for pain, not attitude."

"You don't have to get snippy."

Winnie and Pell rode up in the elevator without another word.

Mr. Phillips opened the door and found the pair standing in the hall. "Hello," he said, with a politeness endemic to his generation.

"Mr. Phillips?" Pell took the lead, fearing how the interview might get derailed before it left the station if Winnie were to take charge.

"Yes."

"I'm Agent Pell, and this is my partner, Agent Winnie. We'd like to ask you a few questions."

"Is it about them?" Phillips leaned out and cautiously peered in the direction of his next-door neighbor's door.

"Sir, do you think we could come in?"

"Certainly. I rarely have company, so I don't have much to offer you but whiskey or Ensure." He escorted the pair to the living room and waved a hand. "Or I can get you some water."

"No, thank you. We just had lunch. Mr. Phillips, we're investigating the theft of some pharmaceuticals. As you've no doubt heard, a truck was hijacked and the drugs were stolen. Some of those drugs showed up in the pharmacy downstairs."

"Yes. I heard about that." As he spoke, Phillips's eyes slid in the direction of Bustamante's condo as though Carmen and Muscia could see through the wall.

"Well," Pell continued, "it has come to our attention that you may have purchased some of those drugs."

Phillips's eyes suddenly grew wide. His lips pressed into a bloodless line.

"I'm not suggesting you did anything illegal. Perhaps you weren't aware they were stolen. We're just interested in finding out who is selling them."

He sighed, his bony shoulders sagged. "It was her." He pointed next door. "She...those women over there said they could get me a good deal. It wasn't a good deal at all. And the worst part was I bought them because I thought they were interested in me."

"Interested in you in what way, sir?" Winnie, who had been taking notes, paused and looked up, not certain she really wanted to know the answer.

"You know. Just because we're older doesn't mean we're not amorous. I lost my wife a few years ago, and I admit, sometimes I get lonely...in bed."

"Sir, would you mind getting the pills you purchased from your neighbor?" Phillips stood. "You're not going to take them, are you?"

Pell nodded. "I'm afraid we have to. They'll have to go into evidence. I'm sorry."

In the bathroom, Phillips removed one of the little blue pills and secreted it in a bottle of aspirin.

Once they'd concluded the interview with Mr. Phillips, the agents regrouped at the end of the hallway in a seating area opposite the elevators.

"This is the break." Pell crossed her legs and unwrapped a stick of gum, which she folded into her mouth. "Juicy Fruit?" She offered the pack to Winnie.

Winnie shook her head. "Or two loose ends, depending on how you look at it. We have an end-user, a pusher, and a designated buy for tomorrow night. Somehow we've got to start connecting these dots."

"Can you believe Barney Fife neglected to interview this Phillips guy?"

The elevator *pinged*, and the green arrow over the door lit up. The doors parted and out stepped Troy Shoat.

His pleasant expression turned black at the sight of the women. "What are you two doing here?"

"Your job," Winnie fired back.

"Huh," Shoat snorted, and headed down the corridor. "Bitches," he said under his breath.

Winnie shot up out of her seat, but Pell was faster and blocked her path.

Using her index and third fingers, Pell pointed to her own eyes then to Winnie's. "Don't let him get to you. We don't have time to duke it out with Junior. Let's stay focused. Which door is he going to?"

The dark-haired agent looked over her partner's shoulder. "He's at the neighbor's, the woman who allegedly sells Viagra."

"Let's go," Pell turned abruptly. They reached Carmen Bustamante's just as Muscia invited him in.

"Hey," Troy started to object.

"Agents Pell and Winnie." Both women flipped open their black leather badge cases. "We'd also like to ask your employer a few questions."

"Wait here." Muscia eyed everyone with equal distrust and closed the door.

Pell smiled congenially. "You have questions, we have questions. You do your interview, and we'll sit in and see if we have anything to add."

Following her partner's lead, Winnie forced a thin smile. "Try to look professional."

Muscia returned. "She just woke up from a nap and is expecting company shortly. Will this take long?"

"Please tell Mrs. Busta…Busta…" He glanced at the name he had written in his pocket notebook.

"Bustamante?" Muscia proffered the correct pronunciation in a low voice.

"Yeah, Mrs. Bustamante." Troy stepped in front of the women. "Please tell her I won't take long."

Muscia turned her gaze on the two women.

"We'll only take as long as it takes," Pell said politely.

"Come with me." Muscia led the way into the interior of the condo, with Shoat in the lead, followed by the FLABI agents.

Winnie turned and mouthed one word, *Bustamante*, then reached behind her back with a closed fist and felt Pell answer her in kind.

Carmen did not stand when her interrogators entered. She eyed each of them as they approached.

"Have a seat," Muscia said, and waved toward the sofa. "She just woke up. It takes her a minute or two to get her bearings."

Troy was the first to speak. "Mrs. Bustamante, I'm Officer Shoat and I'd like to ask you about one of your neighbors, Anita Lemoyne. Did you know her?"

Winnie's eyes glided slowly over to her partner. With the slightest movement, Pell's shoulders lifted. Shoat clearly did not have any evidence and was returning to do the interviews he should have done on the first day.

"Would you mind if I used the restroom?" Winnie asked Muscia. "I just had two cups of coffee."

"Down the hall on the right. First door."

Winnie wasted no time disappearing into the corridor. She slipped by the bathroom and went directly to the end of the hall, where she located an office and what appeared to be a guest bedroom. She deduced that, unfortunately, the master was on the other side of the condo, behind the kitchen. Undaunted, she scouted the office, looking in the closet, feeling under the desk, working quickly with an expert efficiency she had learned from the academy. There were no photos, no records; the room was essentially clean. A quick pass through the guest room turned up empty as well, and she finally was forced to use the bathroom so she wouldn't attract attention. That's when she discovered the toilet lid. It was up, not something one would find in an elderly woman's home. She guessed it had been used recently because Muscia struck her as the kind of caregiver who straightened things and kept them tidy.

Thinking quickly, Winnie darted back to the office, located a tape dispenser on the desk, and headed back to the bathroom. She stood in front of the toilet with several pieces of fresh tape and estimated where a man would touch the lid to lift it. She stuck them on the underside of the toilet lid and then crisscrossed them with more tape to make a patch. She left it in place while searching for something to protect any possible fingerprints. Thinking they were only going to interview two seniors, it had not occurred to either agent to bring an evidence kit. How could they have known Ralph Bustamante's mother was the woman they would end up questioning? But if she could get even one solid print, it would confirm her suspicions that Ralph was involved.

"So, Mrs. Lemoyne ate dinner with you from time to time in the dining room?"

Carmen nodded dumbly, her eyes half closed. Her lips moved as though she were having another conversation, one with herself.

"Other than that, did you spend much time with her?" Shoat pressed. "Maybe play bridge or bingo?"

The voices in Carmen's head seemed to be getting louder. Her eyes roamed the room as though searching for clues to her own insanity.

"One more question and I'll wrap it up. Did Mrs. Lemoyne have any enemies to your knowledge? Anyone who might have taken issue with her at the homeowners association meeting?"

Carmen Bustamante sat motionless.

Winnie returned in time to see Carmen working on her insanity defense and to catch the last of Shoat's ill-prepared interview questions. If she had to pick a winner in the contest, Carmen's bad acting was far better than Shoat's interview. Although, Winnie considered, the older woman was probably more familiar with the legal system and had more experience in dealing with law enforcement than Shoat the younger. But even after factoring this in to her imaginary competition, Winnie still thought Carmen outperformed her rival.

"Okay. I'm done." Troy was anxious to leave. Between having lunch with his old man and now trying to interview another chronically ill senior, his body language suggested that he was uncomfortable around illness. He stood, pocketed his notebook, and nodded toward the older woman. "Thank you, ma'am. I appreciate your time. Hope you get to feeling better." He gave the agents a surly grin as he passed, briskly heading for the door.

Muscia followed him out. When she returned, Pell turned her inquisitive gaze on the dark-eyed aide.

"Muscia, right?"

Muscia's dead-eyed stare didn't waver.

"Does Mrs. Bustamante have any children?" Her pen was still, and she did not want this question to come across as threatening.

For the first time since their arrival, Carmen's eyes flickered.

"Yes." The baritone voice matched the dimensions of the woman.

"It's good to have family around on the holidays." Pell jotted something on the pad. "Muscia, have you heard about any illegal drugs in the building?" The agent hoped the shift from the Lemoyne murder to illegal drugs would throw the caregiver off balance.

But Muscia remained quiescent, her gaze fixed on the agent.

Pell's eyebrows lifted. She trained her Arctic-ice blue eyes into the darkest part of Muscia's pupils. "Would you like for me to repeat the question?"

"No."

"No, you don't want me to repeat the question? Or, no, you don't know anything about illegal drugs in the building?"

"I'm not aware of any drugs except for Mrs. Bustamante's prescriptions."

On her pad, Pell wrote: *She's buying time. She definitely knows something.* Pell laid the pad beside her, knowing Winnie would have a look.

Winnie cleared her throat. "How long have you worked for Mrs. Bustamante?"

"Just over ten years."

"Wow, that is a long time. So you probably know all about her, her past, her husband."

Muscia didn't take Winnie's bait, but sat perfectly still.

"Did you know that she was arrested for poisoning him?"

"She was found innocent."

Winnie smiled. All the while she was considering how many times she would have to pop the behemoth with the Taser to bring her down. It was a lot like trying to figure out how many hours to roast a pig. First, you had to calculate the weight; only then could you figure the hours per pound. She figured Muscia weighed well over two hundred pounds and it all appeared to be muscle.

"Indeed she was. So, where's Ralphie these days?" Winnie changed gears quickly, another tactic designed to fluster either or both interviewees.

"I can provide you with his number," Muscia said, and started to stand.

Pell interrupted. "That's okay, we got it. You know if either one of you decides to cooperate, we'll make certain you're protected. Yes, that's right, Carmen. You don't mind if I call you by your first name, do you? I know this is some kind of act you're putting on. The fact is, you're a mob wife from way back. The Eye, remember, from Jersey? You're no stranger to handling heat. I'm sure the feds were at your house at least once a month back in the day. So you know how to clam up. I'll give you that. But know this, we will find Ralph. His fingerprints are all over this crime. And if you two are covering for him...well, let me just say, they don't have bingo and bridge in Lowell Correctional." Pell stood.

"We know where the door is." As she passed, Winnie gave the caregiver a look that dared her to move.

Not until they were in the rental car did either agent speak.

"He's been there," Winnie said with absolute conviction. She withdrew her hand from her pocket and held in her palm the scotch-tape patch. "I think I've got fingerprints."

"Where—"

"Bathroom. The seat on the toilet was up. I improvised."

"Even if that's positive, no judge is going to give us the go-ahead. And you know better than to get evidence like that. You can't use it in court. So what good is it?" Pell nodded at the carefully guarded tape in her partner's hand, shook her head, and turned the ignition.

"The more you know, the more you know. Let's go to the station and have their crime lab take a look. It doesn't matter if we get the search warrant. It's another piece of the puzzle. At least we'll know for certain if he was there."

"If we take our evidence to the station, Shoat might find out. Right now he's focused on the Lemoyne case. He doesn't have any idea that the two events are probably part of the same case. If he finds out about these fingerprints, you can bet he'll do everything in his power to steal the collar." When she realized that Winnie wasn't agreeing, she looked over at her partner. "Are you listening?"

"It's not as if I have a lot of choice."

"I'll give up the prints if you concede that the last man in that apartment was probably Ralph Junior. And—"

"And?" Pell folded her arms over her chest.

"And now that we have Ralph in the picture, I know we're heading in the right direction. It's all related." Winnie turned to her partner. "What if this Anita woman stumbled on something or threatened them in some way and they had to get rid of her? Someone had to drive her out to the dump site. She wasn't alone. We know that much for certain. I think they were going to kill her but she died first. So we need to be looking for the *capo di tutti* and a reason that Anita had to be silenced. Ralph is the common denominator. He's behind the hijacking, and I'm betting he is responsible for the hit on Anita."

Pell nodded thoughtfully. "That, my friend, is a good working theory. I can get on board with that. You wouldn't think an old folks home would have all this intrigue, but there really is a lot more going on in there than meets the eye."

Winnie nodded thoughtfully. "Maybe that is what Ralph was counting on. Who would ever look twice at a place like that?"

"So now let's concentrate on Paige and the buy tomorrow night. If that goes down like it's supposed to, we'll get our search warrant and have Ralphie in cuffs before he knows what hit him."

Bumping fists, they pulled out of the Highland Terrace driveway.

Chapter 42

THE INTERVENTION

Thursday, December 25, 2008 – 6:00 p.m.

"Hi, girls." Mr. Phillips was quite obviously taken aback by the appearance of the three women at his front door.

"Hi, Mr. Phillips. We're here for your intervention." Charlotte led the charge.

"Good job, Char." Sonny was already regretting her intervention in the intervention.

"Your fly is open. Can we come in?" Charlotte stepped closer when the older gentleman turned to zip up.

"Sure. I'd love some company. I just opened one of those new grills and was reading a recipe for quesadillas. I don't have any tortillas, but I'm thinking whole wheat bread will work just as well. Probably has more fiber, too."

"Yes, that's why we're here. You're buying too many things and you must be stopped," Charlotte continued authoritatively.

"What Charlotte is trying to say," Tricia said, stepping between them, "is there's a good possibility that these companies you're ordering from are taking advantage of you. And quite honestly, wheat bread is nowhere close to a tortilla."

"Young lady, you look like you know your tortillas, so I'll take your advice. How about a grilled cheese, then?"

"Why don't we sit and talk for a bit?" Suddenly, Tricia was in charge of the operation and everyone was heading toward the living room with its spectacular view of the Gulf.

Everyone but Sonny took a seat.

"So, Mr. Phillips, we came over to chat about all the stuff in your guest bedroom. We all know it's none of our business, so you can toss us out any time," Tricia said.

"Fair enough. But it's nice to have some company, especially a room of pretty girls."

"It's just that we are worried about you. That room full of stuff might be a symptom of someone who is trying to compensate for something that is missing in their lives." Tricia read the gentleman's expression as open, so she continued. "I understand that you lost your wife several years ago."

"Yes, she passed away," Phillips said, and folded his hands in his lap.

"Did you two have children?"

"We have two daughters. They live in California. I haven't heard from either of the girls since we had a falling out when their mother was in hospice. I really don't like to talk about that, though. Why is she standing there?"

Tricia glanced over at Sonny, who was now standing on one foot while holding the other foot straight out to one side, gripping the toe of her shoe between thumb and first two fingers. "She has her own issues," Tricia said confidentially.

"She's a yoga-holic and her Vata is out of alignment," Charlotte offered with her own professorial candor.

"I don't know what that means, but would anyone else care for a glass of wine? It's time for my evening merlot."

As soon as the man was out of earshot, Tricia swiveled to face her partner. "Feel free to step in anytime. You're the one who does chakras. I'm just along to interpret, remember?"

When he returned minutes later, Sonny was prepared. "Hey, Mr. Phillips? How's your balance?"

"It's fine now, but after a couple of these" he held up his glass—"I wouldn't want to test it."

"Do you think you can stand on one foot?"

It didn't take long for Sonny to have him moving through his paces. Blissfully unaware of what was going on, the old man complied with all her suggestions: moving from foot to foot, balancing, walking with his eyes closed, rolling onto his toes and then back onto his heels, and finally sitting still as she took him through a guided meditation.

"I think that went quite well,"Tricia said as the three women headed back to the elevator.

For the first time in days, Sonny appeared calm. "Yeah. I think there's hope for him. And whether he realizes it or not, he was doing some grounding and centering. If we spend a few minutes three or four days a week working with him and doing some meditation, I think we can get him through this."

"Well, he won't be buying anything tonight." Charlotte pushed the down button and looked straight ahead.

"You're pretty confident of your sister's talent."

"No, I'm not."The door opened as Charlotte dug into her pocket and produced a handful of credit card slivers.

Tricia sighed heavily, and Sonny silently twisted herself into Garudasana, riding the elevator down on one foot.

Chapter 43

TESS

Friday, December 26, 2008 – 9:08 a.m.

Tess had not slept well. She had stayed up late to catch the eleven o'clock news. By eleven thirty, there had been no report of Christie. This meant one of two things. The girl was either still wandering around or she had succumbed to nature. Throughout the night, Tess had gone to the window to keep an eye on Hector's place. His car never left and the lights had gone off at ten. But this was not enough to quench her worry. She had lain awake planning her next move, thinking of every detail, every contingency. The last thing she remembered was how very important it was to be alert and in control. She would go back to taking her prescriptions the minute she boarded the plane to Italy. But for the moment, she was grateful for her state of mind.

Her sleep had been fitful. Her dreams were filled with religious dignitaries pursuing her through the old neighborhood in Newark. She twisted the sheets and kicked the pillows off the bed, but they chased her till dawn, when she at last surrendered to the fact that there would be no rest until she had closure.

Finally, just after nine, Tess got out of bed, headed straight to the window, and took one look to see if Hector's car was there. It was, so she continued into the shower. Even if he had chanced a visit to her condo, he'd come back eventually. It might even spook him, she grinned. Vengeance was an elixir.

With her hair still wet, Tess retrieved the paper at her door and brewed coffee in the complimentary Mr. Coffee. There was still no indication that Christie had been located. While this brought her a modicum of relief, there was still the matter of bringing enough force to bear on her victims to cause damage without killing them. She was not familiar with the use of drugs; guns had always been her tools of choice. But Tess had decided not to spill any blood. Her revenge would be more memorable and enduring. "Payback is a bitch and so am I," she whispered, and laughed lightheartedly as she collected the vials of diazepam, setting the three bottles in a row. It occurred to her that it had been Hector who took the initiative and signed her up for the Medicare plan which supplied her with three months' worth of the prescriptions. But was it her well-being he had in mind, or his? It was going to be a long day. But once things were in motion, there would be no turning back.

Chapter 44

MILO THE DAY AFTER

Friday, December 26, 2008 – 9:15 a.m.

It was chilly when Milo headed to work for his ten o'clock shift that morning. He had left early so he could spend a few minutes with his father. The young man often visited the grave, finding solace in the simple act of reading the headstone. Coffee mug in hand, he stood before the smooth black granite, his free hand resting lightly on the cold stone. Milo hoped what he had planned for that night would make his father proud. In fact, he aimed to spend the rest of his life making the late Gus Purdie proud. But considering some of the things he'd done last year, he still had some work to do to reach the threshold of redemption. The way Milo figured, he was nearly to the breakeven point. But all that was going to change tonight because he was on a mission. The whole graveside ritual lasted less than five minutes, and Milo climbed back into the cab of his father's Ford F-150 and turned on the heat.

With the lower than usual temperature, Milo had an excuse to wear his black sweat jacket over his official Crukinshank shirt. After work, he was going to put on his black jeans and black Converse high-tops. He would complete the outfit with the black bandanna he'd gotten when he test-drove a Harley-Davidson a few months earlier.

Harley-Davidson didn't just engineer and produce the finest motorcycles in the world; they made bona fide chick magnets. Irresistible, chrome and black metal, the bike he wanted was sex on wheels. He had opened a savings account, and was putting aside a monthly sum to eventually pay cash for the bike. In the interim, he had purchased a leather vest which, the salesman told him, was great for picking up biker chicks. It had a strong, animal smell that Milo liked. He sprayed it liberally with his T-Rex cologne and hung it in his closet with the intention of wearing it to his favorite bar. Apparently Boomer was attracted to the vest as well, and dispatched it the following day. Milo, however, was not deterred by what some would decipher as a bad omen. He was determined to buy the bike and manage the women who would be drawn to the man who rode it.

And while his account was building, he liked to picture a hot babe on the back of his hog, her arms wrapped tight around his waist, her chin resting on his shoulder as the wind whipped through their hair all the way from Florida to California.

This vision was still tripping through his mind as Milo made his rounds at eleven a.m. Nodding and tipping his hat, he imagined the storekeepers and shoppers were watching him go by on his bike, admiring the sleek body, the chrome mufflers, and the roar of his engine.

Before he could fully comprehend what was happening, Milo nodded politely to Perky. On closer inspection, he realized she was holding a seductive teddy up to her chin. Her eyebrows went up and then down, the meaning was unequivocal. The vision of his bike popped like a balloon and suddenly, Milo was back on the concrete aisle that ran the length of the Stone Crab property.

"Hi, Milo," Perky said, as she added a batting of her eyelashes to the production.

"Hey." Milo pretended to look in her storefront. "Everything all right in there?"

"Why don't you come in and see for yourself."

The woman was easily old enough to be his grandmother. To his everlasting chagrin, Milo recalled one of the sins he was still paying for. He had spent several months the previous year working as a male escort. Unemployed and increasingly desperate, his original plan had been to provide his services to middle-aged vixens who could afford an hourly rate of a hundred dollars. And while he had managed to get the attention of several wealthy and attractive women—three, to be exact—the rest of his clients tended to be well past middle age, with an overripe sense of entitlement. It had been one of these clients who died during a particularly grueling session that was nearly twenty minutes past his hour limit. Although the death had been ruled an accident, and Milo's story only appeared once in the police blotter section of the newspaper, there were still women who remembered. And those women, unfortunately, were still talking because the story had just reached the ears of Perky, turning the matronly ex-librarian into a wanton hussy. Milo was well aware he was going to have to work hard to restore his reputation. Moments like this served to galvanize his resolve.

With that thought in mind, Milo put on the sternest look he could muster. When would it end, he wondered, and why didn't women his own age desire him with such ferocity?

Milo continued his beat, periodically glancing at his watch. He needed to be alert, not let his mind wander. Encounters like the one he'd just had with Perky tended to throw him off his game, and he couldn't afford that right now.

The Espresso Barn was a welcome sight. He ordered a double *cortadito* with sugar and resumed his rounds with a spritely bounce in his step.

Chapter 45

NEWS CONFERENCE

Friday, December 26, 2008 – Noon

Troy had called the news conference because the young woman was still missing and he needed the public's help to find her. That's what he told himself, anyway. Over the years, he'd watched his father on camera. For Shoat Senior, it was part of the job, and it didn't hurt to get as much face time as possible during election years. While it wasn't an official election year, Troy thought it was time for his big debut. It might even lead to the whereabouts of the young woman, he thought, as he examined himself in the mirror.

There was a knock at the door and Sheila stuck her head in. "They're all here," she announced.

"It's the men's room, Sheila. But thank you." He patted his hair, although he'd used more than enough gel to keep it in place. "Let's do this." He winked at the man in the mirror, adjusted his sidearm, and headed out to meet his audience.

The podium his father used was in place directly in front of the station so that the gold star on the door provided the backdrop. The reporters were standing by, shifting from side to side under the weight of their camera equipment and microphones.

Troy took a breath, nodded solemnly to the crowd, and took the press release from Sheila's outstretched hand just as they had practiced. The whole event was like a sequence out of his football playbook, from the number of the steps he took to the podium to the timing of lifting his chin and squaring his shoulders. Troy had rehearsed for a solid fifteen minutes, each time reading the short announcement in his head before looking up into the cameras. He placed the press release on the podium and looked out over the field of reporters. His gaze was steady and cool. He hoped his daddy was watching.

"This afternoon we are appealing to the public to help us find a young woman who has gone missing. Miss Christie Wilcox was last seen in Naples Christmas Eve, but when she failed to show up for work, her employer became suspicious. She was last seen leaving the club where she is employed as a neurotic dancer."

Troy's head snapped back as Sheila suddenly clapped her hand over the mic directly in front of him. He turned, confused and cross at the interruption.

"An erotic dancer," she whispered slowly and deliberately.

It took a second for the embarrassment to register and another second for the red to creep out from under his collar and swallow his face. He felt his Adam's apple bobbing as he struggled to pull it together.

"Correction, Miss Christie Wilcox was last seen leaving a club in Fort Lauderdale where she is employed as an erotic dancer. Friends watched her leave the club. Later that day she called her family in Iowa and reported that she was in Naples visiting her boyfriend. She is five foot two, weighs ninety pounds, and has blonde hair and brown eyes. Miss Wilcox has a medical condition. She is diabetic and requires daily injections. If you have seen Miss Wilcox or have any information on her whereabouts, please contact NSD immediately. Questions?" Troy knew his credibility was gone, but pressed on.

The local media personalities clumped together and looked at him as though there had to be something more. Finally, a young reporter spoke up. "Do you know who the boyfriend is?"

"We're working on that lead right now," Shoat assured them. "We will be handing out head shots with the missing woman's description and we'll be posting them around town, along with a description of her car."

Chapter 46

TESS AT HECTOR'S

Friday, December 26, 2008 – 3:15 p.m.

Tess had watched the news conference while sitting on the edge of her bed, aiming her hair dryer at her freshly painted toenails. She had learned three things during the press release. One, the sheriff was an imbecile. Two, Christie was not likely to be a problem. Tess went on to wonder how long it would take the sheriff to figure out that Hector was Christie's boyfriend; ergo, he should top the suspect list. And three, Hector was not watching television. With every passing hour, her assessment about Shoat's ineptitude seemed more accurate as there was no sign of any police interrogation across the street. Once, a black-and-white drove by. It did not slow as it passed. Tess glanced at her watch and shook her head; the local authorities did not have a clue.

At 3:10, Tess slipped a vial of diazepam in one pocket of her jacket and her thirty-eight in the other. She checked her Anita wig in the bathroom mirror, and applied a fresh coat of lipstick. She collected the keys to the Audi, the blazer she had worn the day Anita disappeared, and a bottle of wine wrapped in a brown paper bag. Pinot grigio, Hector's favorite. Heart pounding with anticipation, Tess headed out the door.

It took under a minute to get from her door to the lobby and another minute to drive Christie's minivan across the street. Still no police, and Hector's Vette hadn't moved. Tess entered the screened porch at the front of Hector's unit and rang the bell with one hand while slipping off the wig with the other.

"Hi." Hector was clearly surprised to see Tess standing on his welcome mat. He was wrapped in the navy blue bathrobe she had gotten him for his birthday.

"Feeling better?" Tess forced a look of concern.

"A little. You don't want to get too close. I'm probably still contagious."

"Poor baby. I won't stay long. I'm headed to Carm's for dinner. I just wanted to stop by and see how you're doing, and drop off one of your Christmas presents since we couldn't get together yesterday. Can I come in?"

"Sure. Of course." Hector was thrown off balance by her uncharacteristically polite manner, but he held the door and backed up to allow her in.

"Your favorite," she said, slipping the wine from the paper bag.

"So, what have you been up to?"

"Little of this, little of that." Tess headed into the kitchen. "Do you mind if I pour myself a drink?"

"You don't have to ask. Help yourself. You know where everything is. I'm just gonna put on some clothes." Hector headed in the direction of his bedroom.

Once inside the master bedroom he slipped into the attached bathroom and locked the door. This wouldn't have been his ideal choice for taking out the old broad, but she was here and that was all the opportunity he needed. He would have preferred to do the job in her condo, or at least drive her out someplace. Hector's mind was designing a plan even as he slipped into the jeans he'd worn the day before. Flipping on the fan to cover the noise he was about to make, Hector visualized whacking her from behind and dragging the body into the bathroom. He yanked down his shower curtain and spread it out on the floor. He didn't want any traces of blood or other bodily fluids left on his floor when he finished.

Wearing jeans and a polo shirt when he returned, Hector found Tess holding two glasses of wine. He was holding his pistol with a silencer on the barrel.

Tess stared at the man for several seconds. "So, it's true," she said matter-of-factly.

Hector nodded. "Nothing personal, it's just business."

"Carmen put you up to it?"

He shrugged and nodded.

Tess sighed. "Were you lying about the stomach flu?"

"Yeah. I thought it would be hypocritical to spend the night with you, then... you know."

Tess pursed her lips, considering her next words. She nodded regretfully. "Will you at least have a last drink with me? You owe me that much."

Holding the gun level with Tess's chest, Hector accepted the glass.

"Can we sit down?"

Hector shook his head. She was too smart and might try something. "No. Let's have our drink and get this done."

Tess nodded solemnly. "You need to know something about Carm." As she spoke, Tess tipped the lip of her glass toward Hector's. "*Salud.*"

"*Salud,*" he said automatically, and took a swallow. "What do you want to tell me?"

"First, Carmen is not to be trusted. One day you will be standing in my shoes."

Hector considered this. "Maybe not." He took another healthy drink.

"Then there's the money." Tess sighed dramatically.

"Money?" Hector pinched the bridge of his nose, then pulled out one of his bar stools and sat, keeping the gun aimed at all times. He polished off the last of his glass.

"You okay?"

"What do you care? I'm about to off you and you're asking if I'm okay?"

Tess set her own glass on the bar. "I'm just asking. Listen, Hector, I wanna make a deal with you." She poured him another glass.

"You got nothing to bargain with. I'm getting paid for this job."

"I want you to do it quick. Will you at least do that for me?"

"Tess, baby, I don't owe you dick." He squinted and blinked as though trying to focus.

"In return, I'll tell you where my stash is."

"Why would you do that?"

"Because if something happens to me, Carmen is my next of kin and she'll get everything. You really think I want my hard-earned money going to the one who double-crossed me?"

Hector grinned, revealing the boyish looks that had attracted her early on. "Are you kidding me?"

"No."

"Okay." He held his glass up. "I'll drink to taking your money so Carmen doesn't. Anything special you want me to buy with it?" He laughed and threw back the wine. "A car? Hey, can I have your Audi?"

"You sure can," Tess said solemnly. "The keys are in my bag."

Hector rocked unsteadily on the stool and nearly fell off. He shook his head doggedly, clearly having difficulty focusing. "Man," he said, and swayed.

"Yeah, baby," Tess said mockingly. "I want you to have my car to remember me by. In fact, it's parked right outside your back door. Come here and take a look."

Confused and high as the Goodyear blimp, Hector staggered after her to the back door, where Tess pulled aside the sheer and pointed to the Audi parked in the corner of the lot.

"See! I delivered it to you."

Hector turned to her, his face the picture of confusion. The pistol dangled from his hand. He opened his mouth to speak, but seemed to have forgotten his native language. He dropped to his knees, chin falling toward his chest.

Tess knelt in front of him and gently freed the gun from his hand before he dropped it. "Honey, can you hear me?"

Hector tried unsuccessfully to open his eyes. He nodded once.

"Let's get you on the floor so you don't end up hurting yourself." Tess eased him onto his back. Once he was disarmed and nearly unconscious, she straddled him, and with one swift movement backhanded him back to consciousness. "Did you know that you're not supposed to mix alcohol with diazepam? I didn't either till I read the directions. And just to make sure, I looked it up online. It says alcohol actually doubles the effects. And I put half of one of those little bottles in your first vino. Wait, I'm not done talking." She gave him another vicious slap that left him blinking. "I know about Christie."

Hector made a face as this fact registered somewhere in a faraway part of his melting brain.

"Don't cry. You know there was so much I wanted to say to you, but seeing you like this somehow satisfies me. Don't get me wrong, you were a good lay, but this...seeing you look so pathetic and helpless. It makes me feel like my work is done. So when the cops get here, which should be any time, you're going to get exactly what you deserve." Tess continued her side of the conversation another minute, although Hector was now completely unconscious and would remain so for hours. Even when the drug wore off, it would take him another twenty-four hours to clear the cobwebs from inside his skull.

Holding her ex-boyfriend's hand, she raked her fingernails down his arm, leaving a defensive wound the cops couldn't miss.

Then she pushed herself up, off the inert body, and went to work. When the police searched his condo, the keys to Christie's car would be found in his bedside table, along with the keys to her Audi. Christie's cell phone was out in the open on his coffee table; even the developmentally challenged Shoat should be able to find it. Her own cell phone found its way into the kitchen garbage can. Anita's blazer was under all the clothes in his hamper.

Tess's last order of business was to make the phone call to Carmen. Using his landline, she dialed Hector's cell phone number and located the device in his bedroom. Flipping it open, an idea occurred to her. She scrolled through his list of contacts until she located Carmen's number and then typed one word into the text line. *Done.* She hit send. That had been her trademark word during her employment with Carmen.

Tess glanced at her watch. It had taken less than thirty minutes to complete this half of the mission. On the letter table inside the front door, she spotted Hector's Yankees baseball cap, and for the first time in her career decided to take a souvenir. Then Tess slipped on her Anita wig, tucked the keys to Hector's Corvette into her pocket, and headed out to the parking lot.

Time for a little late lunch, she mused, as she inched the Vette's bucket seat closer to the steering wheel until she could reach the pedals. As she slid the stick into reverse, the transmission protested with a grinding sound. The car shuddered and shut off. On her second attempt, Tess was able to back the Vette out of its parking space and drive the vehicle from Hector's parking lot, across the street, and up to the topmost deck of the Pier Hotel and Tennis Club.

Chapter 47

WINNIE'S MAKEOVER

Friday, December 26, 2008 — 4:00 p.m.

Pell was behind the wheel when she and Winnie pulled into the Stone Crab parking lot. An anxious Paige Chesley sat in the backseat. Coming off alcohol and drugs was difficult enough without the stress of being pressed into service for the Florida Bureau of Investigation as an official snitch.

"Hang in there, Paige. After tonight, you'll be able to start putting your life back together." Pell was watching their suspect in the rearview mirror.

"How about shot of tequila? I feel like I'm gonna throw up. Seriously. I've got to take something."

"I'm going to get out in a second. Why don't you get in the front seat?" Winnie suggested.

"Like that's gonna make it better?"

"Paige? Listen to me. We're doing our best and we need you to do your best if you ever want any kind of life again. That includes getting your kids back. I'll bring you food and a nonalcoholic beverage when I'm done. But you need to be completely coherent when you're in there tonight. There will be no room for error. We need to get this done right the first time, so we can get these people behind bars."

"You're scaring me. You make it sound like they'll shoot me or something."

Both agents clenched their teeth to keep from telling her the truth. There was a good possibility that things could get ugly before they could reach her. She would be bugged and carrying marked bills. But at the end of the day, she was their only hope for catching Ralph Bustamante and his gang. And when the results from Winnie's tape came back positive with Ralph's fingerprints, they knew they were close.

Winnie hopped out of the car and came around to the driver's side. Pell rolled down her window and stuck out a closed fist. They bumped knuckles and Winnie headed into the main entrance of southwest Florida's largest flea market.

Wearing a Florida Marlins baseball cap, Winnie picked up a free newspaper at the main entrance. "I'm in," she said, feigning interest in the centerfold, a layout of tide charts for the upcoming week.

"You're coming in just fine. Take care of business," Pell encouraged.

Surrounded by the smell of fried funnel cakes, hot dogs and popcorn, Winnie made haste to the target, booth 408. After walking nearly a block, she located the storefront, glanced in and went past it, stopping at the storefront across the corridor. Winnie studied a pair of sunglasses as though they were worth more than the ten-dollar price tag. She tried them on, turning the mirror so she could see into 408.

A small Asian woman appeared in her peripheral vision. "Those are very flattering. They make your face look more oval. And they have a special polarizer to protect your eyes from the sun. If you go to the beach you need sunglasses with special UV protection. Uh-oh," the petite woman looked askance at Winnie's stitches. "What happened?"

"Bar fight," Winnie answered self-assuredly. "But you should see the other guy."

The saleswoman did not pick up on the joke and continued to look at her with pity. "I got something for you. Come with me."

"Can't you tell me what it is? I hate surprises."

"This good surprise. You like. I promise."

Not wanting to draw attention, Winnie followed.

"Winnie? What's going on? Talk to me or I'm coming in!"

"Relax. I'm going to take off my earpiece for a few minutes. I'll be online shortly."

Fifteen minutes later, Winnie returned as promised. "Hey. I'm going to pick up some eats. I'll be out in about ten minutes."

Winnie exited the flea market forty-five minutes after she had entered. She carried a brown paper bag and a cardboard drink carrier with three cups.

Pell squinted at the person approaching the car. She had Winnie's walk, and was wearing Winnie's ball cap and clothes, but as she approached, Pell's eyebrows furrowed in confusion. "What the heck happened to you?"

"You mean my new look?" Winnie climbed into the backseat, since Paige was occupying the passenger side. "This really nice woman gave me a makeover for free. I decided to go all the way and get hair extensions while I was in there. I had to pay for those, but it's worth it." She took off her new sunglasses and beamed at Pell and then Chesley. "What do you think?"

"You want to tell her, or should I?" Paige shut her eyes tightly as if to erase the image.

Pell turned around to face Winnie directly. "Have you actually seen yourself in the mirror?"

"Not yet. She only had one of those little mirrors you use when you try on sunglasses, so I didn't bother. But all the women in the makeup place told me I look great."

"You do look great—if you're trying to look like a prostitute," Paige said flatly.

"What?"

Pell turned the rearview mirror toward her partner.

"Uh-oh."

A bright light flashed. When Winnie regained her sight, Pell was pulling up a photo of her on her cell phone. "This should come in handy." Pell laughed out loud.

Winnie slipped on the sunglasses, crossed her arms over her chest and sat back.

"Oh, stop it. Quit pouting. I'll erase it. See? All gone. What did you get for dinner?"

Still smoldering with embarrassment, Winnie handed a bag of food over the front seat. "Tacos and chips, three diet sodas, and a funnel cake for dessert."

"And you think alcohol is bad for you?" Chesley disdainfully re-wrapped her food and returned it to the bag.

Winnie leaned forward. "What about the hair? You don't like the hair either?"

"Honestly it's hard to get past the makeover part. I hadn't really looked at your hair." Pell tried to cover her grimace by looking away. "You're attractive without makeup…particularly when it's applied with a spackle tool. Honestly, Win, you look fine just the way you are. And since I've always known you with short hair, the long tresses will require a little adjustment."

"They're called rasta dreads. And they're very popular." Winnie shook her head from side to side like a shampoo model, illustrating how fabulous hair should look. Tiny white beads at the ends of her spaghetti-thin braids clicked with each turn of her head.

"You kept the receipt, right?"

"Yeah, it's in my pocket. At least it covers my stitches. Finish your dinner and let's get to work. Not much longer to game time."

Both agents peeled back their sleeves, looked at their watches and nodded.

Chapter 48

TESS CALLS THE POLICE

Friday, December 26, 2008 – 4:05 p.m.

"Yes, I'd like to place a delivery order." Tess stood by the window in her hotel room, staring down at Hector's unit. Delaurentis's put her on hold.

The police were taking longer than she would have expected. Perhaps they needed some help, like a big flashing light or a fax. "I'm at the Pier Hotel and Tennis Club, room number two-oh-seven. I'd like a small pepper and mushroom pie, small antipasti salad, dressing on the side, two dozen rolls with garlic butter, and a dozen cannolis." She heard the cash register ringing up a total. "Forty-seven fifty-two." Tess glanced at her watch. They would deliver her order within the hour. She counted out three twenties and placed them on the bar beside the Anita wig.

There was still no movement across the street and the time Tess had allocated for her plan was running out. She needed to make sure Hector was on the sheriff's radar. It occurred to her that they likely did not have much homicide experience. In the time she had lived there, Naples had had fewer than a dozen murders and Tess had been responsible for three of them. She chuckled. Maybe one of the families in Italy would have need of a seasoned button woman.

The call came into the station around 4:10. That's when it was officially logged in. Sheila had stepped away from the switchboard, so the call went to whoever was nearest the phone. That happened to be Officer Bakeley. He was on his way to dinner when the phone rang. Once he took down the information, he folded the paper and headed over to McDonald's for a meal. He did understand that the case was high priority, which was why he used the drive-through and ate on his way to the Villa Del Camino. The urgency of the call did not detract from the taste of his Big Mac. He'd been craving one all day and knew from experience that this itch wouldn't stop till it was scratched. Resistance was futile. He smiled inwardly as he chased the last bite with a handful of fries; his wife was pregnant and he was the one with the cravings.

Too often, when someone went missing, the public was so eager to help that calls and well-intentioned tips flooded in while only a fraction of them turned into valuable evidence. But everything had to be checked out. At four thirty, the cruiser rolled into the Villa Del Camino. He spotted the vehicle in the front lot, just as it had been described. Bakeley rolled around behind the van and checked the digits on the plate against the flyer Shoat had handed out earlier. The numbers matched.

Tess was watching the parking lot when her order arrived. She looked at her watch. The delivery was early, the cruiser was late. She shook her head and mumbled her favorite litany of imprecations as she snatched the money from the bar, along with Hector's baseball cap. She wanted to be there when Shoat arrived, assuming he would arrive at some point. She wanted to see Hector led out in handcuffs, assuming she hadn't overdosed him. She wanted a photo of the whole affair on her phone so that she could relish the moment when she was settled in her new home.

When she finished paying the delivery person, Tess returned to the window. She parted the curtains to let in some light, but kept the sheers closed. The garlic butter came in two plastic containers. She had been given a three-month supply of diazepam and had only used four drops in Hector's wine. It had taken less than five minutes for the drug to take effect with Hector.

Tess pulled a chair up to the table under the window. Two more black-and-whites were in the parking lot now. She flipped open the pizza box and sat back as though watching a movie. A news crew pulled in, then another. The only thing missing was a bottle of Chianti, but she didn't want to miss the scene where Hector was led out in handcuffs.

Apparently they hadn't made the link between Hector and the missing woman. "The diazepam won't last forever," Tess commented, and checked the clock on the nightstand behind her. "Idiots. I'll give you another half hour to figure this out."

A young woman appeared in the doorway beside Hector's condo. She stood for a long time watching things unfold. Then she ducked back in and reappeared in a light jacket. Tess looked on as she walked directly to one of the reporters. They conversed for a moment and then both turned to look at the cops swarming around Christie's minivan.

Tess laughed, "*Cogliones*. The girl just put two and two together and now she's talking to a reporter about it. Are you kidding?"

That's when Tess got the idea to turn on the TV, and see if any of the stations were running the story yet. She dabbed the sides of her mouth with a napkin and flipped on the set, taking the remote back to the table with her. The young woman and the reporter were talking to one of the boys in blue when she returned to her seat. He, in turn, gestured to another cop. Soon everyone—including the other reporter and several neighbors—was talking. Tess flipped to another channel, wanting to be in on the conversation. Nothing.

Then the young woman pointed to Hector's door. There it was, she thought. "*Infine*, finally. Now, what are you gonna do about it?" She burped softly.

As if in response, one of the policemen went to his cruiser. In the light of the overhead lamp, he typed something into his portable computer. Tess watched as he climbed back out and gestured to Hector's unit. He and another officer approached the front door while two more men headed to the rear of the building, each going in the opposite direction to make a full circle.

"Don't worry, he ain't going anywhere." Tess leaned back in her seat, cradling the container of antipasto. She bit off a piece of pepperoncini and chewed. She knew they would have a clear view of him on the kitchen floor if they looked in the back window. She knew that because she had purposely dragged

Hector to the center of the room and positioned him there after re-dressing her ex-paramour.

"This ought to be good." She wished the camera crew and reporters had been allowed to follow the cops around back to capture the sight of Hector in his compromised state. It had not been easy to get Hector's clothes off, and harder still to fit him into Christie's bra and panties, but it was believable enough. Ten minutes went by and Tess could tell from the restlessness of the loiterers that something was going down. Then she heard a siren.

An ambulance pulled into the parking lot and within minutes they were taking Hector out on a stretcher. She couldn't be sure, but it looked like he was unconscious. Hopefully he still had on at least the panties. "I hope he's not dead." Then she began to cackle hysterically, laughing until she was crying. "What the hell kinda hit woman are you? Of course you want the son of a bitch dead." She wiped her eyes and watched as the ambulance pulled out of the parking lot. She checked her watch. *Miracle on 34th Street* would be on in fifteen minutes.

Chapter 49

MILO TAKES HIS BEST SHOT

Friday, December 26, 2008 – 6:25 p.m.

    Milo watched the last of the vendors pack their vehicles and drive away. He made a tour of the parking lot just to be certain. Finally, he returned to the storage area men's room with his clothes for the stakeout. On the way out, he looked at the man in the mirror. A tall, good-looking man with a cool mustache looked back at him. Since he had purposely not shaved that morning, there was just enough stubble on his face to make Milo look as dangerous as he felt. With a well-placed spritz of T-Rex cologne, he was ready. Milo was in ninja mode.

    Dressed completely in black, Milo moved stealthily to the trunk of his car and removed the composite bow and a quiver with three metal-tipped arrows. He had a can of pepper spray in one pocket and his phone, which doubled as a camera, in the other. In the pouch of the sweat jacket, he carried ten plastic ties, in case he had to restrain the perps, and the tiny recording device. His comb fit into his back pocket. Milo was prepared for any and all contingencies as he slipped into the EZ-Go golf cart and turned it on.

Milo's golf cart had been plugged in long enough for a full charge. While he hoped it wouldn't happen, the golf cart could run all night if he needed it to. He remembered the plug when he pulled away and heard it snap out of the wall. Looking back as he sped toward the main entrance, Milo spotted the cord trailing along behind him like a possum tail. Undeterred, Milo drove around the front of the campus with his lights off, until he reached building four, where he slowed. Edging around the corner, Milo was on high alert, looking for any signs of entry. All the locks were in place, the after-hours lights were on. Crickets were the only sound he heard when he tuned in. Even so, he strained to hear the women's voices. But the night was still, dark, and cold, and filled with insects.

Milo was prepared to wait. He backed the EZ-Go to the corner of building three and set the parking brake. The perps were now free to pull up to Grace's booth from any direction. No one would pay attention to a golf cart parked at a loading dock.

With one last look in the side mirror, Milo abandoned the cart, leaving his weapon under the front seat out of sight. His plan was to position himself in the booth beside Grace's, but this time he would have the lock with him. From this vantage point he would be able to record even if he couldn't see anything. Taking three strides across the no-man's-land between buildings three and four, Milo did not bother with the stairs, but swung directly up onto the walkway on the side of the building. He was busy sidestepping his way toward the front entrance when he heard a car approach.

With his body flat against the concrete, he slid far enough to peek around the corner. The rear entrance gate to Grace's storefront was halfway up and the light was on. The perps were already in Grace's place. And the Cadillac he had seen several nights earlier was parked close to the loading dock by the stairs. He slipped the phone from his pocket, aimed at the vehicle and took a picture. Unexpectedly, the flash went off. The light startled Milo, but he had the presence of mind to leap from sight.

He waited a second, listening for footsteps. When none came, he sprinted across the alley to his vehicle. Milo reached his golf cart and ducked inside. Stretching out across the front seat of the golf cart, he cupped his hand over the phone. The photo he pulled up was clear and unmistakable. Milo was pleased.

The license plate on the Caddy was the solid evidence he needed to make a case to Winslow and the cops. He nearly dropped the cell phone when it suddenly started to ring. A photo of his mother appeared on the screen.

"Mom," he whispered, "I'm right in the middle of something. I'll call you back."

"All right, honey. I just wanted to remind you to return my Tupperware when you're finished with it. I have the whole set and want to keep it that way. Don't forget."

"Bye, Mom." He snapped the phone closed and clutched it to his chest, wishing he'd read the manual and knew how to put it on silent mode. Milo could not risk another surprise call. He placed his cell phone on the console. A feeling that the force was with him inspired Milo to see what other evidence he could recover while he still had the opportunity.

He reached under the seat to collect his bow and arrows. It was unlikely that the perps had both ends of Grace's storefront open. It would be enough to use the loading dock for their criminal activities. Armed with his new weaponry, Milo approached the stall for a second time, entering the building from the front entrance. Coming in through the entrance on the main aisle afforded Milo two escape routes, one in either direction. If anyone tried to come in through the loading dock, his plan was to make a hasty retreat into the aisle and double-back via the front of the building.

Indeed, the aisles were lit only by the overhead safety lights, which remained on all night. He made his way to the vacant booth that adjoined Grace's and used his master key to open the locked gate that faced the main aisle. His father would be proud of all the preparation and attention to detail.

From his position in the empty booth, Milo listened to the chatter through the wall that separated his hiding place from Grace's store. Despite his effort, he could not make out the words he wanted to hear. There was just a buzz of people, a collection of indistinct voices. The recording device was in place and turned on. Milo's only move now was to wait. And wait he did, standing flush against the wall, holding his weapon at the ready.

Then he heard the unmistakable sound of the chain in the next booth as the overhead door was cranked up. He sucked in his breath, nodded to himself and rolled right, running flat out toward the front of the building to intercept the three-woman crime wave. Halfway around the building, Milo stopped abruptly as he caught sight of someone else running toward the crime scene. Rather than risk detection, Milo scrambled back to his hiding place in booth 410.

Chapter 50

WINNIE AND PELL GET INTO POSITION

Friday, December 26, 2008 – 6:37 p.m.

After dropping Paige and Winnie on the sidewalk in front of the flea market, Pell had parked the rental next door in the Stone Crab Marina lot to avoid detection. Her earpiece was already in place and she maintained a visual on the two until they reached the first row of buildings.

"This is weird. I just saw a flash," Winnie whispered into the wire that wrapped over her ear.

"What kind of flash?"

"I think someone took a photo, and his—I'm assuming it was a male—flash went off."

"Why would someone be out here taking photos?" Pell wondered out loud. "We'd know if the Feebs were here, right?"

"Definitely. And that was sloppy for someone in law enforcement."

"What about Shoat? Do you think he caught wind of what was going down?"

Winnie snorted, "Not unless you told him."

"Are you in any kind of position to make a move? Where are you right now?" Pell asked.

Winnie replied, "I'm hunkered under the loading dock across from the booth. Chesley is walking that way now. Where are you?"

"Working my way toward you. You see the dumpsters at the south end of the parking lot? I'm at the corner of the building across from them. Where was the flash?"

Winnie stared into the darkness. "Pretty sure it was from the corner of the building. It happened so fast, it's hard to tell."

Pell stated, "It's probably easier for me to double back and come up behind this interloper."

"Yeah. That way, he's caught between us. You better get moving. I don't know how much longer we have to intercept this moron." Winnie heard the sound of Pell running and assumed she was heading around the length of the building. "Let me know when you're in position."

From her hiding place under the concrete dock, Winnie could see a light and the movement of legs under the partially open aluminum door. Occasionally a voice could be heard over the crickets. Two other people entered, stooping to get under the gate.

"Hey," Pell whispered. "Did you notice a golf cart earlier?"

"Yeah. It's been there the whole time. I've also seen a couple of people coming from that direction. Any one of them could have driven up in it."

"How's our girl?"

Winnie located her agency-issued binoculars and peered through them to get a better fix on the situation. She immediately recognized Paige's sandaled feet. "Well, she's in there. I've seen at least eight more people enter, two have left. Punks and losers, mostly, but there are a couple of housewives like Chesley."

"You don't think she'd try to take the money and skip, do you?"

"I guess it depends on who she's more afraid of. Someone as desperate as she is has nothing to lose."

"And she's detoxing," Pell added. She sighed loudly. "Don't let her out of your sight."

"She doesn't know it's marked, right?"

"I'm not even going to dignify that with an answer. Instead, I'm going to see if I can find our photographer." The agent pressed her back against the wall and took a quick look the length of the building. "Winnie, can you take a look at the stall on the corner and tell me if there is a lock on it?"

Looking through the binoculars, Winnie panned the row of stalls. She cocked her head. "Negative. It looks like unit four ten has no lock. If our boy is in there, you better take him down and keep him quiet."

"Just keep an eye on our money." Pell rolled right around the corner, entering the stall—weapon drawn.

Milo had used his ninja senses to blend into the darkness. With his wiry body wedged into the corner nearest the back gate, he was prepared to take out a perp with his bare hands. He leapt forward, assuming a classic karate stance.

For the second time that day, the first being the sight of Winnie's makeover, Pell was surprised. She blinked incredulously. "Who the fuck are you supposed to be?" she hissed as loud as she dared. Her gun was aimed directly at his chest.

Milo rose up on one foot, extended his arms to either side, bringing the fingertips of each hand to touch like twin bird beaks. He had seen the move in *The Karate Kid*, and though he'd never actually tried it out, Milo felt confident he could pull off a solid front kick if he needed to. He thought about launching his attack complete with a bloodcurdling Bruce Lee scream, but at the last second opted for something more practical. "Who the fuck are you?" he whispered with equal ferocity.

Keeping her weapon trained on the man in black, Pell flipped open her badge. "FLABI."

"Uh-oh." Milo lowered his foot and hands. "I work the security detail here. I was checking out some illicit activity next door. You don't want me." He clapped a hand to his chest. "You want the..." He pointed to the adjoining stall.

Pell didn't wait for him to finish the thought. She was reaching for her cuffs when she heard Winnie.

"Abort. They're heading toward the door. They're coming out."

Pell re-holstered her weapon. "It's your lucky night, security man. Get your ass out of here."

"Okay, just know I'm here if you need backup." Milo spoke softly and turned to retrieve his weapon. When he turned back, the agent had vanished into the night.

By the time Winnie finished the word *abort*, her partner was already on the move, nearly out the door. Pell hopped to the ground and rolled under the loading dock. She heard movement overhead and assumed the security man was making his getaway. "Okay, let's do this."

Winnie replied, "Locked and loaded. Over."

Chapter 51

MILO GETS INTO POSITION

Friday, December 26, 2008 – 6:42 p.m.

Using the loading dock for cover, Milo ducked and scurried toward the golf cart. He thought it wise to be in position in case the agents needed assistance. What he did not plan on was a severe leg cramp.

There was no place to stretch out but through the side opening. Hoping no one was looking, Milo shot his leg out of the vehicle, desperately pointing and flexing his toes. Not until the cramp subsided did he realize that he'd bumped the brake. The EZ-Go was appropriately named, he thought, as he swiftly glided toward the Caddy. By the time Milo discovered his blunder and located the brake, he was less than three feet from the Caddy's rear bumper.

Milo eased his leg back inside the cart and leaned up on one elbow to observe. The thought of returning to the booth crossed his mind, but the FLABI agent had told him to leave. In the interest of keeping out of sight, so as not to jeopardize the investigation, he pressed his cheek into the white leatherette. It smelled like Armor All, perspiration, and popcorn. He made a mental note to spray some T-Rex on it as soon as possible. In the meantime, he had a front-row seat to a real bust. His drinking buddies would be so jealous.

Chapter 52

WINNIE AND PELL MOUNT UP

Friday, December 26, 2008 – 6:47 p.m.

Winnie cupped her hand over her mouthpiece. "Pell, get the car, crank it, and be on standby. I'll get Paige. We'll head toward you at the marina."

Moving quickly and deliberately like an apparition through the darkness, Pell's voice was calm and controlled. "Do you have a visual on Paige?"

"Okay. And there she is." Winnie was thinking out loud as she watched Paige exit the stall. "She doesn't see me."

"The money is gone?"

"Yep. And it looks like she's carrying an incredibly tacky purse. It actually looks like something you carry a bowling ball in."

"After what you did this afternoon, I don't think you have any business talking fashion, Miss Makeover."

"Not the time for this, Pell."

"I'm just saying, if I didn't know you, I'd arrest you for prostitution."

"Would you stay focused and quit busting my chops? Okay, Chesley is walking out the same way she came in, but she has company. I'm guessing it's Jose."

Pell said, "Don't get sidetracked. We can pick him up whenever. I'm in the car."

"Okay, I'm backing off. Wait—this is weird."

"What? What's happening?"

"That golf cart that was here earlier just rolled across the alley. What the hell?"

"It's that ignoramus, the cop for hire. I should have cuffed him when I had the opportunity."

"Shoulda, woulda, coulda," Winnie prodded. "At least he didn't collide with the getaway car. Ralphie would have capped him on the spot."

"Just keep a visual—"

"It's got to be one or the other," Winnie said. "The gang is still inside and Paige is about to get past me. Can you see her?"

"No. Not yet."

"Well, I'm not moving from my position, so she'll be your problem shortly."

"She knows to come to the car when it's done. Okay, she's on my radar and she is alone."

Winnie declared, "I see a lot of movement under the door, but no one from the gang has come out yet. Can you get into position in the alleyway between the Caddy and the golf cart? We can sit there completely out of sight until Ralph and his men come out. "

"I have Paige. She's on board and we're rolling." Pell slipped the car into gear and with the headlights off, rolled out of the marina parking area and into the flea market lot.

Pea gravel, while inexpensive and functionally ornamental, is not conducive to stealth or comfort. The Taurus lurched and bumped along until they reached the far end of the alleyway between buildings. The asphalt was poorly graded, so the underbelly of the Taurus scraped before it rolled up onto the smooth surface.

"Almost there. The freakin' golf cart is really in the way. I don't know if I can get around it. I might have to back up and go around the building the other way."

"You can't! They'll see you. Can't you bump it out of the way, push it forward or something?"

"Last time I took driving instructions from you, we not only lost a possible witness, we nearly lost our jobs."

A year earlier, Agents Winnie and Pell had ruined a minivan after riding up on the sidewalk while tailing a suspect. Neither woman realized that minivans lack the clearance for sidewalk driving, an error which cost the agency several thousand dollars and led to an endless stream of woman-driver jokes.

"Fine, go around the building, maybe they won't notice. Back out, and come around again. I don't know where your security guy is. I don't think there's anyone in that golf cart. Okay, I've got someone coming out."

"Is it Ralph?"

"This thing just gets weirder by the second," Winnie noted suspiciously.

"What are you talking about, Winnie? What's happening?"

"Well, a little white-haired lady just got in the Caddy. She's behind the wheel. And here comes another one."

"I'm almost to your position. Is the Caddy moving?" Pell's voice was agitated.

"No, the interior light is on and I swear it's just got two little old ladies." Unless Ralph was already inside, there was no sign of him.

Winnie squinted in the direction of the Caddy and then the Taurus. She considered her options as her partner crept closer. "Sit tight. Let's let everyone get in the car and start rolling. Okay, another passenger just got in, but I don't think it was a man. The light in the Caddy is off, so I can't see much now. I just heard the engine."

Winnie cocked her head, wondering if the drugs for pain were causing her to see things. Why the Caddy was put in reverse she couldn't be clear, but the big GM moved backward before the driver realized her mistake and put the car in drive. As the big sedan pulled forward, there was a sound of bending metal and the golf cart seemed to be following behind. It took Winnie a second to realize that the little vehicle had apparently gotten snagged on the bumper of the Caddy.

As the two vehicles moved toward the exit, Winnie put on a burst of speed, sprinting toward the Taurus. With the rental in motion, the agent jumped through open the passenger door and leapt into the empty seat. She wasted no time buckling her seat belt in anticipation of tailing their suspects.

Chapter 53

MILO'S NIGHTMARE BEGINS

Friday, December 26, 2008 – 6:49 p.m.

Milo exhaled, relieved when he recognized the sound of the stall gate being pulled down. This was followed by footsteps padding down the side stairs just feet away and finally women getting into the Cadillac. The Caddy's eight-cylinder engine growled to life at the same time Frank Sinatra began singing "My Way." At least he thought it was Frank Sinatra. All those singers from the 1950s pretty much sounded alike to Milo. His mother said he had no appreciation for the great balladeers, and after listening to the lyrics about forging through life, Milo realized she was right. Sinatra didn't have a whole lot of rhythm or attitude, but then, his mother didn't appreciate Milo's music either. Milo strained to look over the dashboard without causing his leg to cramp up again. He watched as the two mean women climbed into the vehicle; neither seemed to notice him or the EZ-Go. After a minute, another woman, the size of a football player, got into the backseat. The door slammed and he heard someone say, "That golf cart is pretty close." The engine started up, drowning out the end of the conversation.

In the next instant, his entire body went rigid. Something bumped the golf cart—hard. Milo held his breath, praying the giant in the backseat wasn't trying to push his vehicle out of the way. Soundlessly, he rose up on one elbow. From this vantage point, Milo saw that it was the Caddy; it had backed up without realizing he was there. The driver's head appeared out the side window and Milo ducked out of sight.

"What the hell, Connie. You want me to drive?" someone inside the vehicle said in an unnaturally loud and abrasive voice. The windows went up and there was the distinct sound of the transmission as the gears changed. Milo started to relax until he felt the EZ-Go moving.

He had heard about bumpers locking, but never thought he would be living it. Staying low, he pulled the emergency brake, hoping to dislodge himself. A moment passed before the horror of his situation was accompanied by the smell of burning rubber. He released the brake and began praying that the speed bump at the exit would be enough to free him.

They passed one long alley and then the next. Milo rose up enough to peek out the windshield and saw they were getting close. He closed his eyes tight and willed the golf cart to let go. In the next instant, they were up and over the speed bump and pulling onto Vanderbilt Boulevard. The Caddy began to pick up speed as they approached one of four bridges crossing inlet waterways.

With no idea where they were going, or if the Caddy might be headed toward Highway 41 where speeds went as high as sixty miles per hour, and certain death, Milo's mind began to race. With nothing to lose, he sat up in the seat. Clutching the steering wheel for balance, Milo pressed down on the horn.

Chapter 54

WINNIE AND PELL IN PURSUIT

Friday, December 26, 2008 – 6:50 p.m.

"Paige?" Winnie turned around and handed a manila folder to the woman in the backseat. "See if you recognize any of the people in the photos from the meeting tonight."

Paige located the dome light and flipped it on.

Before anyone could blink, Winnie snapped around and flipped the light off. "No light."

Paige placed the folder on the seat beside her. "Then no photos. I know you two are like preternatural creatures of the night. But I can't see in the dark."

Turning around to face forward, Winnie suddenly clapped her hands on the dashboard. "Well, I'll be damned!"

"This isn't good." Pell was hanging back to give the Cadillac time to put some distance between them. But the golf cart was staying right on its bumper.

"You think that's the photographer?"

"Hell if I know. I had no idea those little carts went that fast."

With a monumental look of incredulity on her heavily painted face, Winnie turned to her partner. "You're kidding, right?"

"Well, I just thought they couldn't do more than about fifteen miles per hour. I mean, who needs to go fast on a golf course, right?" Pell crept out of the parking lot and put on her headlights. The suspects were now a block away.

"It's caught on the bumper, Pell."

Paige leaned forward between the seats to see what they were talking about.

"And you need to put your seat belt on," Pell said over her shoulder. "Buckle up back there or I'll have to pull over."

Winnie's original look of incredulity spread to Paige Chesley. "Okay. But I'm thinking that unless you go over ten miles an hour, I'm not in a whole lot of danger. This little circus is getting pretty exciting."

"Well, excuse me." Pell was growing increasingly irritated. "It's not enough that I feel like a pimp right now with her in the passenger seat, but now I have to deal with an obnoxious witness, too?"

"Wait a second. Listen."

"The guy in the golf cart is blowing his horn," Pell nodded. "Smart."

"Not much of a horn," Paige observed. "Sounds like the horn on my son's bike."

Winnie rolled down her window. "Did you see something just fly out of the golf cart?"

"Yeah." Pell slowed when they drew near the item lying off to the side of the street so that Winnie could open her door and snag it.

Winnie grimly shook her head. She closed her door and held up an arrow. Its metal shaft was bent nearly in half. "Let's go! We don't want to lose them now. You're going to have to break the speed limit, Pell. C'mon, long pedal on the right, push it to the floorboard!"

Chapter 55

TAILGATING THE CADDY

Friday, December 26, 2008 – 6:51 p.m.

"Look behind us." Flo was staring in the passenger side mirror. Connie and Muscia turned around. The sight was surreal. They were being tailgated by a maniac driving a golf cart.

"I didn't know those things went so fast," Connie mumbled, and accelerated. "He's so close I can't even see his headlights!"

"He's blowing at you." Flo scowled. She did not like the looks of this. "I think he wants to pass."

"Well, we're in a no-passing zone. See the double line? He's just gonna hafta wait."

"We have a car full of cash and drugs and you're worried about some *piccado* passing you in a no-passing zone? Geez, Connie, get your head out of your ass, pull over, and let the guy go around."

Flo moved as far as she could to the right, accidentally dropping the front tire off the shoulder of the road and overcompensating with a sharp tug at the wheel. "Uh-oh."

"What?" Connie stared in disbelief in her rearview mirror.

"He ain't passing, he's trying to shoot us!"

"With a bow and a freakin' arrow," Connie finished the sentence.

Muscia had been watching the events as they unfolded. In fact, there was a man aiming an arrow directly at the rear window. "Floor it!" she bellowed, and the driver obeyed. "He's stuck on the bumper. We're going to have to lose him some other way."

"What do you suggest?" Connie began to panic.

"Oyster Pass is coming up. You have to get this car airborne," Muscia answered.

"Hell no. I'm not going to wreck my car because——"

"Do it!" Muscia roared.

Grudgingly, Connie got the Caddy up to eighty as they approached the bridge. When the big GM came over the top, the four-ton car left the asphalt for a split second and then slammed down on the other side in a flurry of sparks.

The golf cart hopped off the roadway, rolled down the short embankment, and disappeared into the tidal current below.

"Keep going. We need to get off the road." Muscia kept her eyes straight ahead, never bothering to look at the aftermath of her decision.

Chapter 56

DIAZEPAM GARLIC ROLLS

Friday, December 26, 2008 – 6:55 p.m.

Tess took the butter containers out of the mini fridge in her room and removed the lids. A container of garlic butter came with every dozen rolls and she estimated the container held at least five ounces. She split a bottle of diazepam between them and considered the implications of what she was about to do. After the dose she had used on Hector, she knew there would be enough to knock Carmen unconscious. The only concern she had was the possibility that Muscia would eat some. That issue was easily resolved by adding the remaining bottle of diazepam before sealing each of the lids.

They had been like family at one time. And that was the only reason Carmen, like Hector, would be allowed to live. As she repacked the butter in the bag in which it had arrived, Tess hoped this final act would be enough to sate her need for revenge and ensure that she would be able to live the rest of her life without having to look over her shoulder.

Armed with the take-out order of rolls and cannolis, she donned Hector's Yankees baseball cap and began to implement phase two of her plan. On the top deck of the hotel's parking garage, she climbed into Hector's car. Revenge was sweet, and she would miss this phase of her life. But Italy was calling to her now.

Tess estimated that this part of her mission wouldn't take more than fifteen minutes from beginning to end, and she wanted to be home in time for *Jeopardy!* Highland Terrace was less than a mile away; even hitting every light she'd be there in six minutes, if traveling at a speed of thirty miles per hour. She looked at her watch, then the clock on the dashboard. "Asshole is two minutes off. He was never cut out for this kind of work," she noted, and put the Vette into reverse.

In fact, the trip took seven minutes. She pulled the baseball cap as low as she dared, slipped on a pair of tinted glasses, and walked to the doorman's podium. He wasn't there, which meant one of two things: he was either in the restroom or parking a car. A small miracle she took as a sign. Tess checked the order, the nondescript aluminum bowls for the rolls and salad and the plastic butter cups, making certain there was nothing that would indicate where they had come from. Even Shoat would ultimately unravel that mystery, but by then she would be long gone. Tess folded the white paper bag closed and wrote: Bustamante – 802 – *Mangia*, Hector!

The doorman came down the hall just as the sliding doors in the front of the building opened.

"Have a good evening," the man called.

Tess recognized the voice and, without turning around, she waved over her shoulder. "Take-out for Bustamante there." Tess slipped back into the night.

As she walked down the circular driveway she pulled up her sleeve. "Eleven minutes. C'mon, Fontana," she scolded herself.

Chapter 57

INTERVENTION PART DEUX

Friday, December 26, 2008 — 7:03 p.m.

"Hi, Mark." Charlotte gave the doorman an awkward wave that looked more like a salute.

The three women approached the elevator where he was standing in wait for the next car.

"Hi, Char. You're looking better than the last time I saw you. How are you feeling?"

Charlotte's eyes went from the white bag to Mark's midsection. Even with a jacket, his expansive girth was hard to miss. "I feel fine. How are you feeling?"

Aware of her focal point, Mark was growing increasingly self-conscious. The lights over the elevator suddenly held great importance. "Elevator is slow tonight." Mark straightened his shoulders and stood a bit taller. "I'm okay. Did you all have a nice Christmas?"

"She had a great Christmas," Sonny intervened, wondering what happened when she wasn't around to act as a buffer between her annoying sister and the unsuspecting population at large. "Pizza?"

Mark blushed. "It's not for me. It does smells good, though. Where are you off to tonight?"

Charlotte said, "We're going to visit Mr. Phillips. He gave us Grill Buddies."

"Would you mind delivering this to Mrs. Bustamante? She's right next door. It's paid for and everything."

"Sure, no problem." Tricia relieved the man of the take-out order.

"I appreciate it. It's just that I hate to leave my station this time of year, what with everybody feeling generous. You know? I worked yesterday and made nearly two hundred in tips."

Tricia replied, "I understand."

"Thanks again." Mark waved and wasted no time getting back to his station in front of the podium.

"Bustamante—they are the women who sold Mr. Phillips the Viagra," Sonny explained to Tricia as she pressed the up button repeatedly and enthusiastically.

"They?"

"The Bustamante woman and her major domo, the biggest woman I've ever seen outside the pages of *The Guinness Book of World Records*. She's, like, ten feet tall and weighs more than a subcompact."

"That's not true." Charlotte's eyes narrowed. "She's probably about six feet tall and weighs a lot less than a subcompact."

"I'm not worried. If they look dangerous, I'll toss the pizza through the door and run."

The elevator chimed; the women boarded.

"This is what we know. Phillips has two daughters. They both live out west. Char found their phone numbers in his address book and recognized the California area code. I think it's best if we call them from his condo—makes it more ligit."

"Have you decided on a treatment?" Tricia asked.

"It will depend on what kind of relationship he has with his daughters and what he needs in order to stop his impulse to buy everything he sees on TV. Char, does that go along with what you're thinking?"

"He needs a puppy."

The door opened, and the three women headed down the hall. "If you're not back in two minutes, we'll call the police." Sonny was only half kidding as she rang Mr. Phillips's doorbell.

In less than a minute, Tricia let herself in.

"No problems?" Sonny asked.

Tricia held up a twenty-dollar bill. "The big woman gave me a tip." She folded it and slipped it into the breast pocket of her guayabera, then patted it for good measure. "I'm thinking about changing careers."

Sonny said, "We were just talking about how we slept last night."

"I made a tasty quesadilla at two a.m. It was quick and easy," Charlotte offered, even as Sonny threatened her with a cease-and-desist look. "Mom got angry because I used the last of the Velveeta, so there was none for breakfast."

"No one cares, Char." Sonny returned her attention to their host. "How about you, Mr. Phillips, did you sleep better last night?"

He had on his gray sweater again, complete with the gravy stain from the day before. "You know, I did. I think that meditation thing we did really helped. I slept like a baby. Didn't wake up till after seven. And I didn't have to take a nap this afternoon."

"Good. Meditation can do wonders. Imagine how you'd feel if you could sleep like that every night."

"And think of all the money you'll save," Charlotte added helpfully.

"How are your daughters? How are they doing?" Sonny was getting into the interview, finding her rhythm.

Phillips's face fell. All the joy that had been there a moment earlier vanished.

"Bad subject?" Sonny continued.

"I haven't heard from the girls in a while." He shook his head, which seemed heavy with worry. His black-rimmed glasses shifted slightly. Out of habit he pushed them back up his nose, closing his eyes and setting his jaw.

"How long is a while?" Sonny urged.

Phillips sighed, but did not answer.

Tricia stepped in. "Do you want us to give you some privacy? We can visit some other time."

He shook his head. "No, I like having company. You girls can stop in anytime. It is always a pleasure to see you." He stood, and with long strides that matched his height crossed to the window. "Must be a year, maybe two, since I've talked to either of my own girls."

Sonny asked, "Do you remember the last time you spoke to either one?"

"Yes." He nodded and drew in a jagged breath. "It was on the day of their mother's funeral, two years ago January."

"Have you tried calling them?"

"I don't want to bother them. You know, they both have full-time jobs and families."

Sonny was beginning to feel like an interrogator. Hesitatingly she asked, "Would you like to talk to them if we can get either one on the phone?"

"I suppose." He sank his hands into the pockets of his sweater.

"Things can change in two years." Sonny felt her right foot inching up as though her body was sensing her tension ahead of her brain and preparing for the tree pose.

"Let me get you their phone numbers." With surprising agility, Phillips got to his feet and made haste to the master bedroom. When he returned, he was thumbing through the leatherbound book. "I can't read my own writing."

Since she was already standing, Sonny extended her hand. "What are their names?"

"Daisy and Lilly. That was their mother's idea. She loved flowers."

They all watched eagerly as Sonny punched in the number before handing the phone over to the elderly gentleman. A shy grin began to take shape on his face, starting at the corners of his eyes. He listened intently, clearly becoming more anxious with each ring. Before too long, his anticipation faded. Phillips handed the phone to Sonny.

She listened: *the number you have dialed has been disconnected*. After repeating this to the others, she said, "Let me try again." She took the address book and couldn't help but notice that the page was empty except for Daisy, his daughter. She punched in the number, and as she waited Sonny discreetly thumbed through the book, where she found the pages mostly empty.

"How about your other daughter? Lilly?" Sonny had to ask after receiving the recorded message for a second time. The only logical deduction they could draw was Daisy had moved and not provided a forwarding number to her father. This probability hung in the air like a bad smell. No one wanted to address it, but it wouldn't go away.

"Okay, I've got ringing," Sonny said excitedly after she dialed the second number.

Mr. Phillips sighed, as hope propped him up again.

"What!" the voice at the other end answered with a hostility usually reserved for sales calls.

"Hi, is this Lilly?" Sonny turned her back to the trio.

"Yes. Who is this?"

"My name is Sonny. I'm a friend of your father's."

"Is he dead?" Her tone was not that of a frightened daughter bracing herself for the bad news. Lilly sounded giddy.

"Um, no." Sonny didn't waste any time getting to the kitchen where she could speak openly. She stepped over a stack of assorted boxes and noticed two more piles on the countertop and a host of other packages haphazardly arranged in the food pantry. The old gentleman was drowning and he didn't even know it.

"Is he sick?" Again the woman on the other end was way too excited.

"No. I'm here with him now. He's fine, healthy and happy, actually."

"Oh." The voice flattened out. "So what does he want?"

As she spoke, Sonny stepped back on her left foot, aligning the arch with the heel of her right foot. Bending her right knee, she sank into Warrior Two. With one arm extended out, fingers reaching toward the wall in front of her, while the other hand held the phone to her ear, she drew in a deliberate breath and exhaled. "I'm trying to figure out what could possibly cause you and your sister not to call your dad at Christmas. And why would your sister move without giving him her new number?" Sonny hated confrontation, but she hated ill-treatment of the elderly even more. And if the conversation continued to deteriorate, at least she was braced in Warrior Two to release the tension as it hit.

"Who do you think you are to judge me, to judge us?"

"I'm a friend of your father's." Sonny pronounced each word slowly and realized her voice had dropped an octave.

"Who are you again? What's your name?" The voice on the other end of the line was heating up as well.

"Sonny."

"Let me set the record straight, Sonny. My father is worth millions, but he's also a selfish and petty little man."

"Oh, so this is about money." Sonny didn't try to hide her disgust.

"Yes, it's about money. What would you do if your father sent you a twenty-dollar shirt from Costco for Christmas—every year? Meanwhile, you're a single mom trying to buy a house on a teacher's salary. At my age, I'm supposed to be thinking about retirement, not how to get another job to pay for my kids' tuition."

Sonny did not like Lilly's tone, but she understood the woman's argument. It wasn't the first time she'd heard it.

"He must have been in his early teens during the Great Depression. His formative years were probably shaped by privation."

Tricia appeared in the doorway and held her palms up. Sonny turned her extended hand so that her thumb pointed down. Tricia nodded and returned to the living room.

"So what?" Lilly snapped. "We're his daughters. That should count for something. Instead, our lives and his grandkids' lives are being shaped by privation."

"I'm not going to argue with you. He is the way he is. I just thought you might be interested to know he is doing fine."

"Well, I think I speak for my sister when I say screw you, and tell Dad whatever you want."

The phone went dead.

Sonny took her time coming out of Warrior Two. Mr. Phillips looked up when she reentered the room. He stood expectantly, but all hope vanished when he realized she was no longer engaged on the telephone.

"Maybe we can do some more of that meditation," Sonny offered cheerfully.

"Or we could try some tai chi," Tricia volunteered.

"Or we can get him a puppy," Charlotte concluded.

Oyster Pass

Chapter 58

SAVING MILO

Friday, December 26, 2008 – 7:04 p.m.

Winnie, Pell, and Paige were captivated by the scene ahead as it unfolded. Unable to turn away, unable to respond, in the dim light of the streetlamp, they watched in horrified helplessness as the Cadillac hurtled up one side of the bridge. They saw the golf cart separate from the bumper, reach the crest of Oyster Bay Pass and lurch sideways. As if in slow motion, the cart continued its trajectory, wheels spinning as it hit the shoulder of the road and disappeared down the embankment.

Had they not stopped to gather the evidence, there might have been a different outcome. But by the time they reached the place where they had last seen the golf cart it had already disappeared into the dark water of the pass, leaving behind a trail of bubbles.

"Call nine-one-one!" Pell called over her shoulder to Paige, as the two agents scrambled down the slope toward the water.

"There it is." Winnie pointed and headed into the chilly water. She waded in as far as she could, then dove forward and began to swim.

Swimming with just as much determination, Pell was a stroke behind. They treaded water long enough to fill their lungs before diving under the surface. The cart was barely visible ten feet down. It was bottoms up, resting on its roof. Beyond that, the water was too dark to see much else. Pell felt along one side until she located the passenger compartment. Reaching in, she swept her long arm from side to side in an effort to locate the unwitting passenger.

Suddenly she felt a foot. Instinctively, Pell gave a tug and found that he was stuck on something. With her breath running out, she pushed off the bottom and rose to the surface. Gasping, she saw that Winnie, too, was up from her dive.

"I found him, but he's stuck on something." Winnie gulped for air.

"Were you by any chance pulling his arm?"

"Yeah. Why?"

"Well, that was me pulling him in the other direction. Let's try again and we'll both grab from the same side. C'mon." Pell slipped under a second time, with Winnie in tow.

Working as a team, they managed to free Milo from the EZ-Go golf cart and get him to the surface. Pell wrapped an arm around his torso and scissor-kicked to the closest patch of dry land.

It was a strip of beach bordered by mangroves on one side. Winnie helped her pull the man to shore. In the distance they heard a siren.

"Pump or blow?" Pell asked, but Winnie was closer to the man's face.

She cradled his head to position it, pinched his nose and blew in a controlled breath.

Instantly, Milo came to life with a cough that originated somewhere deep in his waterlogged body. The explosion of air was followed by a wave of vomit which managed to splatter Winnie.

The young man opened his eyes and saw a dripping wet hooker looking down at him. He blinked, unable to tell if the prostitute was a woman or a drag queen. Groaning, he attempted to sit up.

"Hold on." Winnie pushed him down, making no effort to hide her distaste. "Lay still or I'll sit on you."

Whatever gender the hooker was, it was a mean one, and Milo decided not to move and end up pressed under the creature. "Where am I? What's going on?"

In his last year of high school, Milo had suffered a head injury on the football field. The trauma left him with a soft spot on the back of his head as well as a scale by which to measure all future traumatic events. Right now, his pain level was a seven, with the football injury topping the chart at a ten. He tasted blood and was fairly certain he'd broken his leg. His pride wasn't in very good shape either.

An emergency vehicle pulled onto the shoulder of the road behind Winnie and Pell's sedan. They looked up and spotted the three paramedics looking over the bridge.

"We're down here!" Pell waved. She was sitting on her haunches still trying to catch her breath.

Like a drill team, the crew of two men and one woman hurried toward the victim and surrounded him.

"What's your name?" One of the techs held his eyelid up while she shined a light into first one eye and then the other.

"Bilo," he croaked.

"I don't know what kind of name that is, Bilo, but you're pretty lucky to get out of that alive. Looks like you nearly drowned," the tech said pleasantly. "What's your last name, Bilo?"

Milo thought he heard his name being mispronounced, until he spoke again.

"Burdie," he said, and realized that his nose was broken—again. For the second time in two years, Milo had managed to break his nose. His pain factor rose to a solid nine and fear bumped it to a ten.

"Facial trauma, his nose is all over the place," the female attendant noted matter-of-factly. "You'll have a good story to tell the kids." She patted his arm. "I'm going to slide this collar under your head, and then we're going to get you up on the gurney."

"Leg's broken. I'll stabilize when we lift him." A man's voice came from the foot of the gurney where someone was cutting his pants off.

Another pair of hands began to cut away Milo's jacket. "Bruising on the ribs, right side. Bilo, is this tender?"

The victim moaned.

"Okay, ribs, at least one, broken. Let's be careful, gang. Don't want any punctured lungs tonight."

"Were you taking pictures back at the flea market?" The homely hooker was leaning over him, scowling.

"Umb, yes. Yes." Milo swallowed, gagged, and retched.

She flipped open the leather wallet where she carried her badge and held it so Milo could see. "Florida Bureau of Investigation. And I don't mind telling you that you screwed us up royally."

Milo tried to apologize, but blood from his nose began sliding down the back of his throat. He managed a pathetic gurgle.

"Ma'am," one of the male techs said, and shuddered at the sight of the dripping wet hooker. "Or sir, we need to transport our patient. You can talk to him at the hospital, but right now we need to get him out of here."

Winnie's face darkened. Her eyeliner was running in black streaks down her cheeks and she looked as though she'd be more at home as a cast member of *The Rocky Horror Picture Show* than selling her booty in Naples. "We've got extra blankets," the medic said, and made an effort to appease the agitated drag queen.

A black-and-white had come on the scene and was parked in front of Winnie and Pell's rental. The police officer was talking to Paige, writing her account of the accident in his notebook.

Lower jaw jutting just past her top lip, eyes narrowed, Winnie strode over to the waiting car, badge at the ready.

Pell stopped her. "Let me handle this. Go wait over there. Better yet, I took off my cell and shoes. Would you mind?"

Winnie glowered, then seemed to brighten. "Sure."

Chapter 59

WINNIE FINDS MILO'S CELL PHONE

Friday, December 26, 2008 – 7:08 p.m.

The grass down the embankment had been flattened from the traffic of the rescue. The spit of sand was churned up with the footprints of the rescuers. Winnie returned to the area and stood, hands on hips, facing the open water. The golf cart was out there. Any remaining evidence, like the camera, was probably ruined. And she was too cold for any more physical activity tonight.

Turning, she spotted Pell's things and gathered them up in a bundle. Winnie was heading back up the slope when she heard something. She froze, listening. Then she dropped the bundle she was carrying and hurried toward the sound.

With no guardrail to identify where the golf cart had left the road, there was no way of re-creating the incident. But as Winnie moved toward the sound, she began to piece together the fragments of the story: a piece of chrome, a patch of torn turf, and a path of debris. She came across something that looked like a bow and stood over it, frowning. "That explains the arrow."

Winnie carefully stepped deeper into the debris field. She could see the remnants of a red taillight, broken glass, and there at the edge of the mangrove was a cell phone. Hurrying forward, she snatched up the evidence.

"Hey!" Pell called down.

"Is the black-and-white still there?"

"No. We just wrapped things up. It's just me and Paige. Did you find something?"

"I found a lot of things. I'm going to need the camera. I'm pretty sure I've got the vic's cell phone, too."

"We're gonna have to come back. Right now we've got to get to the hospital and interview that Bilo guy. No one is going to bother the scene before we get back."

Pell met her at the top of the embankment with a blanket wrapped around her shoulders. She held another one for her partner and both women climbed back into their rental car. Paige was in the backseat wearing her now familiar pouty face.

"So, what did you tell the boys in blue?" Winnie asked her.

"Why don't you ask Grendel?"

Pell eased the vehicle onto the asphalt. "I did all the talking."

"Can you go a little faster? I'd like to get there sometime before dawn." Winnie shivered and adjusted the heat. "So, what did you say to them?"

"Just what they needed to know. They think we're a couple of good Samaritans who pulled some guy out of the water."

"How did you explain the golf cart?"

"I didn't. We just saw a vehicle go off the road and jumped in to help him. That seemed to satisfy them. They said we could go to the station tomorrow if we had anything to add, but they're thinking it was a case of drunk driving. That's why we've got to get to him before Shoat does."

Winnie slowly turned toward her partner. In the light of the dashboard, she could see Pell was focused on her driving. "They don't know who we are, do they?"

"Nope."

"That means Shoat hasn't said anything about us being in town. Which essentially corroborates his contempt for us."

"Yep."

"Okay, so why is buttercup back there so pissed off?"

"I told them they should ignore her and erase anything she said."

"Because I'm schizophrenic and bipolar." Paige filled in the rest of the information before huffing and crossing her arms with all the belligerence she could muster.

Pell shot back, "Well, I didn't know what you told them and didn't want to take any chances that you leaked something."

"Meanwhile, your other passenger looks like she took last place in the homeliest hooker contest." To Winnie, she said, "That's why she sent you down to get her stuff. She didn't want you talking either."

"Really?" Winnie was genuinely offended.

"You are kind of scary tonight."

"Screw you, Pell. I'm out there getting puke all over me and giving it my all and you're embarrassed of me. Screw you."

"Yeah, Pell. You suck," Chesley snapped.

The heat blowing from the vents escalated the tension in the car. Winnie finally turned on the radio and adjusted the dial to Christmas music. They drove on wordlessly, each woman fuming over her own wounded ego.

Sitting at a red light en route to the hospital, the mystery-man's phone began to ring again.

"Hello?" Winnie answered, since she was closest.

"I'm sorry, I must have dialed the wrong number," a woman replied.

"No, wait! Who are you trying to reach?"

"Milo. Is he there?"

"No, ma'am, but I'm pretty sure this is his phone. This is Agent Winnie with the Florida Bureau of Investigation. Who am I speaking to?"

"Priscilla Purdie. Milo is my son."

Winnie thought for a second, remembering Bilo Burdie. "Mrs. Purdie, your son is on his way to the hospital. He was hurt in an accident."

"Oh my God." The woman suddenly sounded frail. "Which hospital?"

"Naples Memorial, ma'am. If it makes you feel better, he was conscious and talking when they pulled out."

"Thank you."

The phone went dead.

"The vic's name is Milo Purdie," Winnie noted, drawing the blanket up around her neck.

"Why does that name sound familiar?"

Paige leaned forward and crossed her arms over the back of Winnie's seat. "He's the guy from the Ballyhoo robbery last year. I don't know if you heard about it, but he took out these two gangbangers with a tire iron. That guy is a local hero."

Pell nodded thoughtfully. "Yep. We heard. And you need to put your seat belt on."

"This is one weird little town," Winnie noted as they pulled into the hospital parking lot. "I'm ready to wrap this investigation up and get the hell outta here." She climbed out of the car and headed toward the emergency room with the blanket draped over her head and shoulders.

"You want to wait here or come in?" Pell asked Paige.

When she didn't answer, Pell turned to look in the backseat. Paige Chesley was wearing her second-favorite look: defiance. She took a moment out of filing her nails to glower at the light-haired woman, and then returned to her task as though Pell did not exist.

Inside, the agents were greeted by a young man in navy blue scrubs. A caduceus was sewn on his pocket. "Can I help you?"

"We need to speak with the guy they just brought in, Milo Purdie." Pell was careful to pronounce the name correctly, since Milo's speech was impaired and there was no way to tell how he might appear on an official record.

"Let's have a look-see." His fingers tapped out the name on the keyboard. "Oh, that guy. Hmm. He's in surgery." The nurse continued to read from the computer screen in front of him. "Poor guy. Oh, man, I bet that hurt. Whoa!"

"What?" Winnie and Pell leaned ominously on the counter.

"Nothing," he noted sheepishly. "Patient confidentiality. Suffice it to say, this guy is gonna be knocked out for a while."

"What's your name?" Pell asked politely, providing him with a gentle smile.

"Ted," the man offered uneasily.

"Ted, we're the ones who pulled him out of the water." Pell held open the blanket around her shoulders to reveal her wet clothing. She started to explain the incident, but Winnie elbowed her aside. Her blanket slipped off, leaving a trail of hair extensions on her chest and neck. As she flipped open her badge case one of the extensions landed on the Ted's keyboard.

"He's part of an investigation, *Ted*. Did you talk to him when he came in?" Winnie was inching dangerously close to the nurse.

He looked from her face to the badge, then to the hair extension and back to her face.

"It's called a hair extension, you turd miner." Winnie plucked the offending lock from his work station and flung it over her shoulder.

"Some kind of prostitution ring, no doubt?" Ted nodded knowingly. "You're very convincing, by the way." He returned his attention to the computer screen. "I took his information when he came in. But the story remains the same. Even if the guy could talk to you, which he can't, nothing he said would hold up in court. You all are going to have to check back tomorrow. Even then there is no guarantee he'll make any sense." Ted concluded by rotating the screen so the women could read it for themselves.

"Wow." Pell read down the list of Milo's medical history. "Looks like he's a regular."

Ted shrugged. "Anything else I can help you with?"

Pell handed him a soggy business card. "You can call us when Mr. Purdie is lucid."

Frustrated, the women turned away from the emergency room nurses' station.

"We need to secure his room." Pell shivered and ducked into her blanket. "I hate to call Shoat, but we need someone watching him till we pick up Ralph."

"They don't know he's here."

Pell bit her lip and considered the pros and cons. "They might. And we can't risk the investigation because of our egos. I'm gonna give the locals a call and have them send someone over, at least till tomorrow. Maybe by then we can get someone from our team down here."

"Whatever," Winnie snarled.

"I think it's time for someone's pain pill."

Winnie was about to offer one of her classic expletive monologues when Pell stopped suddenly. "Oh, no."

"What?"

Pell began to hurry toward the exit. When she reached the parking lot, she broke into a sprint. The blanket fluttered behind her like a superhero's cape as she raced toward the rental car. Instinctively, Winnie did her best to keep up with her partner, but the events of the evening, along with her head injury, prevented her from going too fast. She reached the vehicle as Pell slammed the flat of her hand on the roof.

"Son of a bitch!" Pell shouted with uncharacteristic hostility, and smacked the car again.

Winnie peered in the window and saw Paige stretched out on the backseat. The woman's eyes were slits, and she appeared much the same way as the day they'd found her in the lawn chair, with the exception of the cat coiffure.

Winnie asked, "Is she alive?"

"Yeah. She just flipped me a bird."

"She looks dead," Winnie observed. Paige slowly lifted her arm and pressed her middle finger to the window where Winnie was standing. "Oh." Winnie tried the door handle and discovered it was locked. "Are you kidding?"

Pell replied, "Yes. This is all an elaborate joke to lift your spirits."

"Those are my pain meds, aren't they?" Winnie spotted the empty bottle on the floorboard, its lid nearby. "So how many pills were left?"

Pell closed her eyes and recalled the history of the pill bottle. "We started the day with four. You had one at lunch. So three."

"Pell, we can't interview her like this."

"We are so screwed. I should have left you here to interview her while I went in. What the hell was I thinking? An hour ago, we had two solid leads, now we've got one in surgery and a toasted junkie in the car who has locked us out. We're gonna have to call a locksmith. I'm gonna have to pay for it, too." Pell buried her face in her hands. "We can't let the chief find out about this."

Pell's rant was interrupted by a sharp rap. She looked over the top of the car. Winnie was holding her loafer, using the heel on the glass.

"Paige, so help me, there will be nothing left of you to identify if you do not open this door right now."

The woman's brain was steeping in a soothing fog. She wasn't fazed by Winnie's threat. To show her absolute contempt for the angry agent, Paige gave her a sultry look and lifted her shirt to reveal the waistband of her pants, where the butt of the gun protruded.

"Is that Betty?" Pell squinted, trying to identify the weapon.

Indeed, the gun was none other than Betty the Glock. Winnie insisted that, with all the money she had invested in her personal weapon, she should have a name. She honored the weapon with the name of her favorite comic book character. Now Betty was in the hands of a would-be felon.

Winnie's face was mashed against the side window. Her eyes sprang open, impossibly wide, and the pounding became frantic. "You put her down this minute. Do you hear me, Paige? Put that gun on the floor right now!" Winnie bellowed like a water buffalo ready to charge.

Suddenly, Winnie was looking down Betty's barrel. Even as Paige appeared to be slipping deeper into her mind-altered state, she held the weapon unsteadily and pointed it in Winnie's general direction.

"Uh-oh," was all Winnie got out before dropping flat on the ground. The weapon roared. With her hands clapped over her ears, she looked under and saw Pell on the ground looking back, and it was not a happy look.

"Since the police are coming anyway, we might as well ask them to protect the Purdie guy. As soon as we finish explaining how someone in our protective custody managed to shoot out a window with your gun." Pell emphasized the word *your*, as if clarify any confusion about who Betty's mommy was.

From inside the car there came a loud *thunk* which sounded like a heavy metal object falling to the floorboard.

"I'll look," Pell volunteered, since Paige would have to have a very contorted grip in order to fire in Pell's direction. She peeked over the edge of the window. Indeed, Paige was well along into her drug-induced bliss and Betty had slipped from her hands.

Both women got to their feet and scanned the parking lot for onlookers. Across the street, Dairy Queen diners had clearly heard the gunshot, but did not seem to know exactly in what direction it had come from.

"At least we can get in the car," Winnie noted, as she reached through the shattered window and found the handle.

"Don't—" Pell tried to warn her a split second before the car alarm went off.

Chapter 60

TESS CALLS POLICE - POLICE CALL FLABI

Friday, December 26, 2008 – 7:17 p.m.

It was time for the next phone call. Donning the Anita disguise one more time, Tess went down to the lobby. There was one courtesy phone at a well-lit table by the door. But it was in full view of the desk clerk. She headed in the opposite direction, toward the rear of the building. "These things used to be everywhere," Tess mumbled, as she crossed the marble tile looking left and right. The bar and restaurant were doing a brisk business, forcing her to reconsider leaving the building. "*Che palle*," she muttered, and stepped into the cold night air. And there it was. Attached to the restrooms, on the other side of the pool, was a perfectly beautiful pay phone.

"Nine-one-one, what's your emergency?"

"I'd like to report something suspicious going on in unit eight-oh-two at Highland Terrace on Gulf View Boulevard."

"And who am I speaking with?"

Tess heard Barry Manilow's famous "Copacabana" ballad over her shoulder as the door from the lounge swung open and a couple appeared. Tess huddled closer to the phone. "Um," she cleared her throat, "this is Lola."

"Lola, what is your last name?"

"Smith," Tess answered smugly.

"Suspicious in what way, Ms. Smith?"

"I just heard a loud thump and glass breaking."

"Okay. We'll get someone over to check it out."

"Bye now." Tess hung up and wiped the handle of the phone before replacing it.

As she walked back toward the warmth of her room, she wished she could take in the Carmen Bustamante double feature, but she was tired and could read about it in the paper tomorrow on her way out of town.

Chapter 61

MUSCIA
FINDS
FINANCIAL
FREEDOM

Friday, December 26, 2008 – 7:20 p.m.

No one made mention of the golf cart incident, per Muscia's strict instructions. She knew they wouldn't because they were more afraid of her than of Carmen. Instead, they all filed in to Carmen's condo and acted as if things had gone precisely as planned. Flo and Connie put the money in the middle of the bridge table to be counted and recorded. Connie pulled out her log book and calculator. The process took time, as each bag had to be dumped and checked before getting tossed. Then the money had to be counted twice. Once the amount was verified, it was bound in a brown wrapper destined for Ralph's laundering operation. Muscia kept an eye on the proceedings even as she set out a light dinner buffet at the bar.

Tonight she used paper plates instead of the good china, most of which was still in the dishwasher from the day before. She put out a plate of cold ham leftovers from Christmas dinner, a cheese platter from one of the girls in the numbers pool, potato salad and pickles from the deli, the rolls and cannolis from Hector, and three champagne glasses to celebrate a successful evening. When she finished, Muscia looked around to make sure she hadn't forgotten anything.

"Hey, where's the garlic butter?" Flo asked, as she slipped her hand under her plate to support an extra helping of potato salad.

"I have to heat it up. Sit down. I'll bring it out to you." Muscia's voice was low and her words clipped. She was in no mood for attitude.

Although Flo heard her, she did not pick up on Muscia's tone and continued her chatter. "Yeah, 'cause that's the best part. Carmen, you buy the rolls?"

"Hector. Hector sent them up," Carmen said. She was pleased that he had sent a small token of his appreciation for his new position. Tess had trained him well. She nodded approvingly as she fixed herself a plate.

"Golly, that was sure nice of him. Is this ham from yesterday?"

"Hey, Flo, could you leave some for the rest of us?" Carmen prodded, jabbing her plastic fork in her friend's back end.

"How about the cannolis?"

Carmen took the spoon for the potato salad from Flo's grip. "Hector. Hector sent over a whole order from Delaurentis's. Now, would you take a roll and get out of the way, already?"

"What a nice a fella. I see why Tess likes him. He's a great guy. That reminds me, has anyone seen Tess?"

Muscia dutifully put a cup of garlic butter in front of each woman. "There's one for each of you. Does everyone have a drink?"

"We're good." Carmen waved her away with the fork she had used earlier to prod Flo along. "I'll call you if we need anything."

And so Muscia gave one last look of warning to Flo and Connie before she flipped off the kitchen lights and headed to her bedroom to read. She would have stayed there until it was time to put Carmen to bed had she not heard the sound of glass breaking.

She swung her legs over the side of her bed into waiting slippers, snapped up the pistol on her nightstand, and ran toward the sound. She saw Flo's body first.

It was sprawled across the hallway by the buffet. Rolling her over, she discovered the old woman had a pulse and was breathing. Stunned, Muscia took in the sight of Connie and Carmen, facedown in their plates.

Like Flo, both women's pulses were strong and they were breathing without difficulty. Muscia noticed Carmen's broken glass on the terrazzo floor; red wine that looked like blood ran into the grout and nearby rug.

Muscia stood to her full height and folded her arms across her bosom. All three had quite clearly been poisoned. Her first thought was Ralphie. Maybe he had finally figured out the only way he would ever move up in the business was to take out his mother. If that was the case, it was time to get the hell out.

"How ironic," Muscia said out loud.

As she scanned the room trying to make sense of what she was seeing, an idea began to take shape.

The take from their latest collection was laid out on the table in neatly bound stacks. When Muscia searched the remaining purses, she found piles of loose cash still waiting to be counted.

Muscia went back to the guest bathroom, removed the laundry bag of cash that Ralphie would pick up on his way back through town, and put it in a plastic garbage bag, along with the stacks of money on the table. Leaving the remaining cash in the purses, Muscia tied off the garbage bag, using a dish towel. She removed the garbage from under the kitchen sink and carried both plastic bags to the garbage chute at the end of the hall and dropped them in, knowing that collection day was still two days away.

Fifteen minutes later, she left the unit, boarded the elevator, and went down to the second floor. She found what she was looking for near the stairs. In one swift movement, Muscia drove the butt of her gun into the glass fire alarm. And with perfect poise, a straight spine, and head lifted to her full imperial height, Muscia Bolineaux walked away without looking back.

Chapter 62

WINNIE AND PELL ARE CALLED

Friday, December 26, 2008 – 7:28 p.m.

"I kind of wish we hadn't taken Ramon back to the high school. We could use a little help right about now." Winnie was standing at the rear door of the rental, her arms hooked under an unconscious Paige. She walked backward, dragging the ex-debutante's limp body out of the back of the car. "I say we handcuff her for the duration."

"I don't think she's given us much of a choice." Once Paige was out, Pell bent down and collected half the weight, draping Paige's arm across her shoulders. "I wonder if they'll put her in witness protection."

"Let's just get her upstairs right now, okay?"

"You don't think we need to get her to a place that specializes in detox? You and I aren't doing a very good job of keeping her drug free, and we've only had her for three days. It's like she's trying to kill herself."

"Pell," Winnie panted, "that is not part of our job. We are supposed to get the bad guys off the street. Paige here——"

At the sound of her name, Paige moaned.

"See, she's okay. Getting Ralph Bustamante behind bars is definitely part of our job description. And Paige's testimony is going to help us make that happen. I'm anxious to take a look at that guy's phone and see how he fits in."

"I still can't believe you found it. Nothing short of a miracle."

With an arm draped over each agent's shoulders, Paige Chesley's inert body was dragged up the stairs and over the threshold of the hotel room she shared with Winnie. They lowered their witness turned prisoner onto her bed. While both women had their firearms, their handcuffs were in the glove compartment, so Pell secured the unconscious woman to the bed with regulation plastic ties.

"That'll hold her. I honestly think we did the right thing by pursuing the suspects. We couldn't take time to get Paige's testimony without forfeiting the pursuit. It was an either/or situation, and I think we made the right call."

Exhausted, Winnie dropped onto her own bed and closed her eyes. "It doesn't matter what we think. The chief will be the ultimate decider. And there is no way to predict how he'll react when he finds out about this. What we need to do is make the bust sooner rather than later." She pulled Milo's cell phone out and flipped it open. "You wanna see if you can work this thing?"

Pell took the phone and sat on the edge of the bed. "Here's a record of his recent calls, incoming and outgoing. His mother's number is the last thing in, of course. And here is his contact list. We'll check all these. Hey, this is interesting."

"What do you got?" Winnie propped herself up on one elbow.

"He's got a camera on this thing." Pell pulled up the last photo and turned the screen to her partner. "Got 'em."

"Nice job, Agent Pell," she said, and bumped knuckles with her partner. "I'll call HQ and have them run the plate."

"How about I make the call and you take a shower? Get what's left of that makeover off."

With uncharacteristic calm, Winnie rolled off the bed and headed to the shower. "Wow, I really do look like something from *Night of the Living Dead*."

"C'mon, get going. I'm heading next door to clean up when I'm done with this call. I've got seaweed in my hair."

Winnie had one leg in a fresh pair of sweatpants when the call came in on the hotel room phone. "Hello?"

"Hey. Is this Winnie or Pell?"

"Winnie. Who is this?"

"Well, this is Sheila from over at the sheriff's office."

"Hey, Sheila."

"Did you all have a good Christmas?"

"Pretty good. How about you?"

"Yes, I did. My husband got me a new tractor. I do all the yard work and he said he was tired of seeing me out there with the push mower. I can sweat up a storm even in the winter. We got three acres, you know."

"Listen, Sheila, I'd love to catch up, but Pell and I are headed out the door," Winnie lied.

"Well, real quick, I wanted to let you all know we just now got a tip a few minutes ago from a female caller about something suspicious going on over at that rich-people's old folks home where you all are investigating the drugs and all. Now, ordinarily I wouldn't do this, but Troy isn't here and he isn't answering his cell phone. He went over to Lauderdale to interview some of that girl's co-workers at the club where she worked. And everyone from the station is down at that condo where they found that missing girl's boyfriend. They're saying he is a suspect, you know."

"Have they found the girl?"

"No. Not yet. But they found some things at the boyfriend's place, including the girl's keys, and it looks like her van never left the parking lot. Anyhow, I thought you all might want to take this call, seeing as how you're on the case over there. Could be a lead, you never know."

"Okay, we'll take it. What's the number?"

"Got it right here, eight-oh-two."

Winnie gasped. "Thanks, Sheila. We're on our way." She put the phone in its cradle. "Pell! Get your ass in here." She slipped into her navy blue FLABI sweatshirt. There wasn't time for the uniform.

Pell was coming in the adjoining room wearing her FLABI sweats as well. She hopped on one foot as she wrestled the other into a sneaker. "I just received confirmation on the plates. The car is owned by someone at Highland Terrace. We got him now."

"And I just got a call from Sheila at the police station. Something is going down at Bustamante's place." Winnie didn't bother to tie her shoes before she sprinted for the door.

They crossed the parking lot with as much haste as two women who had recently pulled a man from the Gulf and provided him with CPR could. Without the relief of her pain meds, Winnie's head injury was taking its toll. She focused and dug deep into her reservoir of self-discipline. Tonight could be a genuine career maker for both agents and she was not about to give in to her pain.

"What did Sheila say?" Pell asked.

"A call came in not long ago about something suspicious in eight-oh-two."

"Holy shit! You think he killed his own mother?" Pell aimed the key fob and unlocked the car.

"You probably don't need to use that anymore," Winnie reminded her, gesturing to where there had been a window at one time.

"Chief is gonna be pissed," Pell said as she cranked the car, throwing it in reverse in one swift motion.

"Not nearly as pissed when we give him Ralph Bustamante. Do you have anything to take the edge of this effing headache?"

"There is a bottle of ibuprofen in my ammo case. Sometimes I need one or two when I come off the range. Help yourself." Pell handed the black zippered case to her partner.

"It's empty." Winnie shook the container.

"Paige! That low-life junkie took every last one."

"Never again, Pell. We are never babysitting another addict. I don't care if she knows who was behind the Kennedy assassination—never again."

Guzeman's Scooter

Chapter 63

WINNIE AND PELL STORM THE GATES

Friday, December 26, 2008 – 7:42 p.m.

The first siren could be heard from a distance, but Pell could not immediately tell which direction the emergency vehicle was coming from. She and Winnie were headed south on Tamiami Trail when she spotted the light in her rearview mirror. They pulled onto the right shoulder as the fire truck raced by, rocking their vehicle. Within seconds, two more trucks appeared, along with a rescue truck.

"Wow," Pell commented as she pulled back into the slow-moving traffic. "Do you see smoke?"

"No, but it's dark."

"Surely we'd see the flames from a three-alarm fire. Don't you think?"

"We have our own drama to deal with right now. Focus."

Pell squinted and leaned over the steering wheel. "Isn't that where we turn?"

Red and blue lights flashed, clearly visible through the royal palm trees that lined the circular driveway in front of Highland Terrace. The fire department had already cordoned off the driveway, along with the cul-de-sac in front of the complex, and waved the agents away from the area.

Forced to park a block away, Winnie and Pell trekked back to Highland Terrace where they stood, watching the residents pour through the lobby doors.

"What do you think?" Pell folded her arms across her chest.

"I don't smell smoke. I don't see flames. I think this might be Ralph's idea of a diversion."

"C'mon." Pell headed toward an officer positioned between them and the front door.

The man held up his hand, his fingers splayed, his face a mask of resistance. "Not tonight. As you can see, we're—"

Without slowing down, the women flipped open their badges and stepped around the man, who could only mutter his consternation under his breath. They continued their march to the front door, where they were finally forced to stop by the onslaught of residents fleeing the building. Like the great spring animal migration crossing the Mara River in Africa, the condo owners swarmed out and down the sidewalk as though survival of their species depended on reaching the driveway. All the while, the fire alarm shrieked in the background, intensifying the fight-or-flight response.

Winnie and Pell were forced to stand aside and let the throng flow.

"Think there is any point in going around back?" Winnie asked.

"I think if he parked in the underground garage he'd have to come this way. Why don't you take a position by the fountain and I'll take the door."

Winnie walked briskly to her detail. The stream of humans did not abate. They came walking with canes, in wheelchairs, on electric scooters. They came with nurse aides and spouses. They hurried across the driveway, past the fountain, and down into the cul-de-sac, where they huddled under blankets supplied by the fire department.

A news truck appeared, disgorging a reporter and camera person before being waved away. Chum in the water, Winnie thought, the sharks will come, holding microphones up to the frightened residents as though the sound of the alarm and threat of fire wasn't enough trauma.

She was making up her mind about how to approach Carmen and her body-guard, if they happened to get by her partner, when a woman in a Jazzy Scooter surged through the opening and headed right for her. Speeding across the brick paving stones, Winnie thought she looked familiar. As the driver bore down on her, Winnie remembered her from the hall, where she took out several feet of plaster above the baseboard and nearly tipped over rounding the corner to the elevator. Winnie stepped right and then left as the woman barreled straight for the fountain. She figured the inexorable collision would stop the woman, but on impact, the slight woman bounced up from her seat and landed back in place. She shook her head, no doubt getting her bearings again. The crash had little impact on her, as evidenced by the scarring on her bumper. She simply pressed the throttle in the opposite direction and backed away from the obstacle in her path.

Winnie realized immediately that the woman was not just uncoordinated, she was blind. "Stop," Winnie commanded, and thrust out her hand, palm open.

The driver's head swiveled on a spindly neck, looking for the owner of the voice. Her thick glasses magnified her brown eyes, giving her the look of a praying mantis when observed up close. Still she could not focus completely on Winnie, so the agent took a step in her direction.

"You either need to get some new glasses or stop driving so fast. You're going to hurt someone."

Before Winnie could reach her and locate the off switch, the large eyes narrowed into thin slits. Without further warning, the woman's bony thumb mashed the throttle forward. Winnie cleared the bumper but grimaced as one of the tires rolled the 250-pound machine over her feet. "Son of a..." She pressed her fist to her mouth and bit down to prevent her usual litany of profanity. "I will catch up with you. You will not get away with this!" Winnie limped after the hit-and-run assailant but couldn't catch her. "I know who you are!"

Pell pushed her sleeve up to check the time. The fire chief was in clear view, standing in the lobby, talking on his walkie-talkie. She exhaled sharply and reached for the handle of the door, which was open as people continued to pour out.

"Hey!" she shouted, as she recognized Mr. Phillips and the caregivers from the hospital.

Sonny headed the group off to one side. They waited as Agent Pell maneuvered through the throng of people as though she were wading through a rushing river.

"You just came from the eighth floor?"

Sonny nodded.

"You see or smell any sign of fire?"

Sonny shook her head. "No. Nothing."

"I don't suppose you noticed anything unusual about the Bustamante place?"

Tricia spoke for the first time. "I handed some take-out food to the big CNA a while ago."

"The door was cracked when we just went by," Charlotte said flatly.

Pell cocked her head. "Those doors are heavy they close automatically, don't they?"

"Yes," Charlotte said. "They're made to close like a hotel door. The only way they stay open is if you put something in the way, like a door stopper or a fork."

"Fork?" Pell was confused.

"Don't ask," Sonny warned.

"A shrunken head or a deck of cards," Charlotte continued.

"She gets the idea, Char."

"Did you see anyone coming out?" Pell went on with her inquiry.

"I didn't. But then, I wasn't really looking." Sonny turned to Tricia, who also shook her head.

"One more question: how long have you all been here?"

"We got here about an hour ago. We've been with Mr. Phillips the whole time."

"Did you happen to notice anything unusual?"

"That's two." Charlotte held up two fingers.

"What?" Pell scowled.

"Two questions," Sonny noted. "Ignore her. She'll drive you bat shit."

"Bad yogi. I wonder how your students would feel if they knew you talked to your sister that way," Charlotte scolded.

"We didn't see or hear anything out of the ordinary, unless you count the five-hundred-decibel fire alarm."

"Gotcha. Thanks for your time."

It had taken the fire department four minutes to empty most of the residents. A few stragglers continued to exit the building, but the mass of homeowners was already outside and assembled nearby.

Pell noticed her partner sitting on the edge of the fountain. Winnie's shoes and socks were off. One foot was in the water and she appeared to be examining the other.

"Dare I ask what you're doing?"

Winnie looked up angrily. "I was hit by a woman in one of those electric scooters. I wanted to make sure nothing was broken."

Pell nodded and scanned the crowd. "And?"

"I think I'm okay. I can wiggle my toes. I soaked them in the cold water to prevent swelling, and that seemed to work."

"Well, it looks like they got most of the people out and I still don't smell smoke."

As if on cue, the fire alarm became silent.

"You feel like taking a look inside?"

Winnie nodded, redressed her feet, and hobbled after her partner.

The fire chief was in the lobby when they approached. He looked up and shook his head. "We'll begin letting folks reenter when we've finished checking every floor. Please wait outside."

Out came the badges. Like a well-oiled machine, the two women snapped open their leather cases in unison. "FLABI. We're investigating some suspicious activity in this building."

He sighed, "You might be interested to know that the alarm on the first floor was pulled."

"There's no fire in the building, though, is there?" Pell already knew the answer.

"No, ma'am. We've been on nearly every floor and haven't found anything. It looks like a false alarm at this point."

"Elevators working?"

"Yes, ma'am. But in the interest of safety, would you use the stairs? I don't want anything to boomerang back on me in case we do have something. What floor are you going to?"

"Eight." Pell stared him down.

He nodded and turned away. A typical reaction to her gaze.

It was Pell who reached the eighth floor first. She had left Winnie on the third floor landing, telling her that she wasn't going to wait. Despite Winnie's protests not to go in alone, Pell loped up the stairs. She was slightly winded when she reached the fire door and paused to catch her breath. She listened for her partner but heard nothing.

The hallway was empty, the floor was quiet; everything was essentially normal. The door to the Bustamante unit was ajar, just as Charlotte had described. Pell rapped on the door. "This is Agent Pell with the Florida Bureau of Investigation. I'm coming in and I'm armed."

Pell entered, firearm first. She pressed her back against the foyer wall and moved down the entry hall. The kitchen was to her left and she chanced a quick look around the corner, halfway expecting to be met by the giant CNA. But the kitchen was empty.

The light in the living room was on and Pell was sidestepping her way toward the room when the door behind her opened. She swung her weapon and stared down the barrel at her partner, who was now standing on one leg.

"It's broken, Winnie whispered, and pointed to her left foot.

Pell gestured for her to stay put, but as soon as she turned back to the living room, she heard a hop on the parquet floor behind her. Two more steps brought her close enough to the living room to peer in. And then she saw them.

All three women were facedown, one on the table and two on the floor.

"Get nine-one-one up here ASAP." She ran to the first victim and found a heartbeat. "This one is still alive." She rolled Carmen onto her back, looking for signs of a struggle or foul play, but found nothing.

The next body was in similar shape, alive and very relaxed, without any sign of trauma.

The third victim was face down in a plate of food. Pell carefully lifted the head and saw that the woman was blue. There was no pulse and her skin was cold. "This one didn't make it. Looks like she suffocated in the potato salad." She gently eased the corpse onto the floor.

"I'm thinking this is pretty incriminating." Winnie checked the contents of one of the handbags from the Stone Crab pickup hours earlier. "Oh, and what's this?" She used a pen to lift a snub-nosed thirty-eight from the table where the women had been sitting. "It looks like Ralphie has poisoned his own mother and her buddies."

Pell straightened her legs and stood slowly. "Where is the big caregiver?"

Winnie paused and considered. "We should track her down, find out what she knows, where she was when this was happening. Will this night never end?"

Two members of a rescue crew assisting with the bogus fire entered the Bustamante condo.

"We're over here," Pell called. "This one is gone, but those two are still kicking—so to speak. Listen, Winnie, why don't you have a seat and let me collect the evidence? See if the EMTs can set you up with some crutches, or at least an Ace bandage, until we can get you to the hospital."

"Funny." Winnie sat back on one of the bar stools and watched the EMTs assess their patients. "Yo, Pell. Let me go check out the driver of the vehicle."

Pell appeared from the bathroom where she had located a pair of latex gloves. Winnie turned on the swiveling bar stool and watched as her partner opened and closed drawers. "Watch the cash," Pell said under her breath, and gestured for Winnie to turn around. "I'm trying to find some baggies so I can start collecting evidence."

"At least let me go talk to the driver," Winnie called over her shoulder.

"The car is registered to a Connie Columbo. She's in four-oh-six."

"No, she's not." One of the EMTs looked up from a prone figure on the floor. "She's right here." He lifted the limp arm to reveal a medical alert wristband.

The agents turned and stared at the victims receiving medical attention. Two more crews had arrived on the scene to help load the two live women. The third was already zipped into a black body bag and awaiting transport to the morgue.

The young man held up his clipboard. "Yes, ma'am. This is Constance Columbo," he said, and pointed to the first woman on the stretcher. "Not sure who this one is." He aimed his pen at Carmen.

"That would be Carmen Bustamante," Winnie volunteered. "This is her unit."

The EMT nodded and jotted the name on his clipboard. "And according to the license we found in her wallet, the unfortunate one in the bag is Florence Bondi. Everyone has been ID'd and we'll be transporting shortly." He tucked the clipboard under his arm.

As Carmen the Nose Bustamante was being wheeled out of her condo, her eyes flickered for a second and she managed to mumble, "*Siamo fottuti*," before once again falling into a stupor.

Winnie's head snapped back. "Holy shit."

Pell looked up from her task. "What?"

"I think I know what happened."

The agents stared at each other across the room as the EMTs struggled to lift the corpse of Florence Bondi onto the gurney. Pell followed them to the door and closed it.

"You know what she just said?"

Pell shook her head. "I took French in school."

"My first language is Spanish, then English, then Italian. She said, 'We're fucked.'"

Pell blinked and scowled in incomprehension.

Winnie let out a short laugh. "Ralph wasn't using his mother, she was using him. The *capo di tutti* isn't Ralph. It's Carmen."

Chapter 64

CHRISTIE FOUND BY CANADIANS

Saturday, December 27, 2008 – 8:02 a.m.

"We have breaking news this morning. It involves the story of Christie Wilcox who was reported missing Christmas Day. We have confirmed a report that the missing woman was located about an hour ago. Miss Wilcox was found by a family from Ontario. They were visiting the area and pulled into a picnic spot off Tamiami Trail for an outing. That's when they discovered the young woman in the park's restroom, where she had apparently spent the night. She was not conscious when discovered. However, we have learned that Christie is now in critical condition but she is awake. Doctors at Miami General, where she was taken, say that Christie suffered a reaction from her diabetic condition.

Now to our live crew at Villa Del Camino, where authorities have discovered evidence in at least two other disappearances, including the recent abduction of Anita Lemoyne. The man who lived here, Hector Rinaldi, has been charged. His condo is now a crime scene. Selma, what can you tell us about the suspect?"

"He's a fifty-seven-year-old local man with a long history of run-ins with the law. Hector, Rinaldi"—the reporter consulted her notes and looked up again— "has been living at the Villa Del Camino for five years. Neighbors said he is quiet and helpful, carrying groceries for the elderly couple upstairs, helping out at the annual community garage sale. But according to police records, Hector Rinaldi is no angel. He did time in New Jersey's infamous Rahway Penitentiary in the eighties. From there he was picked up in Fort Lauderdale for solicitation. Police have spent the last hour in his condo collecting evidence. Rinaldi himself was found unconscious yesterday, apparently the victim of his own overdose. He was taken to Naples Memorial last night and was later released into police custody. Right now, he waits in a jail cell for his bond hearing later this morning."

The camera returned to the studio, panning in on the anchor who looked genuinely concerned, but only because she spent hours practicing the expression.

"Sometimes you just don't know who you're living next door to. Thanks, Selma. In other news, there is unrest in the Middle East..."

Chapter 65

SONNY AND TRICIA

Saturday, December 27, 2008 – 8:05 a.m.

Tricia was awakened by the sound of the phone ringing. Sonny's half of the bed was empty, and after a few more rings, she realized that Sonny wasn't in the condo. Next came the very recognizable voice of Elizabeth Delaney. Although Tricia couldn't make out exactly what she was saying, Elizabeth sounded more animated than usual.

In the kitchen, she found her favorite mug beside a half-full pot of coffee and the red light blinking on the answering machine. Somewhat disappointed that Sonny hadn't made each of them an espresso in the new *macchinetta* she had gotten for Christmas, Tricia sighed as she poured the remainder of the coffee into her cup. She hit the playback button and poured a splash of cream into the black brew.

"Hello? Hello? Hello?" Elizabeth chirped. "I'm calling to give you a heads-up. Apparently you all made quite an impression on Mr. Phillips. He called your sister this morning and told her that he can't remember the last time he slept well two nights in a row. He gave the manager at Highland Terrace your number and she is supposed to call you to discuss arranging a meditation class. Tricia? I'm thinking it wouldn't be a bad idea to mention that you teach tai chi. Oh, and have you seen the news? It looks like..."

The machine shut off, and Tricia secretly wondered how long it had taken before Elizabeth realized the line was dead.

In the living room, Tricia flipped channels until she found one describing the day's headlines. As soon as she heard the top story, she yanked her fleece jacket off the coatrack, slipped into her leather sandals, and went in search of her partner.

Knowing Sonny, she would have seen the news and headed straight to the water's edge. Tricia figured this, because that is exactly what she would have done under the circumstances.

In fact, Sonny was seated cross-legged just out of the tide's reach not far from the rear entrance of the condo. Tricia knelt down beside her and looked toward the horizon where Sonny's gaze was fixed.

"Did you come to keep me warm?"

"Yes. Well, that and I wanted to find out if you heard the news." Tricia tried to read her face.

Without taking her eyes from the Gulf, Sonny let out a long, slow breath. "Yeah. I got up early. Couldn't sleep. My vata was all over the place. I didn't want to wake you so I went out on the balcony to meditate, but I couldn't stay focused. Finally I gave up, made some coffee, and turned on the news. After seeing that guy in handcuffs, I felt so peaceful."

Tricia put her arm around Sonny's waist "No more vata?"

"Maybe a little." A hint of a smile appeared on Sonny's lips.

"So who'd have thought Collier County was so dangerous? Anita really was murdered. And the same guy tried to kill the erotic dancer? I'm still trying to comprehend everything. "

Sonny nodded. "Apparently there was another victim in between. He was charged with killing another old lady from Highland Terrace, but they haven't found the body. The only bad news is Char will probably have to testify."

"Anything to get this guy behind bars, right?"

"Yeah. It all had to do with some crime ring at Highland Terrace. The woman living next door to Mr. Phillips was the alleged ringleader. You wouldn't think things like that happen in a retirement center."

"She probably got bored playing shuffleboard and bridge." Tricia slipped her sandals off and dug her toes into the sand. "Your mother called, too." This announcement was met with resounding apathy. "She says you should expect a call from someone at Highland Terrace regarding setting up a meditation class."

"No."

"It can't hurt to listen."

Finally Sonny turned to face her. "Yes it can. They'll talk me into something I'll regret. I can't get involved with anymore seniors. Too much bacteria. And don't even get me started on the smells." Sonny wagged her head with renewed determination. "Germs, bodily fluids..."

"We'll be like that one day." Tricia interrupted her.

Sonny shivered at the thought.

"And you'll wish for someone like you to come in and take care of you," the darker woman pressed.

"Where will you be?"

"You mean, will we still be together? Absolutely."

"What'll we be doing at that age?" Sonny pressed herself into Tricia and reached for her hand.

Tricia smiled, "I don't know for sure, but I'm looking forward to it."

EPILOGUE

Carmen the Nose Bustamante and Constance Columbo were both found guilty on charges of racketeering and murder. The RICO Act was used to confiscate the money found at the scene, all monies from the sale of the condo, and other property. They are currently serving life sentences in upstate Florida.

Ralph Bustamante could not be connected to any of the criminal activity and had to be released after questioning. Upon returning to Fort Lauderdale, he assumed control of the family business. But his reign as *capo di tutti* was short-lived; less than a month after his newfound status, a freak boating accident took his life.

Hector Rinaldi was convicted of the murders of Anita Lemoyne and Tess Fontana. After learning of her fiancé's double life, Christie Wilcox took the witness stand for the prosecution. She used the proceeds from the sale of her engagement ring to purchase a newspaper stand near the club where she once stripped. She enjoys a thriving business.

Smiling Tess Fontana nearly made it across Alligator Alley in Hector's Corvette. Unfamiliar with the horsepower and rusty on the use of a stick shift, she accidentally overshot her rest area exit and plunged into one of the many area canals. Her body and the vehicle were recovered months later when a fisherman reeled in the Anita wig. Troy Shoat believed hers was the body of Hector's second murder victim and closed the case. He went on to lose the election to his challenger, but remains in the Naples Sheriff's Office.

Milo Purdie became a minor witness for the prosecution and was helpful in putting the remaining members of the Bridge Club behind bars. An even more important witness, Grace, was placed in Witness Protection and vanished overnight. Milo regretted never having dinner with her, but was glad to have played a part in bringing an end to her nightmare. He knew it would have made his father proud.

The Bustamante Gang trial was broadcast nationally, and upon learning that a company employee was involved, the president of Crukinshank Security tuned in. Milo was promoted to a substation, where he spends his days indoors watching residential communities via live video surveillance in air-conditioned comfort.

On the day Boomer's pups were scheduled to be given up for adoption, Milo claimed the litter and is raising them in hopes of creating a new line of hybrid security dogs. His letter to the American Kennel Club, pitching the pit bull and shih tzu mix as the first ever bull-shihtz breed, has yet to be answered.

Muscia Bolineaux waited twenty-four hours before returning to recover her money from the garbage bins. She was never charged. Fearing a reprisal from Ralph Bustamante, she left the country on a private charter boat bound for the Cayman Islands.

Paige Chesley moved to Los Angeles, where she is working on a reality series of her life as a drug dealer.

Winnie and Pell remain in the Organized Crime Unit of the Florida Bureau of Investigation, where they continue to serve and protect.

Agida - slang for heartburn
Buon natale — Merry Christmas
Capiche — do you understand
Capo di tutti — boss of all bosses
Cazzo — dick
Che palle — what balls
Cogliones — idiot, prick
Comare — a married man's female lover
Cugine - a young tough guy looking to be made
Felice Anno Nuevo — Happy New Year
Goomah - a mafioso's mistress
Infine - finally
Mangia - eat
Oobatz - Derived from an Italian expression used to describe someone/thing as nuts/crazy/insane
Poraccione - pig
Siamo fottuti — fuck me or we're fucked
Stugatz - testicles
Stunad — stupid
Tie vaffanculo — fuck you

CPSIA information can be obtained
at www.ICGtesting.com
Printed in the USA
LVOW01s1333090916

503941LV00026B/439/P